SEX,
CULTURE,
AND
JUSTICE

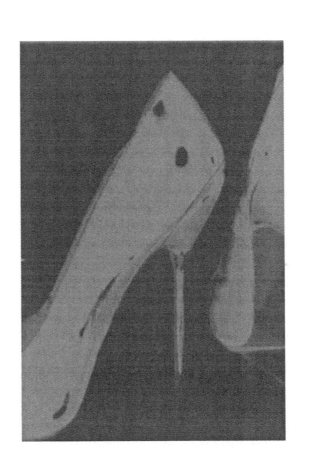

SEX, CULTURE, AND JUSTICE

THE LIMITS OF CHOICE

CLARE CHAMBERS

THE PENNSYLVANIA STATE UNIVERSITY PRESS
UNIVERSITY PARK, PENNSYLVANIA

Library of Congress Cataloging-in-Publication
Data

Chambers, Clare.
Sex, culture, and justice : the limits of choice /
Clare Chambers.
        p.   cm.
Includes bibliographical references and index.
ISBN 978-0-271-03301-3 (cloth : alk. paper)
1. Feminist theory.
2. Sex role–Philosophy.
3. Feminine beauty (Aesthetics)–Social aspects.
4. Body, Human—Social aspects.
5. Social norms.
6. Autonomy (Philosophy).
7. Liberalism—Philosophy.
I. Title.

HQ1190.C43 2007
306.4'613—dc22
2007025808

The Pennsylvania State University Press
is a member of the Association of American
University Presses.

It is the policy of The Pennsylvania State
University Press to use acid-free paper.
This book is printed on Natures Natural,
containing 50% post-consumer waste, and
meets minimum requirements of American
National Standard for Information
Sciences—Permanence of Paper for
Printed Library Material, ANSI Z39.48-1992.

CONTENTS

ACKNOWLEDGMENTS

Although writing a book can be a lonely experience, it cannot be done alone. I have relied on a great many people and places while writing this book, and I am profoundly grateful to all of them.

Some chapters of *Sex, Culture, and Justice* have been previously published elsewhere, although in each case the version that appears here has been revised or extended. An earlier version of Chapter 2 appeared as "Masculine Domination, Radical Feminism and Change," in *Feminist Theory* 6, no. 3 (December 2005). It is reprinted by permission of Sage Publications Ltd., all rights reserved. An earlier version of Chapter 4 appeared as "All Must Have Prizes: The Liberal Case for Interference in Cultural Practices," in *Multiculturalism Reconsidered: Culture and Equality and Its Critics* (Polity Press, 2002), edited by Paul Kelly, and is reprinted here by permission of Polity Press. An earlier version of Chapter 5 appeared as "Are Breast Implants Better Than Female Genital Mutilation? Autonomy, Gender Equality and Nussbaum's Political Liberalism," in *Critical Review of International Social and Political Philosophy* 7, no. 3 (Autumn 2004), and is reprinted here by permission of Taylor & Francis Ltd. I should like to thank the editors and publishers for permission to use those works here. I should also like to thank the staff at Penn State University Press. In particular, Sandy Thatcher was enthusiastic about the book from the start and supportive at every stage. Cherene Holland kept everything running smoothly and to schedule, and Andrew Lewis provided excellent copyediting and editorial suggestions.

My work on *Sex, Culture, and Justice* began while I was a graduate student at Nuffield College, University of Oxford. During that time I was very fortunate to have research funding from the UK Economic and Social Research Council (ESRC), for which I am very grateful. I am also grateful to the other members of Nuffield College—fellows, students, and staff—for the excellent practical, intellectual, and emotional resources they shared with me during the sometimes challenging doctoral process.

I was also fortunate to have two wonderful supervisors, Lois McNay and David Miller, who spanned what sometimes seemed like a conceptual void between Continental and analytical political philosophy. Having two such different supervisors offered great rewards. But it also brought the difficulty that, if one of them liked a piece of work, the other usually wouldn't. I never decided quite how best to resolve this problem, but hope that at least parts of *Sex, Culture, and Justice* please both of them, for they each contributed an enormous amount. David and Lois continue to offer support and advice, and I am indebted to them both.

I continued work on the book during a two-year lectureship in the Government Department of the London School of Economics and a further two years as Mary Somerville Junior Research Fellow at Somerville College, University of Oxford. In both places I enjoyed the help and intellectual stimulation of excellent colleagues, for which I am very grateful. I should also like to thank my new colleagues in the Philosophy Faculty and Jesus College, University of Cambridge, for their welcome and encouragement.

Parts of *Sex, Culture, and Justice* have been presented at various academic events: the Nuffield Political Theory Workshop, the Oxford Political Theory Seminar, the London Political Theory Group, the LSE Political Philosophy Research Seminar, the LSE Philosophy Department annual conference at Cumberland Lodge, a roundtable on Brian Barry's *Culture and Equality* at Birkbeck College, a one-day conference organized by the Royal Institute of Philosophy and the Open University, the Political Studies Association annual conference in Leicester, and the European Consortium for Political Research annual conference at Marburg. Comments raised and questions asked at these events have been enormously helpful, and I should like to thank all the participants.

Sex, Culture, and Justice has also been explicitly shaped—and, I think, improved—by comments from a great many individuals who have been kind enough to provide them. I have hugely appreciated the comments and support of Ruth Abbey, Mike Aronson, Michael Bacon, Brian Barry, Andrea Baumeister, Richard Bellamy, Thomas Christiano, Jerry Cohen, Phil Cook, Liz Frazer, Michael Freeden, Miranda Gill, Geoff Harcourt, Andy Harrop, David Held, Kimberley Hutchings, Ben Jackson, Stevi Jackson, Paul Kelly, Cécile Laborde, Gerry Mackie, Martin McIvor, Derek Matravers, Matt Matravers, Steve May, Tariq

Modood, Monica Mookherjee, Michael Otsuka, Avia Pasternak, Anne Phillips, Oonagh Reitman, Jonathan Seglow, Birte Siim, Judith Squires, Marc Stears and Stuart White. Dan Butt deserves a special mention for liking an early version of Chapter 5 so much that he came to hear me present it twice, and for insisting that it is sometimes desirable purposely to limit one's own autonomy. I don't think I would have finished this book if I hadn't applied Dan's principle when writing it.

Some people have been kind enough to read the entire manuscript at one time or another, and I should like to give them special thanks. Lois McNay and David Miller did so several times during its doctoral incarnation, and Sue Mendus and Adam Swift were rigorous and constructive examiners. Cécile Fabre provided characteristically detailed and challenging comments while being unfailingly supportive. Katherine Eddy and Zofia Stemplowska responded to my plea for readers to see whether the manuscript made sense after rearranging some chapters; Katherine did so with great speed, and Zofia did so in great detail: a perfect combination. Ruth Abbey and Avigail Eisenberg were anonymous (at the time) reviewers of the manuscript. Each gave comments that were far more detailed and useful than anyone is entitled to expect of anonymous reviewers. In particular both Ruth and Avigail made suggestions about the structure of the book that helped to deal with problems I had previously identified but been unable to see how to solve, and responding to their more specific challenges was a real pleasure. Finally, Ann Cudd was one of the last to read the manuscript, and her comments were interesting, encouraging, and helpful. Attempting to respond to all these critics has been sometimes difficult but always exciting and never unpleasant, and I hope I have managed to resolve some of their concerns (I know I have not resolved all of them).

Since this is my first book, I have accrued a great many personal debts. I shall not attempt to list them all, but will mention two categories. First, many former teachers have helped me develop a love of political philosophy and of academic life. I should like to thank them all, and particularly Nigel Bowles, Mark Evans, Marc Stears, and Tony Ward. Second, many people gave me great emotional help while I was writing this book. In particular, Lu Harley, Jennie Parvin, and John Parvin have been constantly understanding, tolerant, and generous. My father, Keith Chambers, was always available with tea and crumpets, practical advice on everything from car ownership to travel deals, and a groan-inducing pun if times got rough. My mother, José Chambers, has been an enormous influence and inspiration, and an unfailing source of support. I am hugely thankful to both my parents.

Finally, I must thank Phil Parvin. Phil has helped me through innumerable intellectual and emotional crises, and has also brought me great happiness. Phil is an excellent political philosopher, and his ideas shaped many of those of *Sex, Culture and Justice*. Not least, it was Phil who first encouraged me to consider theories of multiculturalism, and this book would have been very different if he had not. Phil insists, against my occasional assertions to the contrary, that I would have finished the book without him. He may be right, but I am extremely glad that I did not have to try.

INTRODUCTION

I've had [cosmetic] surgery. . . . There comes a point when something bothers people enough that it affects the way they live their lives every day, and that's the time they have cosmetic surgery. Most don't have it to be ultra-glamorous. The average person has it to feel normal. To have what society perceives as a normal-sized nose or bust.

—LINDSAY MULLINS, quoted in James Meek, "Prime Cuts"

You have to learn how to wear [Manolo Blahnik's stiletto-heeled] shoes; it doesn't happen overnight. But now I can race out and hail a cab. I can run up Sixth Avenue at full speed. I've destroyed my feet completely, but I don't care. What do you really need your feet for anyway?

—SARAH JESSICA PARKER, quoted in Rebecca Tyrrel, "Sexual Heeling"

In 2002, several newspapers reported the case of Myriam Yukie Gaona.[1] Gaona was described as a former stripper with no medical qualifications who had posed as a cosmetic surgeon in Mexico for several years. She had injected substances into thousands of people, mostly women, to reduce or augment their breasts, stomachs, buttocks, and calves. Many of her patients were attracted with promises that, after the procedures, they would conform to an artificial and idealized standard of beauty: one patient, Maria Concepcion Lopez, says that she visited Gaona because "'she said she'd make us look like Barbie dolls.'"[2]

The injections were successful at first. More and more patients were drawn to visit Gaona's surgery by word-of-mouth, seeing the apparently amazing results that other women had achieved. One woman even took her husband and her daughter along for injections. However, patients increasingly began to complain of serious medical problems,

---

1. See Jo Tuckman, "She Said She'd Make Us Look Like Barbie Dolls"; Agencies via Xinhua, "Mexican 'Beautykiller'"; Alicia Calderon, "Fake Plastic Surgeon Accused of Harming Hundreds in Mexico."
2. Tuckman, "Barbie Dolls."

including aches and pains, lumps that burned when the weather was sunny, and skin that turned black and dead. Medical investigations found that Gaona had been injecting people with mixtures of industrial silicone (usually used to seal windows and doors), baby oil, vegetable oil, and motor oil. Patients had to have mastectomies, have limbs amputated, and undergo agonizing surgical procedures to drain their bodies of congealed globules of silicone and oil. By December 2002, over 400 alleged victims had received remedial medical treatment, over 160 women and one man had filed legal complaints, and Gaona was awaiting trial for impersonating a medical doctor, causing serious injury, and administering drugs without a license.

In Britain a year earlier, an Oxfordshire Community Health NHS Trust conducted a survey asking 164 women about their footwear habits and preferences. The survey found that one in five women wore high-heeled shoes in order to please her boyfriend, husband, or boss, and that one in three women liked wearing high heels. More than 80 percent of women said that they would not change their style of shoe to improve a foot problem. The Head of Podiatry Services at the Trust, Philip Joyce, predicted that three out of four women would have foot problems by the time they were sixty, often as result of wearing high-heeled shoes. "We have tried for years without success to persuade women to wear the dreaded sensible shoes," he told the Telegraph. "High heels have a long history of social status, sexuality and power. It is not really surprising, by the time girls are four years old they know that Disney's high-heeled glass slipper does not fit the ugly women."[3]

Most liberals would interpret these two cases very differently. The first, the case of Myriam Gaona, is contemptible in many easily definable ways, and a clear affront to the rights and freedoms of the women and men who suffered at her hands. Her actions, after all, were built on deception. According to the allegations, Gaona lied to her patients about her medical qualifications, displaying fake medical certificates in her offices. She also lied to them about her procedures, claiming that she was injecting "citrics" and "collagen" rather than industrial silicone and motor oil. It is clear, from the liberal perspective, that those women and men who suffered crippling and life-threatening injuries at Gaona's hands are victims of a serious injustice. It is also clear that Gaona should never have been allowed to perform the injections, and that she ought to be prosecuted.

3. Celia Hall, "Sexy High Heels Are Worth the Agony, Say Women."

On the other hand, we might think that the women in the Oxford-shire foot survey are victims of no such injustice. They were not de-ceived into buying high-heeled shoes. They do not wear high-heeled shoes in the mistaken belief that the heels are not damaging to their feet, since 80 percent of the respondents said that even an actual foot problem would not cause them to change their habits. Liberals would, I imagine, argue that such women are exercising their freedom to choose what to wear on their feet, and to decide whether the aesthetic advantage of high-heeled shoes outweighs the risk of foot problems. No liberal would suggest that the manufacturers of high-heeled shoes ought to be prosecuted, or that injustice has been done.

But are the cases really so different? Gaona's lawyer, Jose Julian Jordan, does not think so. The *Shanghai Star* reports him as saying, "Here, injecting someone isn't a crime. If you tell me, 'I want volume here, I want to reduce this,' and a doctor tells me the treatment is correct and you are already an adult, I'm not cheating anyone, I'm helping with what you've asked me to do."[4] Of course, Jordan's claim is somewhat disingenuous—in Gaona's case, the treatment certainly wasn't "correct," and Gaona was not a doctor. But he raises an issue of crucial relevance to liberal thought: if an adult wants to undergo a dangerous procedure, or take part in a harmful practice, with what legitimacy does the state prevent them from doing so? If people may legitimately decide to wear high heels despite the danger to their feet, should they not also be allowed to decide to undergo industrial silicone injections? If Gaona had told her patients that she had no formal medi-cal qualifications, and that there was a risk of injury from her injec-tions, would she have been doing anything wrong?

In this book, I suggest that there are in fact many similarities be-tween the cases of the Mexican and Oxfordshire women, and that lib-eral theory is not well equipped to deal with those similarities. Both cases involve women who voluntarily risk harming themselves, albeit to different degrees and with different levels of information, in order to conform to standards of beauty. Both cases, in other words, involve women taking risks in order to conform to social norms. Moreover, both cases illustrate women attempting to conform to social norms, not only to please others, to avoid sanctioning from others, or to gain their approval, but also to please themselves. Both the Mexican and

4. Agencies via Xinhua, "Mexican 'Beautykiller.'"

the Oxfordshire women want to look attractive, and feel happier about themselves when they do. But their desires to please themselves and others by conforming to beauty norms is not an isolated, individual decision or preference. It is defined and regulated by the social context that they live in, exemplified by *Sex and the City*, Barbie dolls, and the Disney version of Cinderella.

Most liberal theory, I argue in this book, is built on conceptual premises that prevent it from criticizing this process adequately. As a result, the liberal values of freedom and equality are compromised. Liberal theory tends to support and protect people's freedom to make harmful choices that threaten their well-being or their equality, rather than protecting their freedom to resist inequality and supporting them in doing so. As such, liberals can end up protecting inequality and social constraint. Feminist theory has generally been much more successful at analyzing and criticizing cases such as the two just described. In part, this greater success is because feminist philosophers, in theorizing the nature and variety of women's oppression, have been much more willing than liberal philosophers to take on the issue of social construction and the limits it places on individual autonomy. In particular, feminists have been more willing to adopt certain ways of theorizing about social construction and autonomy. I suggest, then, that theories of social construction can usefully be used to develop a normative approach that more adequately addresses inequality and unfreedom.

In the course of the book, I draw on the work of feminist theorists, and particularly on feminist work that highlights the position of women in the private sphere. Much of what is lacking in liberalism is illustrated by paying attention to this sphere. If we consider the workings of personal relationships within patriarchal society, and particularly the supposedly appropriate roles of women, it becomes clear that many liberal policies that aim to maximize freedom and equality actually perpetuate systematic inequality.[5] Moreover, many feminists find the combination of theories of social construction with liberal values particularly fruitful. Analysis of the social construction of subjects can be similar to feminist arguments concerning the entrenchment of gender difference despite formal equality, and liberal normative arguments are crucial to the feminist critique of patriarchy.

___

5. This point has been made by many feminists, but see particularly Susan Moller Okin, *Justice, Gender and the Family*.

The book also reacts to theories of multiculturalism, which can be seen as drawing on both liberal and social constructionist arguments. Multiculturalism appears to challenge the liberal commitment to universal values, a challenge that is also posed by social construction, by highlighting cultural differences and particularities. And yet culturally sanctioned inequalities, in particular gender inequalities, highlight the need for universal liberal normative claims. Liberals and feminists cannot achieve freedom and equality if these values are allowed to remain culturally particular. The challenge, then, is to combine a liberal feminist commitment to universal values with an awareness of the ways that culture structures our identities and relationships.

Social Construction

Consider the following words of an anthropologist named Fran, speaking in the late 1970s:

> I don't particularly like my breasts right now. They're just too saggy and large according to the ideal of body proportions. . . . In many cultures sagging breasts are a sign of *beauty* and are sought after. . . . Most tribal societies don't favor upright breasts. That is mostly a Western cultural ideal. From a tribal society's point of view, we always want to look *immature* (*laughs*) and there's a lot of truth in that. . . . You'd think that with all the information I've been exposed to I'd feel better about myself. But when your whole upbringing and your culture have made you internalize these fetishes as ideals, there are just too many pressures working on you. I am a product of my culture.[6]

Fran is one of the women featured in Daphna Ayalah and Isaac Weinstock's *Breasts: Women Speak about Their Breasts and Their Lives*, for which ordinary women of all ages consented to having their breasts photographed without any makeup or airbrushing. Some of the women have had breast implants or reductions. Some have had mas-

---

6. Fran, an anthropologist, in Daphna Ayalah and Isaac Weinstock, *Breasts*, 136; emphasis in the original.

tectomies. Some were lactating. Accompanying the pictures are testi-monies given by the women about their feelings toward their breasts. They talk about their insecurities about their bodies—their "tremen-dous anxiety and self-consciousness"[7]—and their desire to conform to a normalized ideal.

Perhaps the greatest contribution of the book is the direct evidence it provides that, despite women's worries, there is no such thing as "normal." Or, to put it another way, the category of "normal" encom-passes enormous diversity. Most of the women pictured have natural breasts, unremarkable and yet utterly astonishing at the same time, for unenhanced breasts are so rarely seen. Despite the ubiquity and visibil-ity of the photographed breast, in its natural form it is concealed. This point is made clear by women's reactions to Alayah and Weinstock's photographs prior to publication: "The one observation that most women made during their brief exposure to the photographs was about the variety of breasts. 'I always thought breasts looked pretty much the same. How amazingly different they all are. They seem to have differ-ent characters—like individual faces.'"[8]

Although the book is nearly thirty years old, explicitly intended as part of the second wave of feminism, the women in it could just as easily be speaking today. Susan Bordo urges us to recognize that "now, in 2003, virtually every celebrity image you see—in the magazines, in the videos, and sometimes even in the movies—has been digitally modified. Virtually every image. Let that sink in. Don't just let your mind passively receive it. Confront its implications."[9] The enormous rise in the number of women undergoing cosmetic surgery empha-sizes that, despite decades of feminism, women still feel compelled to conform to some ideal standard. The UK Breast Implant Registry re-corded 9,731 patients receiving new cosmetic implants in 2004. In other words, in the United Kingdom a woman receives her first breast implants every single hour, twenty-four hours a day, 365 days a year. Between 1993 and 2004, the Registry records 68,177 women having a total of 185,952 cosmetic breast implants.[10] The American Society for

7. Ibid., 13.
8. Ibid., 15.
9. Susan Bordo, *Unbearable Weight*, xviii.
10. In addition to the 9,731 women who had new breast implants in 2004, 961 women had replacement implants. Numbers of first cosmetic breast implants reported have risen from 474 patients in 1993 to 9,731 in 2004. Statistics from the UK Breast Implant Registry, *Annual Report 2004*. The Registry is a voluntary record, meaning that actual figures will be higher than recorded.

Aesthetic Plastic Surgery reported 364,610 cosmetic breast enlargements in 2005—up 9 percent from 2004. That figure amounts to more than forty-one operations every hour.[11]

In attempting to understand and criticize phenomena such as breast implants, feminists can turn to a combination of liberal normative values with a theory of social construction. Social construction enables feminists to understand how it is that patriarchy persists in liberal societies and despite formal equalities: as Fran notes, norms of gender inequality are deeply rooted within individuals and social structures, and cannot be uprooted without radical change. Such an understanding is crucial to the feminist claim that gender inequality persists despite formal, legislative equality. Liberal normative values provide a program for change: they suggest that we should aim for freedom and autonomy even from within the confines of social construction, and that we should also aim to increase gender equality.

However, several problems arise when attempting to reconcile liberal values with theories of social construction. How can the recognition that all social forms constrain people, by constructing their sense of what is possible or appropriate, be reconciled with the liberal desire to emancipate individuals from norms that limit their autonomy? Does social construction rule out autonomy? Moreover, if normative values themselves are the product of social construction, how is it possible, both philosophically and epistemologically, to criticize our own values? In particular, how is it possible to maintain that liberal normative values are more than the situated and relative values of a particular time and place, just like the beauty norms of different cultures that Fran describes? On what grounds can we argue for liberal or feminist change?

In general, we can identify three key issues arising from a feminist reconciliation of liberalism and social construction: how we should understand the thesis of social construction, the (im)possibility of universalism in the context of social construction, and the appropriate liberal response to difference. These issues inform the rest of the book. The first issue, how to understand social construction, is tackled in Part

11. American Society for Aesthetic Plastic Surgery, at http://www.surgery.org/. The society also reports a 444 percent increase in cosmetic procedures in the United States in 2005, as compared with 1997. In 2005, women were the patients in 91.4 percent of cosmetic surgeries. For women, breast augmentation was the second most popular procedure after liposuction.

One, in which I develop an account that draws on both the poststructuralist work of Michel Foucault and Pierre Bourdieu and the feminist approaches of Catharine MacKinnon, Seyla Benhabib, and Nancy Hirschmann. The second and third issues, of how to combine universal liberal normative values with an awareness of social construction and the fact of difference, are the main focus of Part Two. In the remainder of this chapter I consider the varied liberal uses of choice, and the work of some of the liberal feminists who have attempted to reformulate them.

Liberalism, Feminism, and Choice

In this book I combine a liberal approach to normative values and reasoning with a feminist awareness of social construction and gender inequality. This combination is not in itself original: many feminists have attempted to retheorize or utilize liberal values. In part, feminists have felt the need to reconfigure liberalism rather than merely use it intact because of the historical fact that liberalism's grand claims to provide universal freedom and equality often have not delivered those things for women (and various other social groups). As Catharine MacKinnon asks, why has liberalism "needed feminism to notice the humanity of women in the first place, and why [has it] yet to face either the facts or the implications of women's material inequality as a group, has not controlled male violence societywide, and has not equalized the status of women relative to men[?] If liberalism 'inherently' can meet feminism's challenges, having had the chance for some time, why hasn't it?"[12]

One consequence of feminists' need to engage philosophically with liberalism, rather than merely adopt and apply it, is a greater awareness and development of theories of social construction. To understand why it is that patriarchy persists despite formal legal equality, feminists have had to analyze how gender inequality is so deeply entrenched in social norms that individual free choice cannot overcome it. Different liberal theories give different weight to choice, and are differently mindful of social construction. In general, the greater the weight given to choice, the less the attention paid to social construction; for as I

---

12. Catharine MacKinnon, " 'The Case' Responds," 709.

argue throughout this book, an adequate understanding of the latter illustrates what is wrong with the former.

A brief survey of contemporary liberal thought illustrates the variable relationship between choice and social construction. At one extreme are those liberals, or libertarians, who ignore the implications of social construction and consider individual choice to be the final and unproblematic beginning of normative theory, with some process or pattern of preference-satisfaction at the end. Examples are thinkers such as Robert Nozick and Chandran Kukathas, who focus only on the extent to which individuals are able to choose and act atomistically and pay no consideration to how society forms people's preferences or to how people's preferences affect society. A different form of liberal theory, which nevertheless has some connection to libertarian thought, is luck egalitarianism. Exemplified in the work of theorists such as Ronald Dworkin, G. A. Cohen, and Richard Arneson, luck egalitarianism (in very general terms) is the view that equality requires that individuals are compensated for disadvantage that results from certain forms of luck. However, if individuals have made choices that led to their disadvantage, then they are deemed responsible and may not claim compensation. Luck egalitarians may take account of some forms of social construction, recognizing, for example, that individuals' choices may be perverted by the influence of others. However, it is crucial to the luck egalitarian project that a sphere of responsible, individual choice can be identified, and that this sphere is thereby immune from considerations of justice.

An alternative and familiar use of the concept of choice in liberal thought is through the device of freedom of exit. This idea states that certain sorts of inequality which would otherwise be unjust become just if the individuals concerned are able to leave the group or social arrangement responsible for the inequality. If they remain within the group, they are assumed to have consented to or chosen the inequality, thus making it compatible with justice. This device is used by a wide range of theorists, from the libertarian theory of Kukathas to the far stronger egalitarianism of Brian Barry and the liberal feminism of Ayelet Shachar and Marilyn Friedman. There are two main reasons for this diversity of support for freedom of exit. First, it demonstrates the fundamental relationship between liberalism and choice. Few liberals have felt able to deny that individuals' self-regarding choices can be just, and have thus been loath to criticize hierarchical social groups if membership appears voluntary. Second, the doctrine of freedom of exit is versatile since it can be coupled with various different degrees of awareness of social construction. For libertarians such as Kukathas the nature and conditions of the choice to remain within a disadvantageous relationship are unimportant, while for feminists such as Friedman it is necessary to ensure that the choice is free from certain sorts of social construction. Thus, although Friedman agrees that "cultural practices that violate women's rights are nevertheless permissible if the women in question accept them,"[13] she places various constraints on the sorts of conditions that must be in place if a woman's acceptance is to count. I discuss the strategy of freedom of exit in detail in Chapter 4. Its key problem is that even an account such as Friedman's cannot escape the fact that cultural practices are inevitably reinforced by the sorts of social norms that undermine an individual's ability to make the sort of "free" choice that justice would require.

Another strategy for focusing on choice while placing various conditions on the nature and circumstances of that choice is deliberative democracy. In the liberal tradition this idea has been developed in the work of thinkers such as Jürgen Habermas, John Dryzek, and Amy Gutman. Seyla Benhabib's version of deliberative democracy, which she terms "discourse ethics," is useful, since it is developed along distinctly feminist lines. According to discourse ethics, democratic deliberation and the policies that result from it must proceed in accordance with three principles: egalitarian reciprocity, voluntary self-ascription, and freedom of exit and association. The general idea is that when discourse is constrained in these ways, it is proper to follow those policies and principles that are agreed upon, and which thus have been chosen by the participants. The constraints are needed, in part, because of the problem of social construction: if we allow choice to rule unchecked, we risk being bound by decisions that result from various forms of social domination or oppression.

However, there is considerable tension in this desire to prioritize choice while also constraining it. For example, it is unclear how much egalitarianism is required by Benhabib's discourse ethics. In places, it appears as though egalitarianism is brought about if and only if deliberation demands it, since Benhabib states that "discourse ethics does not present itself as a blueprint for changing institutions and practices;

---

13. Marilyn Friedman, *Autonomy, Gender, Politics*, 188.

it is an idealized model in accordance with which we can measure the fairness and legitimacy of existing practices and aspire to reform them, *if and when* the democratic will of the participants to do so exists."[14] The problem with this approach is that it is disingenuous to talk about or wait for the emergence of a democratic will in circumstances of inequality, for there can be no truly *democratic* will until equality is already established and protected.

Perhaps, then, equality is to be stipulated in advance. This is the implication of other parts of Benhabib's work. Her first principle of discourse ethics is egalitarian reciprocity, which states that "members of cultural, religious, linguistic and other minorities must not, in virtue of their membership status, be entitled to lesser degrees of civil, political, economic and cultural rights than the majority."[15] Moreover, Benhabib assumes that one dissenting voice against inequality establishes a democratic will for its abandonment.[16] These provisions solve the problem of inequality but they do so while leaving little role for the majoritarian choice, which was the original reason to favor discourse.

There are similar problems with Benhabib's second principle, voluntary self-ascription: "An individual must not be automatically assigned to a cultural, religious, or linguistic group by virtue of his or her birth. An individual's group membership must permit the most extensive forms of self-ascription and self-identification possible."[17] But it is impossible for an individual not to be ascribed to a linguistic group by virtue of birth, for if an individual is to express a preference about her group membership, she must already have learned a language that she did not herself choose. Benhabib may mean simply that such group memberships must not be ascribed by virtue of birth once and for all, but if that is the case, it is not clear why she labels the principle "voluntary self-ascription" rather than "freedom of exit." Indeed, the idea of "voluntary self-ascription" does not sit easily with the idea of social construction. It is a laudable aim to enable individuals to be the authors of their own lives. However, there is at least a tension between the idea that individuals can be "self-interpreting and self-defining" and the view that they are "constituted through culturally-informed narratives."[18]

14. Seyla Benhabib, *The Claims of Culture*, 19.
15. Ibid., 115; emphasis in the original.
16. Ibid., 116.
17. Ibid., 19.
18. Ibid., 132.

Overall, then, though Benhabib's founding assumptions (strong universalism combined with sensitivity to cultural particularism and an awareness of social construction but a refusal to submit to cultural relativism) and her conclusions (in general, a firm commitment to egalitarianism and autonomy) are laudable, and in line with my approach, her method of discourse ethics is less successful.

Deliberative democracy—or in Rawlsian terminology, public reason—is also a feature of another variety of liberalism that feminists have retheorized: political liberalism. Political liberals attempt to combine the liberal commitments to both universal equality and individual choice by employing a political/comprehensive distinction, according to which freedom and equality must apply in the political sphere, to individuals *qua* citizens, but need not apply to the sphere in which individuals choose and live out their comprehensive conceptions of the good. It is compatible with political liberalism, then, if individuals live in hierarchical groups, as long as those hierarchies are not carried over into citizenly activities such as voting or adhering to the law. In effect, political liberalism involves a restriction of the scope of equality: rather than applying to all aspects of life, equality is required only in the political sphere.[19]

Political liberals also try to avoid privileging any particular substantive moral position by basing their liberalism on the notion of consensus. Political liberals argue that people who hold many different conceptions of the good can nevertheless agree on liberalism as the best *political* doctrine, and that this agreement can be based on different things for different people. Liberalism prevails, then, without a particular conception of the good prevailing. However, the problem with this approach is that we have no guarantee that liberalism and liberal values will be the result of the overlapping consensus, if the outcome of that consensus is not stipulated in advance. While political liberalism claims support from a variety of comprehensive doctrines, rather than on universal acceptance of substantive liberal values, there are in fact claims to universality behind the values on which it rests that undermine its claims to accommodate choice. Feminist political liberal Drucilla Cornell, for example, writes that "political liberalism must find a way to justify a liberal and thus tolerant attitude toward non-

---

19. This facet of political liberalism is complex, particularly as regards gender equality, and I consider it in greater detail in later chapters.

liberal, yet decent, nations. Otherwise, political liberalism can rightly be charged with being illiberal because it imposes a view of the good associated with Western ideals of democracy that other countries and cultures do not accept."[20] Cornell's claim is that political liberalism ought to tolerate decent cultures that do not conceive of their members as equal.[21] Nonetheless, she asserts, "There certainly is basis for optimism that nations could reach an overlapping consensus that one of the universals that must be recognized by all cultures is the equivalent evaluation of feminine sexual difference."[22] But if the ideals and values of different cultures are what is doing the work rather than an antecedent notion of the universal value of gender equality, there is surely more evidence of an overlapping consensus on women's inferiority. Most if not all societies are highly and hierarchically gendered: even liberal societies have not fully embraced women's equality, as Cornell agrees.[23] It is therefore difficult to see how an overlapping consensus on women's equality could emerge in dialogue between actually hierarchical liberal societies and explicitly hierarchical nonliberal societies. As with discourse ethics, political liberalism's attempt to take account of the fact of social construction and difference through the mechanism of choice results in a conflict with its other normative value of equality. One or the other will have to give way: either equality takes precedence regardless of the actual views and choices of those involved in dialogue, or the results of the dialogue are taken to be the requirements of justice even if they entrench inequality.

Will Kymlicka has a different strategy for combining the liberal commitment to choice with an awareness of social construction. He argues that particular cultures within liberal societies provide the context within which individuals can make choices and exercise autonomy, and that they therefore require protection. Without a cultural framework, Kymlicka argues, individuals do not have the raw materials from which to forge autonomy: "Freedom involves making choices amongst various options, and our societal culture not only provides these options, but also makes them meaningful to us."[24] Kymlicka combines

20. Drucilla Cornell, *At the Heart of Freedom*, 153.
21. This understanding is derived from Rawls's use of the idea of a decent nonliberal people in *The Law of Peoples*.
22. Cornell, *At the Heart of Freedom*, 163–64.
23. Ibid., x.
24. Will Kymlicka, *Multicultural Citizenship*, 83.

this claim with a strong argument that liberals must value autonomy. He discusses the conflict between the values of autonomy and toleration, a conflict that is exemplified in the dilemma of whether liberals should tolerate cultures that suppress individual autonomy, and argues that what distinguishes liberalism is precisely its commitment to individual rather than group autonomy.[25] Liberals must therefore tread a delicate line: on the one hand, they must protect individual autonomy from illiberal cultural groups, but on the other hand, they must protect cultures, since their continued existence is a prerequisite for autonomy.

I endorse much of Kymlicka's argument as outlined in the previous paragraph. As Part One shows, I agree that autonomy is developed in a social context, and that the nature of an individual's ability to choose is shaped by her particular cultural memberships. I also agree with Kymlicka that liberalism must be committed to individual autonomy as opposed to group autonomy, as will become clear throughout Part Two. However, Kymlicka's strategy for treading the delicate line between group and individual protection is problematic, for several reasons. It is not always easy to tell precisely what Kymlicka's normative policy proposals are. At times he appears to favor a strong universalist liberal approach, such as when he argues that an individual must have "the freedom to move around within one's societal culture, to distance oneself from particular cultural roles, to choose which features of the culture are most worth developing, and which are without value,"[26] and when he argues that we should "seek to liberalize"[27] illiberal cultures and nations. Elsewhere his proposals are rather more limited. Despite endorsing the need to liberalize, Kymlicka cautions that "there is relatively little scope for legitimate coercive interference."[28] This limitation is not confined to the sphere of international intervention: according to Kymlicka, even within one state, a national minority (as opposed to an immigrant group) which is illiberal should nonetheless be permitted to govern its own affairs as it sees fit. Even though a "national minority which acts in an illiberal way acts unjustly," still the most the majority state should do (barring extreme cases such as torture or slavery) is "speak out" or offer "various incentives" to change.[29]

25. Ibid., 158.
26. Ibid., 90–91.
27. Ibid., 94.
28. Ibid., 167.
29. Ibid., 168.

The general distinction that Kymlicka makes between national minorities and immigrants, with the former given greater scope for illiberality than the latter, is problematic because it relies on the concept of choice. This reliance does not sit easily with Kymlicka's own account, since not only do his arguments about the cultural context of choice undermine the extent to which choice can be a legitimator of culture (a theme that runs throughout this book), but also choice does not function in the required way when discussing groups that persist through generations. Kymlicka wishes to show that immigrants have a greater obligation to assimilate and liberalize than national minorities because the former and not the latter *chose* to enter the liberal society. The normative role of this sort of choice is so strong that it may even justify allowing certain groups, such as the Amish and the Hutterites, to impose the usually forbidden internal restrictions on their own members, on the grounds that these groups historically agreed to be part of wider liberal / American society only on condition that such group autonomy was allowed.[30] But this approach contradicts what Kymlicka rightly identifies as liberalism's insistence that the correct unit of analysis when protecting autonomy is the individual and not the group.

We can identify two types of things that an *individual* member of a group might consent to: first, her membership in the group or in the wider state, and second, the particular practices of, or restrictions imposed by, the group or the wider state. Kymlicka's claim is that previous members of groups such as the Amish consented to membership in American society only on particular conditions (namely, the ability to impose certain practices on their members in perpetuity). In order to consider these historical agreements as binding, Kymlicka must argue:

1. internal restrictions are valid if group membership is consented to (something like the freedom of exit claim criticized earlier);
2. the choice to be a member of a group is more important than being able to choose the particular practices of a group (without this claim then freedom from internal restrictions would be more important to the Amish than their choice or otherwise to be citizens of the United States);
3. agreements made by ancestors are binding on descendants—

30. Ibid., 170.

even if those agreements explicitly constrain the descendants' autonomy;

4. and it is unjust if an individual is a member of a group or state to which she has not consented or whose terms she has not agreed (and thus unjust if the Amish must assimilate into U.S. society on terms which they did not agree).

Each of these claims is problematic, although not all problems can be discussed now. The first has already been criticized, and is investigated at length in Chapter 4. The second is a complex claim that forms the basis for discussion over several chapters in Part Two. The third is highly controversial and the subject of an emerging literature that cannot be engaged with here;[31] suffice to say that Kymlicka does not argue in its favor in *Multicultural Citizenship* and so the case is still to be made. The case needs to made, however, if the fourth is to work. For once we consider the individual as the unit of autonomous choice, it seems that *no one* has consented to membership in their initial cultural group (which, according to Kymlicka, shapes an individual's very ability to choose and which they can rarely or barely leave), and *no one* has consented to membership in their state except *first-generation* immigrants, settlers, and state-builders. In each and every category of group, the only individuals who can conceivably be considered voluntarily to have chosen membership in the group and consented to its terms are the first generation (more realistically, certain privileged members of the first generation). But if, as Kymlicka's account implies, it is unproblematic for descendants of immigrants and national *majorities* to be members of a state to which they did not consent (perhaps on the condition that the state is liberal), it must be similarly normatively unproblematic for national minorities and groups with historic agreements to be compelled to liberalize. Certainly, it does not make sense to hold back on the requirement to liberalize on the grounds of individual choice.

Once again, then, a liberal argument that recognizes the cultural construction of choice ends up relying on choice to make crucial normative distinctions, and problematically uses choice to assess the justice of a culture that has been shown itself to shape the very ability to

31. See, for example, David Miller, "Holding Nations Responsible," and Daniel Butt, *Rectifying International Injustice.*

choose. I do not wish to suggest that choice and autonomy play no normative role: I agree with Kymlicka that some commitment to autonomy is necessary for liberalism. But I do argue that arguments based on choice cannot justify certain sorts of restrictions that are imposed on individuals or disadvantages that they may suffer.

Part Two thus considers alternative liberal ways of approaching the connection between sex, culture, and justice. I consider different liberal and liberal feminist ways of understanding the connection between choice and justice in the context of social construction. Although this book cannot hope to offer a comprehensive analysis of contemporary liberalism, it considers a range of views, focusing on those liberals who, for varied reasons, share something with my approach. My intention is to show that while each form of liberalism goes some way toward securing universal freedom and equality in the face of social construction, no one approach goes far enough. In their place I offer my own.

PART ONE

THEORIES OF SOCIAL CONSTRUCTION

1

CREATIVITY, CULTURAL PRACTICE, AND THE BODY: FOUCAULT AND THREE PROBLEMS WITH THE LIBERAL FOCUS ON CHOICE

In Part One I consider the phenomenon of social construction in more detail, and outline how it impacts on liberal assumptions, through the work of thinkers who are neither liberal nor usually engaged with by liberals. In this chapter I discuss Michel Foucault, and show how a Foucauldian approach undermines the notion of choice as what I call a normative transformer: a concept that transforms an unjust situation into a just one. I argue that Foucault's work highlights three problems with the liberal focus on choice. First, because choice is individual, liberalism's focus on choice marginalizes its social location in culture. Second, because choice is mental, liberalism's focus on choice marginalizes the role of physical embodiment. Third, because liberalism conceives of choice as the absence of (state) constraint, liberalism's focus on choice ignores the creative elements of power.

My discussion centers on the gendered shaping of bodies in patriarchal societies. In this chapter I focus on female genital mutilation, routine secular male circumcision, and female appearance or "beauty" norms. Foucault's work examines in detail the role of the body in maintaining social norms. Although Foucault does not develop a specific theory of gender, and seldom relates his ideas to gender hierarchy,[1] many feminists have adapted his work on the body, in particular, to the analysis of gender. Moreover, the issue of the shaping of bodies serves to illustrate many aspects of Foucault's theory, including subject formation, power, and genealogy.

Foucault has been influential for many feminists because his approach to power and his focus on the body engage with feminist con-

---

1. This fact has led many feminists to criticize him for perpetuating the androcentricity of political philosophy. See Lois McNay, *Foucault and Feminism*.

cerns. His idea of power is helpful to feminist analysis of patriarchy since it addresses ideas of social construction and history in a way that can illuminate issues of gender. Many feminists have engaged with his work, whether to adopt his methods or to criticize them.[2] In general, they have focused on his theory of power and discipline. In this chapter I discuss that work, but I also investigate how the Foucauldian concept of genealogy can assist feminist and liberal analysis.

Discipline and Female Appearance Norms

A crucial element of Foucault's conception of power is his recognition that it can both repress *and* create. Modern political philosophy, and certainly liberal political philosophy, focuses overwhelmingly on the repressive elements of power, particularly as manifested in the state. Instead, Foucault focuses on "the new methods of power whose operation is not ensured by right but by technique, not by law but by normalization, not by punishment but by control, methods that are employed on all levels and in all forms that go beyond the state and its apparatus."[3] Foucault explains why these methods of power are "new" in *Discipline and Punish*, which charts the shift in systems of punishment since the Middle Ages. This shift takes two closely related forms: a shift from an overt focus on the body to an overt focus on the soul (although, as will be seen, Foucault asserts that body and soul are connected in important ways), and a shift from a largely repressive to a more creative power. It is Foucault's contention that, first, power currently operates more significantly through creation than through repression and, second, that power is more effective the less it focuses on crude repressive mechanisms. In other words, a focus on power as a repressive force misses a great deal of power, and misses the most effective power. This argument has significant implications for liberalism because it demonstrates how the liberal concern to limit the repressive elements of power (explicit state laws and institutions) both ignores and leaves intact the creative elements of power (social construction of options, preferences, and subjects), which are, in fact, the most effective. In

2. For a list of such work, see Caroline Ramazanoğlu, *Up Against Foucault*, 3. See also McNay, *Foucault and Feminism*.

3. Michel Foucault, *The Will to Knowledge*, 89.

other words, limiting the repressive power of the state merely alters the form that power takes. It need not, in itself, increase autonomy.

Foucault describes the Panopticon, a prison designed by Jeremy Bentham. The Panopticon consists of cells arranged in a circle around a central watchtower. Each cell has a barred door covering the whole of the internal wall, and a window to the outside that illuminates the cell. As a result, surveillance is very efficient: each cell can be seen from the central watchtower. Guards do not need to walk down corridors, look through peep-holes, or lift flaps. Moreover, the Panopticon has another feature that renders it even more effective: the central watchtower has blinds at the windows (an updated version would be a one-way mirror), ensuring that the prisoners never know whether or not the guard is looking at them. Without the blinds, a prisoner would know when the guard was looking away and could use the opportunity to misbehave; with the blinds, the prisoner must always behave, for a guard may always be watching. What this means, Foucault explains, is that the prisoners become self-policing. There does not need to be a guard present, enforcing compliance, because the prisoners become their own guards. The surveillance of the prison guard becomes an internal self-surveillance, and obedience becomes unconscious and habitual. To begin with, prisoners are self-policing because they are consciously afraid that a guard might be watching, but over time, they obey without conscious fear or reflection. Crucially, obedience becomes habitual at the level of the body: Foucault wants to escape the Enlightenment distinction between the mind and the body and demonstrate that the body plays a role in ensuring our compliance to social norms. Power is embodied when certain forms of behavior feel right to us, when our bodies "naturally" take on the correct position for a certain situation.

The Panopticon illustrates, for Foucault, the general operation of power in modern societies.[4] Power is transformed from a repressive to a creative force: "The exercise of power is not added on from the outside, like a rigid, heavy, constraint, to the functions it invests, but is so subtly present in them as to increase their efficiency by itself increasing their own points of contact."[5] Power is not a repressive force coming from outside the individual, constraining her actions, but a creative force manifested in the individual's everyday life. As in the Panopticon,

4. Michel Foucault, *Discipline and Punish*, 205.
5. Ibid., 206.

social norms do not need to be enforced by the explicit attention of others. Instead, enforcement and the corresponding surveillance is internalized by each individual, and is reinforced whenever the individual acts in compliance with the norm, or interacts with others in accordance to social expectations. This reinforcement is the product of two processes: the threat of surveillance and thus sanctions for nonconformity (for example, feelings of embarrassment or shame at acting inappropriately in a given social situation, fear of not fitting in), and sheer force of habit. Foucault contends that power works to create individuals, to form them as subjects, and that it does so at the level of the body as well as the level of the mind. When the body has been conditioned to obey a rule or act in a certain way, there is no need to seek compliance at the level of the mind as well, for compliance has been made habitual and does not need to be consciously directed.

A premise of this argument is that the human body itself, in the particular form it takes in any one society, is the product of social forces, the product of power. The notion of the female body as created rather than natural is familiar to feminism, as documented by writers such as Germaine Greer, Andrea Dworkin, Susan Bordo, Judith Butler, Naomi Wolf, and Sandra Lee Bartky.[6] Indeed, Bordo reminds us that the feminist understanding of the cultural construction of the body extends back at least as far as Mary Wollstonecraft.[7] As an example of feminist work on the body, consider Greer's *The Female Eunuch*. Greer anticipates Foucault in her discussion of the female body and its distortion by regimes of power, writing, "The new assumption behind the discussion of the body is that everything that we may observe *could be otherwise*."[8] Greer means two things by this claim. First, the significance we give to parts and forms of our bodies is precisely that, a significance given by us, not one that we find in our bodies via "objective" observation. More radically, it is Greer's contention that the very shape and form of our bodies is affected by gendered norms of behavior. Because girls and women are discouraged from undertaking vigorous exercise and weight training, they do not develop prominent mus-

---

6. Germaine Greer, *The Female Eunuch* and *The Whole Woman;* Judith Butler, *Gender Trouble;* Naomi Wolf, *The Beauty Myth;* Sandra Lee Bartky, "Foucault, Femininity and the Modernization of Patriarchal Power"; Bordo, *Unbearable Weight;* Andrea Dworkin, *Woman Hating.*

7. Bordo, *Unbearable Weight,* 17.

8. Greer, *Female Eunuch,* 17; emphasis in the original.

cles. Because they are discouraged from expressing themselves through physical violence, they lack the strength and skill to do so, whether in attack or defense. Clothing and appearance norms have similar effects. As Greer argues:

> There have been great changes in the history of feminine allure in the approved posture of the shoulders, whether sloping or straight, drawn forward or back, and these have been bolstered by dress and corseting, so that the delicate balance of bone on bone has been altered by the stress of muscles maintaining the artificial posture. . . . If I had been corseted at thirteen, my rib-cage might have developed differently, and the downward pressure on my pelvis would have resulted in its widening. Nowadays, corseting is frowned upon, but many women would not dream of casting away the girdle that offers *support* and *tummy control*.[9]

Greer's claim is not merely that different ways of life have an effect on our bodies, but also that different social norms, different ideas about how men and women ought to behave, shape us physically. It is because women's bodies are shaped by the result of human, social factors that it is most appropriate to think of them as shaped by power. Women's bodies are shaped in these ways not as a neutral or undesired side effect of productive work (such as when a manual worker's hands become rough or a computer operator suffers repetitive strain injury), but as a result of compliance with *normative* rules that directly dictate appearance. Women's bodies are supposed to be distorted in these ways, and the distortions are valued in and of themselves.

Similarly, Naomi Wolf argues that beauty norms dictate not just appearance but actions:

> The qualities that a given period calls beautiful in women are merely symbols of the female behavior that that period considers desirable: *The beauty myth is always actually prescribing behavior and not appearance.* Competition between women has been made part of the myth so that women will be divided from one another. Youth and (until recently) virginity have

---

9. Ibid., 36–37; emphasis in the original.

been "beautiful" in women since they stand for experiential and sexual ignorance. Aging in women is unbeautiful since women grow more powerful with time, and since the links between generations of women must always be newly broken. . . . Most urgently, women's identity must be premised upon our "beauty" so that we will remain vulnerable to outside approval, carrying the vital sensitive organ of self-esteem exposed to the air.[10]

Again, we see the interplay between embodiment and power: social norms are transferred onto our bodies, and our bodies in their new forms act out these social norms, perpetuating them by example. It is this constant perpetuation of power at the micro, local level that Foucault wants to capture. As Foucault puts it in *The History of Sexuality*, power is omnipresent "not because it has the privilege of consolidating everything under its invincible unity, but because it is produced from one moment to the next, at every point, or rather in every relation from one point to another. Power is everywhere; not because it embraces everything, but because it comes from everywhere."[11] Power, then, is not confined to those moments when an identifiable senior figure imposes a formal requirement, but manifests itself every time there is any form of social interaction, be it interpersonal or between the individual and an objectified manifestation of culture. For example, the power of female appearance norms is not confined to the formal settings of the beauty pageant or modeling agency, but also manifests itself when women receive (and give) comments on their appearance, or when they observe others' appearance and cast them as regulatory norms for themselves ("The average person has [cosmetic surgery] to feel normal")[12] or when they observe images of ideal female forms on advertising billboards, on television, and in magazines or films. Each transmission of female appearance norms is an instance of power.

The process by which we come to embody social norms of gendered behavior can also be understood in Foucauldian terms. Bartky shows how female appearance norms are enforced through a huge array of disciplinary practices a woman must master: dieting, exercises specifically designed to create an appropriate female figure (such as the "Legs,

10. Wolf, *Beauty Myth*, 14; emphasis in the original.
11. Foucault, *Will to Knowledge*, 93.
12. Lindsay Mullins, quoted in James Meek, "Prime Cuts."

Bums and Tums" aerobic class), posture, deportment (such as sitting or moving so to preserve modesty when wearing a skirt, or looking away from a strange man in the street), skincare, hair removal, hair styling, and makeup.[13] These practices are disciplinary in that they dictate minutely and precisely how the body must move and appear, require constant repetition, which makes them habitual, and are maintained and enforced through (the threat of) surveillance. It is central to Foucault's work that modern power does not come from a single, hierarchical source: power is not enforced by a conscious, dictating ruler. Instead, surveillance comes (and is perceived as coming) from all around: from schools (enforcing gendered uniform and appearance), parents (insisting that girls wear skirts and then telling them to sit in a "ladylike" position),[14] friends (comments on new outfits, makeup, weight loss or gain), the media (even broadsheet newspapers have makeup columns in their weekend magazines), the cosmetics companies and so on, all of whom encourage or admonish women as regards their bodily form. At the extreme, this surveillance is formalized: beauty pageants award marks for adherence to minute and specific rules of appearance and bodily deportment. Bartky puts this point memorably: "In contemporary patriarchal culture, a panoptical male connoisseur resides within the consciousness of most women: they stand perpetually before his gaze and under his judgment."[15]

Occasionally, advertisements prove to be explicit examples of this process. One such advertisement, for Clarks shoes and boots, bears the slogan "Life's one long catwalk."[16] It depicts two women going about their everyday lives: one is refueling her car and the other is carrying plates as if waitressing. However, the women have been cut-and-pasted from these settings and placed into another: they are on a fashion catwalk, and their footwear is being observed and judged by an array of fashion journalists. The suggestion is that women should always take care over their footwear since, even if they are merely engaging in mundane chores, they must imagine that they are under stylistic scrutiny. A recent advertisement for Dove deodorant is an even more striking example of panoptical advertising.[17] The product claims to moistur-

---

13. Bartky, "Foucault."
14. See, for example, Shere Hite, *The Hite Report on the Family*, 87–88.
15. Bartky, "Foucault."
16. "Life's One Long Catwalk," *Sunday Times*, 5 October 2003, "Style" Section, 21.
17. "So No-one Sees Your Underarms, Right?" *Marie Claire*, November 2003, 246.

ize and beautify armpits. In response to the putative objection that armpits are not subject to panoptical surveillance, the product was supported by a series of advertisements showing women wearing sleeveless tops and raising their arms to perform various work-related tasks, such as changing a lightbulb. The slogan challenges women: "So no-one sees your underarms, right?" Both advertisements alert their target audience—women—to the fact that their bodies are on constant show and subject to constant evaluation, and counsel them to take the necessary steps to prepare for this ubiquitous surveillance.

Everyday rules of female appearance also illustrate the connection between power and pleasure. Women comply with appearance norms to an extent because doing so is, in myth and reality, pleasurable. The L'Oreal haircare products' advertising slogan, "Because I'm worth it," epitomizes this phenomenon. Although hair styling is tedious, repetitive, time-consuming, expensive, and prone to failure (think of the phrase "a bad hair day"), L'Oreal's message is that it is self-indulgent and luxurious to apply a set of products to your hair, wash them off with another set of products, and reapply them, day after day. Although high-heeled shoes are uncomfortable, difficult to walk in, and damaging to the skeleton, still women "treat themselves" to yet more pairs, salivating over the newest model. In an episode of the hugely popular comedy drama *Sex and the City*, the character of Miranda complains that walking to her new Brooklyn home from the subway station in her high heels hurts her feet. When her husband suggests that she carry her heels and wear sneakers for the walk, she sharply rejects the suggestion. "You can take me out of Manhattan, but you can't take me out of my shoes," she snaps.[18]

If Miranda loves her shoes, then what is wrong with her wearing them? If in any case, on Foucault's account, she could never avoid the capillary, all-encompassing reaches of power, on what basis could we condemn her high heels? How, indeed, could we distinguish between a person who follows a socially formed preference and one who is coerced to comply? Again, we see that free choice alone cannot be the arbiter of justice, for a Foucauldian analysis shows us that our choices are much less free than we think. We do not have to be acting under

18. *Sex and the City*, episode 91, season 6, "The Cold War," HBO. All the show's characters are devoted to their feet. Episode 83 of season 6 is even titled "A Woman's Right to Shoes." Sarah Jessica Parker, the actress who plays Carrie, shares her character's love of crippling stiletto heels.

the commands of a dictator to be acting in response to power. In our everyday lives, we encounter a host of factors that encourage us to act in certain ways, to form our bodies in certain ways, and to want certain things. High-heeled shoes aren't inherently, naturally sexy. On a man, even one with feminine, slender legs, the general consensus is that they look ridiculous. The distortions they produce in the male body are not seen as attractive—even though they are the same distortions that are revered in a woman. The fact that we find high heels attractive on a woman is entirely dependent on how our society constructs beauty, and this, in turn, is strongly affected by our social norms of gendered behavior. Practices are contingent on the set of social norms (or power/ knowledge regime) they support and from which they derive.

It does not follow that Miranda suffers from "false consciousness." From a Foucauldian perspective, power is not transmitted primarily through ideology, through mistaken beliefs, but through practices that are self-validating: they have no external criteria of validation. Miranda's shoes *are* beautiful, that season in New York. But they would not be beautiful without the accompanying system of discipline and sur-veillance that contrives to make them beautiful, and without this sys-tem, there would be no reason at all for her to love high heels and every reason for her to dismiss them as ridiculous—just as men do for themselves.

Without free choice or autonomy as a legitimating factor, then, we turn to equality. This move is discussed in much greater detail in Part Two. Briefly, however, the problem with disciplinary appearance norms is not just that they are different for men and women, and not just that they are more exacting and expensive (in both time and money) for women, but that their effect is to cast women as inferior. As Wolf argues in the extract quoted earlier, the ideal of youthfulness is a way of deriding female power and experience. High heels render women unable to walk or run easily. Moreover, compliance does not bring women power and respect, but rather ridicule from men who see women as being obsessed with trivia—sometimes expressed in the boredom or contempt which men may display when asked to comment on a new item of clothing, hairstyle, or waist size. Finally, beauty norms are impossible to achieve for most if not all women: most women could never be as thin or as flat-stomached as the models they try to emulate, no cream can prevent skin from becoming wrinkled, shampoo does not make hair permanently super-shiny and gravity-defying, breasts that are both large and pert are somewhat oxymoronic. Real women are not beautiful when compared with the standards expected of them. And, as Greer puts it, "Every woman knows that, regardless of all other achievements, she is a failure if she is not beautiful."[19] The disciplinary power inherent in female appearance norms, then, contributes to and perpetuates women's inequality in a way that is unjust.

The main liberal objection to the Foucauldian account of power operating through internalization is not to deny that such a process can be identified, but to deny that it represents anything more pernicious than free choice—albeit under a set of social constraints within which all of us have to operate. If, as Foucault maintains, power is everywhere, it loses its pejorative sense. If everything is power, there is no longer any distinction between a so-called free choice and a pleasure-endowed internalized norm; Foucault may refer to an action as the latter, but we might just as well refer to it as the former. It makes sense, so the criticism goes, to refer to acts that are not the product of conscious coercion by another individual as freely chosen because that reference distinguishes them from those which are. Differentiating the two enables us to see that the most important projects for a program of political liberty lie with identifiable, preventable, illegitimate constraints. As Janet Radcliffe Richards puts it, "We may argue with perfect justice that women are as they are because of social influences, but that is not enough to show that the choices they are making are not their own real choices."[20]

It might seem tempting to caricature the debate between liberalism and theories of social construction as a debate of two extremes. Foucault's claim that power is everywhere appears to entail that there is no such thing as a free choice or an autonomous subject, which would leave him no normative resources with which to condemn pernicious forms of power or domination, and no basis on which to distinguish influence from coercion. On the other hand, liberals appear to view all choices as free, autonomy as a matter of noninterference, and power as extremely limited in its effects, which leaves them with no normative resources to criticize choices that are the outcome of unjust influence. Neither caricature is entirely accurate. As I pointed out in the introduc-

19. Greer, *Whole Woman*, 19.
20. Janet Radcliffe Richards, *The Sceptical Feminist*, 115.

tion, some liberals, such as Martha Nussbaum, recognize the importance of social norms in forming preferences. Will Kymlicka claims that "liberal egalitarians rightly insist that society can only legitimately hold people responsible for their choices if their preferences and capacities have been formed under conditions of justice."[21] However, Kymlicka makes it fairly clear that his statement is more wishful thinking than statement of fact, and remarks that "liberals need to think seriously about adopting more radical politics."[22]

Foucault's position is also not quite so clear-cut. As Nancy Fraser argues, Foucault's position on normative values is ambiguous. At times it seems that Foucault rejects all normative argument and values, but elsewhere he appears to reject only *liberal* normative argument and values, and in some places he in fact relies on liberal normative argument and values. Fraser concludes that "Foucault's work ends up, in effect, inviting [normative] questions which it is structurally unequipped to answer."[23] As an example, consider his arguments about the relationship between power and freedom. Although *Discipline and Punish* depicts power as "a centralized, monolithic force with an inexorable grip on its subjects,"[24] Foucault insists in a later article that "power is exercised only over free individuals, and only insofar as they are free."[25] With the latter statement, Foucault wants to distinguish a situation characterized by power, which is fluid and retains the possibility for resistance, from a situation of slavery or victory, in which the dominant has won the battle and the victim has no chance to resist. This distinction is similar to Hannah Arendt's distinction between power and violence. For Arendt, power always operates with the consent of those who submit to it. The president of the United States, for example, is powerful only insofar as the citizens of the United States do not revolt and remove him from office: they consent, in their inaction, to his power. If they were to revolt, so that the president could maintain his role only through use of the armed forces, the president would have no power over them, but merely (resources of) violence.[26] Similarly, what

21. Will Kymlicka, *Contemporary Political Philosophy*, 93.
22. Ibid., 96.
23. Nancy Fraser, "Foucault on Modern Power," 142.
24. McNay, *Foucault and Feminism*, 38.
25. Michel Foucault, "The Subject and Power," 221.
26. Hannah Arendt, "Communicative Power." Note that, on Arendt's view, the president would still need the consent of the army in order to undertake such action, and so would still have to rely on power rather than on violence alone.

is distinctive about power for Foucault is the room it leaves for resistance, its indeterminate nature—an indeterminacy that results in part from the fact that power is creative and not (merely) repressive. As power operates by suggesting forms for human subjectivity, it can always be overruled by alternative forms. Thus we could understand Foucault not as ruling out the notion of the autonomous subject, but rather as examining the ways in which the autonomous subject submits to power. The rejection of the autonomous subject should be understood in the sense that, for Foucault, the subject can, at most, choose which norms (or, in Foucauldian terms, which regime of power/knowledge or discourse) to endorse. The individual cannot escape power entirely. In most cases, the individual will not even reflect on or consciously choose to endorse norms at all, but will remain unquestioningly within the normative context in which she was formed.

Nonetheless, Foucault's early work in particular gives the impression that power is a homogenizing, deterministic force that cannot be escaped. Such an impression is problematic because individuals living in liberal societies do not experience their lives as determined, and because liberal societies do indeed allow for more variety than Foucault's account might imply. For example, while all women do face pressures to be beautiful and to comply with appearance norms, there are in practice a variety of images, each with their own set of norms, that women can aspire to. A woman might aspire to look glamorous, with heavy makeup and elaborate clothes and jewelry, or she might aspire to a sporty look, requiring a toned physique, simpler clothes, and "natural" makeup. While both images are derived from gendered society, Foucault's account does not seem to explain how it is that women can internalize both, or how it is that an individual woman comes to internalize one image rather than another.

Bordo sounds a note of caution here. Although it is true that there is a variety of different images of the ideal female body, she argues that it is dangerous to focus on these multiple interpretations of beauty or to suggest that they foster diversity. The array of images of beauty on display in the popular media may contain some minor differences, but overall such images homogenize and normalize.[27] They homogenize because, while some deviations are permitted, fairly strict parameters of age and ethnicity are maintained. For example, one enormously

27. Bordo, *Unbearable Weight*, 24–25.

popular form of cosmetic surgery among Asian women involves inserting a crease in the eyelid to replicate Western facial features.[28] Beauty
images normalize because all images function as models for comparison, against which women should and do assess and attempt to modify
themselves.

Bordo is right to caution against an overly optimistic interpretation
of beauty norms as fostering diversity and autonomy. However, we
do still need a way of understanding how diversity develops, why an
individual situates herself at any given point, and how resistance and
change are possible. In the next chapter, I suggest that Bourdieu's work
shares many of the strengths of Foucault's analysis, but deals more
directly with these issues. It is a central claim of this book that we can
and should recognize the significant limitations on individual autonomy highlighted by a Foucauldian understanding of power and social
construction while, at the same time, continuing to strive for a society
in which autonomy is respected under conditions of equality. In other
words, everything may be a pleasure-endowed internalized norm, but
some pleasure-endowed internalized norms are better than others. We
need to take seriously liberal normative values, and the parts of Foucault's work which urge resistance to forms of domination, but we
must not complacently reduce all resistance to individuals' free
choices.

Genealogy and Genital Surgery

Although most feminist Foucauldians have focused on Foucault's account of power and discipline, another aspect of Foucault's work—
genealogy—is useful for feminism. Most basically, genealogy is concerned with the *development* of a set of norms and practices. The
premise of genealogy is that even the most specific and everyday practices provide an insight into the operation of forms of power and domination. As a result, changes in practices and norms indicate shifts in
patterns of domination. Moreover, Foucault argues that the genealogical method demonstrates that a central site for the inscription of these
norms is the body. Modes of domination operate, in part, through ideas
about how the body should be and practices that affect its shape.

28. For discussion of the connection between cosmetic surgery and racial dominance, see
Eugenia Kaw, "Medicalization of Racial Features."

Consider, for example, the case of genital surgery or circumcision, a practice that affects approximately 13 million boys and 2 million girls per year worldwide.[29] Female genital mutilation (FGM) is perhaps the clearest example of a female appearance or body norm that is fundamentally about the way women are supposed to act rather than how they are supposed to look—illustrating Foucault's claim that domination "establishes marks of its power and engraves memories on things and even within bodies."[30] In most societies in which it is practiced, FGM is designed to secure fidelity and suppress female sexuality. Efua Dorkenoo argues that FGM is often practiced for "psycho-sexual" reasons—beliefs about the nature of female sexuality which imply that it must be curtailed. She argues:

> The Mossi of Burkina Fasso, the Bambara and the Dogon in Mali believe that the clitoris would be dangerous during childbirth when contact with the baby's head would cause its death. In some areas, notably Ethiopia, people believe that if the female genitals are not excised, they will grow and dangle between the legs like a man's. . . . From these myths it can be seen that the clitoris is viewed as a "rival to the male sexual organ and is, as such, intolerable to men." Among the Bambara this is expressed in its extreme form by the belief that, upon entering an unexcised woman, a man could be killed by the secretion of a poison from the clitoris at the moment of contact with the penis. . . . In other instances society is quite direct about curtailing women's sexuality. Very frequently, the reason offered by both women and men for mutilation is "the attenuation of sexual desire." . . . In societies where a man has several wives, it is said that since it is physically impossible for him to satisfy them all, it helps if they are not too sexually demanding. It also supposedly reduces the chance of women straying.[31]

Sometimes, this misogynistic view of female sexuality is expressed via the idea that a woman's genitals are not dangerous but dirty. Dorkenoo

29. George Dennisten et al., *Understanding Circumcision*, v.

30. Michel Foucault, "Nietzsche, Genealogy, History," 85.

31. Efua Dorkenoo, *Cutting the Rose*, 34–35. See also Gerry Mackie, "Ending Footbinding and Infibulation," 1004.

notes that "in some African countries where FGM is practiced—Egypt, Somalia, Ethiopia—the external female genitals are considered dirty. . . . Yet in practice infibulation clearly has the effect opposite to that of promoting hygiene: urine and menstrual blood cannot escape naturally resulting in discomfort, odour and infection."[32]

Interestingly, this latter justification of FGM is similar to the justification for routine secular male circumcision in countries where it is widely practiced, such as the United States and South Korea. Ritual male circumcision in the Jewish and Muslim religions is not justified by any real or supposed effect on functioning, but is a symbolic, aesthetic act representing the covenant between Abraham and God.[33] Routine, secular male circumcision,[34] however, is justified by the somewhat paradoxical assertion of two beliefs: that the foreskin serves no function (so that there is no harm in removing it) and that the foreskin functions harmfully (so that it ought to be removed). Both sets of claims are highly controversial. The claim that the foreskin serves no function takes the form of denying that it plays any role in male sexual pleasure. Against this claim, some studies show that the foreskin is highly sensitive, so that removing it decreases sexual pleasure.[35] More moderately, a study of South Korean men who were circumcised after becoming sexually active found that, while 80 percent of men reported no change in their sexual pleasure, "of those who did report a difference, it was roughly twice as likely for a man to have experienced diminished sexuality than improved sexuality."[36] In relation to the positive claim, that circumcision has beneficial effects, it is argued that uncircumcised men are more prone to a variety of problems. According to Michael Katz, medical opinion on precisely what these problems are has shifted in the United States. Whereas the focus in the nineteenth century was on the prevention of what Dorkenoo calls psychosexual "problems" such as "Onanism [masturbation], Seminal Emissions, Enuresis [involuntary urination, particularly while asleep], Dysuria [painful or difficult urination], Retention [the inability to discharge

32. Dorkenoo, *Cutting the Rose*, 40.

33. See Leonard B. Glick, "Jewish Circumcision."

34. In other words, circumcision performed on babies or young boys not in response to an actually existing medical problem or to adhere to a religious rule or tradition.

35. See J. R. Taylor et al., "The Prepuce," 291–95; Nicholas Carter, *Routine Circumcision*; Billy Ray Boyd, "The Loss."

36. Myung-Geol Pang et al., "Male Circumcision in South Korea," 69.

urine, faeces or semen], General Nervousness, Impotence, Convulsions [and] Hystero-epilepsy," current justifications focus on different problems of health and hygiene, such as "Prevention of phimosis [a condition in which the foreskin is too tight and cannot be drawn back], Prevention of penile cancer, Prevention of cervical cancer, Prevention of urinary tract infections, Prevention of sexually transmitted diseases [and] Prevention of AIDS."[37] Katz's list accurately represents the reasons given in one recent Australian book aimed at parents, *In Favour of Circumcision,* which adds that circumcision is more hygienic for both the circumcised man and his partner, that "being circumcised will result in better sexual function, on average," and that "being circumcised will result in a penis that is generally regarded as more attractive."[38] The final claim rests on a vicious circle: a norm should be followed since, as it is generally followed by others, noncompliance is deviant and disadvantageous.

Katz considers the available research, and argues that contemporary claims are as scientifically suspect as those from the nineteenth century, so that neither adequately explains circumcision. For example, the research on the connection between penile cancer and circumcision is somewhat inconclusive. It seems that the most invasive forms of cancer *are* more likely in uncircumcised men, but the disease is extremely rare, too rare to merit precautionary amputation.[39] As the title of his paper argues, "The Compulsion to Circumcise Is Constant: The Reasons Keep Changing." In other words, medical justifications of routine male circumcision are post hoc rather than genuinely explanatory. The motivation to circumcise is, for Katz, social rather than medical.

If we compare this evidence on routine secular circumcision (RSC) with research on FGM, we see that contemporary FGM combines those justifications of male circumcision which are outdated with those which are still prevalent. Whereas American views of male sexuality have moved from the notion that male desire is immoral to the notion that intact male genitals are unhygienic or dangerous to health, African

37. Michael Katz, "The Compulsion to Circumcise Is Constant," 55–56.

38. Brian Morris, *In Favour of Circumcision,* 88.

39. The incidence of penile cancer among *un*circumcised men in the United States is only 0.002 percent, while the risk of "clinically significant complications" from circumcision is 0.19–1.5 percent. Contracting penile cancer if uncircumcised is thus 750 times less likely than suffering a significant complication, and only ten times more likely than dying, from circumcision. See Michael Benatar and David Benatar, "Between Prophylaxis and Child Abuse," 38–39, and S. Moses et al., "Male Circumcision," 370.

views of female sexuality combine both. FGM, like RSC viewed over the last two centuries, aims not merely to change people's bodies, but also thereby to change their *behavior* and their *preferences*. By mutilating a woman's genitals so that intercourse is extremely difficult and painful, FGM is designed to ensure both that a woman *cannot* and will *not want* to engage in sexual intercourse with anyone other than her husband (intercourse with the husband being part of marital duty rather than motivated by female pleasure). It is central to the practice that the woman's desire for intercourse, as well as her capacity to engage in it, is limited. Because the clitoris has no function other than to give the woman sexual pleasure, myths of its danger to men and babies effectively censure female sexual desire. If the only purpose of FGM were to ensure behavioral compliance with modesty norms, then other practices such as confinement would suffice.[40] FGM focuses on limiting not just a woman's ability to act on her desires, but the desires themselves. Similarly, RSC in the nineteenth century aimed at reducing the temptation for men to masturbate by reducing their penile sensitivity. However, the current justification for RSC involves a complete repudiation of this rationale, for as we saw, it is crucial to the current doctrine of routine secular circumcision that the foreskin be seen as irrelevant to sexual desire. For men in Western societies in the late twentieth and early twenty-first centuries, the aim is to increase or preserve penile sensitivity and sexual pleasure, not to reduce it. Thus, while contemporary and nineteenth-century discourse share the notion that the foreskin and thus the intact penis is dangerous to health, they sharply diverge on the question of whether and to what extent sexual desire is healthy. As Foucault puts it, "Rules are empty in themselves, violent and unfinalized; they are impersonal and can be bent to any purpose."[41] The rule that men ought to be circumcised can be bent to serve the purpose of either restricting sexual desire or increasing sexual hygiene—whichever purpose is deemed necessary by the relevant society.

This brief account of FGM and RSC is a form of genealogy. But why is genealogy in general, and of genital surgery in particular, relevant to feminism and liberalism? Two elements of the genealogical method

---

40. Indeed, Dorkenoo argues that FGM makes it easier for a woman to fake virginity or fidelity, since a reinfibulation looks just like the original one (*Cutting the Rose*, 35–36).

41. Foucault, "Nietzsche, Genealogy, History," 85–86.

are of most importance to my argument: its aim "to conceive culture as practices," and its focus on power/knowledge regimes and discontinuities in them.[42] For Foucault, as Nancy Fraser puts it, "The functioning of discursive regimes essentially involves forms of social constraint."[43] In other words, genealogy contributes to an understanding of how social and cultural practices limit individual autonomy, constraining our options, our self-understandings, and our preferences.

The first aspect of genealogy, the aim to "conceive culture as practices," is perhaps the most important in this regard. The genealogical method emphasizes the intense relationship between practices and cultural norms and interpretations, so that a study of practices serves as a study of a culture. Practices such as FGM and RSC cannot be properly understood outside their cultural context—without knowing what practices are trying to achieve, how they fit into cultural beliefs, we cannot make sense of them. The nature and accepted justification of a practice echoes the normative beliefs that are prevalent in the culture and the behaviors that are prescribed and proscribed. Thus FGM, for example, epitomizes the cultural evaluation of female sexuality and culturally prescribed female behavior. These cultural evaluations are applied not only by individuals to others but also by individuals to themselves. FGM and RSC shape not only what is done to individuals but also their own self-perceptions. Thus in South Korea, for example, RSC was unknown before the start of American trusteeship of the country in 1945 but had become massively popular by the 1960s. Although the practice was entirely new to the country, once the discourse of RSC was entrenched the circumcision rate rose to over 100 percent of newborn baby boys, meaning that it was not confined to newborn babies. Many adult men choose to undergo circumcision in order to conform to the new discourse surrounding their sexuality.[44]

A Foucauldian approach explains why choice cannot suffice as a normative transformer: the simple fact of individual choice cannot render an outcome just, even against a background of liberal equal opportunity. The fact that culture is interwoven with practices means that, in choosing to perform a particular practice, an individual is participating in a social form. While not completely dominated or determined, the

42. Fraser, "Foucault on Modern Power," 135.
43. Ibid.
44. Pang et al., "Male Circumcision in South Korea," 65.

individual does not have control over that social form: she does not control its meanings and symbolizations. Moreover, she does not control her desire to participate in it. In other words, Foucault's approach raises both of the questions that inform this book: first, whether free choice is possible at all in the face of social construction, and second, the extent to which the options from which an individual can choose are themselves just. Practices are never followed in isolation. As such, their normative nature, just or unjust, is not determined by an individual's decision to participate in them. Their justice or injustice is crucially related to the role they play in the relevant culture. This is not to say that choice plays no normative role. Where practices do not epitomize and transmit inequality, it will usually be up to the individual to choose whether or not to follow them, and coercion may render the practice unjust. Choice does not, however, *suffice* to render an outcome just: there are circumstances in which a chosen practice remains unjust, and this is because practices are inherently social and thus do not depend on individuals' choices.

This point may be clarified by considering a question that liberals often ask in discussions of the issues raised in this book: "If a woman wanted breast implants (for example) *for herself,* because she liked the way they look and feel, and not to please a man or to submit to patriarchal norms, would that be alright?"[45] Indeed, many women who do have breast implants claim that the surgery is for themselves, not for their husbands, boyfriends, or men in general.[46] Foucault's insistence that practices are always cultural suggests several points in response. Choosing to have breast implants regardless of the desires of actual men is not the same as choosing to have them immune from patriarchal norms. It would be impossible to say that a woman's desire for breast implants were independent of patriarchal norms unless she lived in a nonpatriarchal society. Her motivations, the meaning of the practice, and its effect on other people could not possibly be immune from patriarchal influence otherwise. Practices are cultural: they do not submit to the meanings that an individual wants them to have, either for herself or for others. We can see this by considering the extreme

45. I use the example of breast implants because that is the issue that most often prompts the question. I have been asked it almost exclusively by men (which might illustrate either the improbability of its premise or the predominance of men in political theory). One could ask the same question about RSC or FGM.

46. Kathy Davis, *Reshaping the Female Body,* 127.

oddity of a woman who did want to have breast implants in a society in which large breasts carried no meaning, one in which women's bodies were not objectified and sexualized and in which large breasts were not considered more attractive by society as a whole. Why on earth would anyone want to have surgery to insert heavy and dangerous alien objects into her body if there were no social meaning to, or social payoff from, the practice? A woman who did want to have breast implants in such a society would be like someone who wanted to have cosmetic knee implants in contemporary Britain. With no (unequal) norm suggesting the attractiveness of large knees there would be no injustice involved.[47] Still, the desire would be extremely perplexing, and people who had that desire would be extremely rare.[48] Indeed, the example seems implausible. Without cultural meaning, a practice does not make sense: one might say it does not exist as a practice. Until breast implants seem as peculiar as knee implants, we cannot say that a woman chooses to have them for reasons divorced from patriarchy and thus that her decision is irrelevant to justice. By extension, all choices take place in a cultural context, and depend in large part on that context for their meaning. Individual choice does not override cultural injustice.

The second part of genealogy is its orientation to discontinuity in discourses or power/knowledge regimes. A discourse or a power/ knowledge regime can be thought of as a set of social norms, a system of beliefs and practices that are upheld and assumed in a culture. With the example of RSC in the United States, we saw that the focus on disorders relating to "excessive" sexual desire was replaced by a supposedly more objective focus on physical disorders that threaten life rather than morality.[49] In Foucauldian terms, this is a discontinuity in discourse, or in power/knowledge regimes. The phrase "power/knowl-

47. In relation to the argument I make in Part Two, there would therefore be no need to prohibit the practice on grounds of justice. There might be a justification to prohibit it on simple paternalistic grounds, if the practice were sufficiently dangerous.
48. By "cosmetic knee implants" I have in mind surgery designed to make the knees larger or more knobbly. I specify this since, as Zofia Stemplowska helpfully pointed out to me, there have been unverified reports that celebrities such as Demi Moore and Nicole Kidman have had cosmetic surgery to make their knees less fatty and/or saggy. See, for example, Simpson, "Demi Completes Cosmetic Makeover."
49. This is, of course, a difficult distinction to draw, since disorders of sexual desire were seen as clinical disorders, and were thought to give rise to physical bodily disorders such as convulsions and bed-wetting. Indeed, the idea that contemporary justifications of RSC focus on threats to health and not morality makes sense only from within the contemporary power/ knowledge regime, which helps to illustrate the point.

edge regime" signifies Foucault's contention that knowledge is not objective, scientific, and absolute, but rather that it is necessarily contingent and value-laden. This claim can be understood in two senses. First, even supposedly scientific findings are influenced by normative considerations: the questions asked and the answers sought result from a normative viewpoint.[50] In the nineteenth century, for example, society was regulated according to a system of "scientific knowledge" purporting to understand and regulate physical problems of excessive desire and their relationship to the intact penis. At present, American society is regulated according to an alternative power/knowledge regime, purporting to understand and control physical problems such as cancer and AIDS and *their* supposed relationship to the intact penis. It now seems fairly obvious to us that the nineteenth-century scientific "knowledge" justifying circumcision was deeply flawed, and more a reflection of contemporary morality than of reliable evidence. Katz believes the same is true of twenty-first-century "scientific" justifications. He surveys the current clinical findings on the benefits of circumcision, and writes, "My conclusion from the examination of all these arguments is that no cogent justification has been brought forth in support of routine prophylactic circumcision. What motivates its proponents is uncertain, but their commitment remains unwavering, and they change their arguments as each one offered fails."[51] In South Korea, to take another example, doctors who advocate RSC mistakenly believe that it is practiced in countries which they see as technologically, medically, and economically advanced. Thus the majority of doctors believe that RSC is practiced in Sweden and Denmark, and that Japan but not North Korea has high levels of circumcision. In fact, only 1–2 percent of newborn boys are circumcised in Sweden and Denmark—hardly routine—and neither Japan nor North Korea practice RSC. South Korean doctors' advocacy of RSC is thus based in part on a normative view of its connection with progress, a view which contradicts the facts.[52]

In a fascinating discussion of a form of FGM or female circumcision

---

50. This point is often made concerning the funding of medical or scientific research by private companies: the problem of the research being biased toward the interests of the funding body is a very real one. See Lise Lkjaergard and Bodil Als-Nielsen, "Association Between Competing Interests and Authors' Conclusions," 249–52.

51. Katz, "Compulsion to Circumcise," 58.

52. Pang et al., "Male Circumcision in South Korea," 74.

in the United States, Sarah Webber similarly argues that an apparent *discontinuity* in the reasoning behind the practice can be explained by *continuity* in gender discourse. Webber states that removal of the clitoral prepuce was practiced in the United States from the late nineteenth century to the early twentieth century so as to *reduce* female sexual response and prevent masturbation and nymphomania, and from the late nineteenth century to the 1970s so as to *increase* female sexual response and facilitate female orgasm during marital sex in the missionary position. She argues that this apparent discontinuity in justification actually conceals a continuity: "The history of female circumcision in the United States is the history of an operation used to direct female sexuality into culturally and medically appropriate behavior: missionary-position heterosexual sex with the husband."[53]

The second way in which knowledge is power-laden is that once a certain knowledge is in place, it has normative implications. If a connection is found between the foreskin and penile cancer, it follows that circumcision ought to be practiced, and that normative sanctions exercised by doctors, friends, and the media can be applied to parents who do not circumcise their sons. The discovery of AIDS, to take another example, prompted a shift in sexual morality, one in which promiscuity, casual sex, and homosexual sex were (re-)cast as immoral in certain discourses.[54] Genealogical analysis involves seeing each set of knowledges, each discourse, as a regime of power, a way in which norms and practices complement and support each other. A discontinuity in practices, or a discontinuity in the justification and "evidence" in support of one particular practice, represents a shift in the form of social constraint. A shift in knowledge is never inconsequential from the point of view of constraint. Rather, it reconfigures the form of the constraint.

Foucault's conception of genealogy is crucial to liberalism because it illustrates the problems with the liberal tendency to consider an individual's freedom in isolation from the discourses and norms surrounding her. By reducing questions of justice to questions of choice, liberals effectively deny the importance of culture to practice, the importance of power in perpetuating practices, and the role that practices play in

53. Sarah Webber, "Cutting History, Cutting Culture," 66.
54. See, for example, Lynne Segal, "Lessons from the Past"; Simon Watney, "AIDS, 'Moral Panic' Theory and Homophobia"; and Timothy F. Murphy, *Ethics in an Epidemic*.

perpetuating regimes of power/knowledge. Saying that an individual chooses to participate in a practice is to say only that she was not coerced, in a Hayekian sense.[55] The difference between choice and coercion is normatively relevant: in many cases, an otherwise unproblematic act becomes an injustice if coerced. But this distinction does not begin to exhaust the normative questions concerning the practice, or to capture the extent to which an individual has acted autonomously. In order to understand the implications of a practice for justice, we need to understand the role that the practice plays in a general social context, its position in a power/knowledge regime. We need to understand the part that the practice plays in constructing the practitioner as a subject: the implications that the practice has for the status, role, and advantage of the individual, as they appear to herself and to others. To assert that breast implants, FGM, or RSC are merely a matter of individual or parental choice is to deny the place of those practices in the wider normative context, and to ignore the intricate ways in which the practices are perpetuated by power and powerfully perpetuate themselves.

Three Problems with Liberalism

This brief analysis of Foucault's work highlights three problems with liberalism and the liberal focus on choice.

First, the liberal focus on choice is a focus on the mental, ideological, and intellectual at the expense of the physical, practical, and everyday. For liberals, the main consideration tends to be the thoughts of the individual concerned, her beliefs and her expressed preferences. Consequently, liberalism is not particularly sensitive to the ways in which power and injustice reside and are perpetuated in the physical and the everyday. Inequality, in other words, is not confined to the beliefs of individuals, but extends to their habitual, physical actions. Social norms are embodied in individuals. Their compliance is habitual and physical, not (only) self-consciously decided upon. Compliance with norms does not, then, necessarily indicate consent, and dissent does not necessarily enable disobedience. A parent who has her son rou-

---

55. By "coercion in a Hayekian sense" I mean intentional interference exercised by one human being over another. See F. A. von Hayek, *The Constitution of Liberty*.

tinely circumcised may not have considered why, and an active feminist may still wear high heels.

Second, the liberal focus on choice is a focus on the individual at the expense of the social. While the relevant normative question for the liberal is "does this particular individual want to follow this practice, and what does it mean for her?" a Foucauldian approach alerts us to the inherently social nature of practices. As a result, it demonstrates that individuals' choices can never be assessed in isolation from the cultural context in which they take place, and a particular practice cannot be considered in isolation from the meaning it has for the community as a whole. More specifically, the justice of a practice or a choice is not usually determined by the individual who initiates it, but relies in large part on the role it plays in the overall system of (in)equality. Liberal focus on the individual fails to notice how individual actions fit into social structures of (in)justice.

Third, liberalism tends to conceptualize power as a negative, repressive force, one that constrains individuals by ruling out alternatives. Hence the liberal focus on state nonintervention as the guarantor of liberty. If power is repressive, then state power simply stops individuals from pursuing their goals. If we remove state obstacles to individual choice, then we remove power and increase freedom. A Foucauldian analysis alerts us, however, to the significance of power as a creative force, one that suggests ideas and forms subjects. Even if we were to eradicate all repressive power, we would leave creative power untouched. Individuals would still act in response to social norms and constraints, but since people are shaped by creative power, those constraints would be internal to them. Even when there is no guard in the panopticon's watchtower, the prisoners still conform to the prison rules. So too with the state: even if it conformed to liberal neutrality, individuals would still conform to the rules of their community. The third problem with liberalism, then, is that it disregards the creativity of power. As a result, the injustice transmitted through such power is ignored.

2

MASCULINE DOMINATION, RADICAL FEMINISM, AND CHANGE

Pierre Bourdieu and Catharine MacKinnon are two major theorists of social construction whose analyses of gender appear at first glance to be diametrically opposed. Consider the following excerpt from Bourdieu:

> I have always been astonished . . . that the established order, with its relations of domination, its rights and prerogatives, privileges and injustices, ultimately perpetuates itself so easily, apart from a few historical accidents, and that the most intolerable conditions of existence can so often be perceived as acceptable and even natural. And I have also seen masculine domination, and the way it is imposed and suffered, as the prime example of this paradoxical submission.[1]

For Bourdieu, then, gender appears to be if not immutable then at least extraordinarily resistant. For MacKinnon, in contrast, gender seems to be a much more fluid, transcendable discourse:

> When one gets to know women close up and without men present, it is remarkable the extent to which their so-called biology, not to mention their socialization, has failed. The discovery that these apparently unmanageable dictates of the natural order are powerful social conventions often makes women feel unburdened, since individual failures no longer appear so individualized. Women become angry as they see women's lives as one avenue after another foreclosed by gender.[2]

---

1. Pierre Bourdieu, *Masculine Domination*, 1–2.
2. Catharine MacKinnon, *Toward a Feminist Theory of the State*, 91.

This apparent difference may go some way toward explaining why Bourdieu and MacKinnon are seldom read together. In fact, however, the two approaches have much in common. Both portray gender and gender inequality as overwhelmingly socially constructed, and they share some of the most useful features of Foucault's approach but have fewer problems: unlike Michel Foucault, Bourdieu and MacKinnon explicitly theorize both gender and change.[3] Their theories are by no means identical. But both approaches are instructive for our purposes since they provide a framework for analyzing gender in terms of both social construction and normative critique.

Both Bourdieu and MacKinnon claim to have negotiated a path between the extremes of determinism and voluntarism. It is partly this claim that has led some feminists to consider Bourdieu's work on gender, and to question whether it might offer a corrective to the more deterministic moments of the more popular Foucault.[4] However, despite his claims to the contrary, Bourdieu seems to deny the possibility of women's agency—a key problem for feminists. I argue that while Bourdieu's work is useful for understanding the entrenchment of gender, the strategies he proposes for change are not well suited to changes in gender systems even on his own terms. I suggest that Bourdieu's account is more conducive to change if we supplement it with a strategy for change endorsed by MacKinnon: consciousness-raising. Combining features of both approaches helps us to theorize both the entrenchment and the rejection of gender hierarchy.

Constructing Gender Inequality

In *Masculine Domination,* Bourdieu asks why gender inequality has persisted throughout history despite significant social change. In general, Bourdieu is concerned with the question of why it is that many forms of domination persist with relatively few challenges: left to themselves and in the normal course of things, individuals will not disrupt

3. For a comparison between Foucault and MacKinnon, see Vanessa E. Munro, "On Power and Domination"; and for a comparison between MacKinnon and liberalism, see Denise Schaeffer, "Feminism and Liberalism Reconsidered."

4. See, for example, Lisa Adkins, "Reflexivity"; Terry Lovell, "Thinking Feminism with and Against Bourdieu"; Lois McNay, *Gender and Agency* and "Gender, Habitus and the Field"; and Veronique Mottier, "Masculine Domination."

structures of domination, such as patriarchy, from which they suffer (or benefit). Even if they have read and agreed with key feminist texts, most women do not stop wearing makeup, taking on the lion's share of the housework and childcare, wearing restrictive and uncomfortable clothes and shoes that emphasize sexual availability, or being attracted to men with characteristics of dominance such as a powerful physique or job. Even if we believe that our desires are indeed the product of the norms and expectations of a patriarchal society, still we do actually *like* makeup, high heels, and men who are tall, buffed, and wealthy.[5]

A central reason for the success of patriarchy, Bourdieu argues, is its ability to naturalize its distinctions. At the heart of any system of hierarchy is the distinction made between those who occupy different hierarchical positions. The system of masculine domination owes its success at least in part to its provision of "natural," biological explanations for hierarchy. This point was also made within the liberal tradition by John Stuart Mill in *The Subjection of Women*. In response to the claim that sexual inequality is natural, Mill asks, "Was there ever any domination which did not appear natural to those who possessed it? . . . So true is it that unnatural generally means only uncustomary, and that everything which is usual appears natural."[6]

The naturalization of gender hierarchy is reinforced in several ways. Women *are*, according to the patriarchal story, different from men in that they have different bodies and different biological functions. They *must be* different from each other so as to reproduce; the differences could not be wished away, for without sex differences we would have no means of perpetuating the species. Moreover, these differences *justify* different positions on a hierarchy in that they dictate different behaviors for men and women regarding matters such as childcare, breadwinning, and courtship, which affect the wider social positions of the sexes.

Instead, Bourdieu argues that the categories of gender are constructed and not necessary.[7] Gender differences start with the socially constructed and thus contingent division of people into two kinds according to their bodies, and specifically their genitals. To say that this

5. For examples of this process, see Simone de Beauvoir, *The Second Sex*, 694–95; Laura Sanchez and Elizabeth Thomson, "Becoming Mothers and Fathers," 766; and Pepper Schwartz, *Love Between Equals*.

6. John Stuart Mill, *The Subjection of Women*, 127–28.

7. Bourdieu, *Masculine Domination*, 11–12, 15.

is a contingent division is not to say that everyone could in theory have the same genitals, or that there is no biological difference between men and women, but it is to say that differences between genitals need not be socially significant. Christine Helliwell describes a tribe in Indonesian Borneo, the Gerai, for whom differences in work, not differences in genitals, are the determinants of a system of classification comparable to gender.[8] Although there are people with different genitals in the Gerai tribe, this fact is not seen as particularly significant, and certainly not as the determinant of gender. While there is a correlation between different genitals and different genders for the Gerai, this correlation is contingent and not necessary. In Western societies, for example, it is overwhelmingly women and not men who provide the primary care for babies in their first weeks of life. However, genitals and not childcare are the determinant of gender: a person with a penis who is the prime caregiver for a newborn baby is still a man. For the Gerai, in contrast, it is the work that is determining—a person who performs certain tasks in rice cultivation is a man, even if that person has a vulva. Helliwell herself was categorized as a man for some time after her arrival in the tribe as a result of the work she was able to do, despite the fact that everyone in the tribe frequently observed her genitals when she urinated in the stream used for that purpose. Thus, "As someone said to me at a later point, 'Yes, I saw that you had a vulva, but I thought that Western men might be different.'"[9]

Genital difference, then, does not necessarily signify different roles or identities. But once the difference between genitals has been instituted as socially significant, it is justified by reference to the naturalness of the distinction. In other words, in answer to the question "Why are genital differences socially significant?" the answer given would be something like "because there are differences in genitals." Moreover, this difference is further idolized by its naturalness. If we ask, "Why are there differences in genitals?" we will receive the answer "because that is how nature is," which is something like saying "because it couldn't be any other way." This circular reasoning leads, Bourdieu argues, to symmetry between the subjective and objective elements of domination. Subjectively, people believe that there are significant differences based on genital differences. Objectively, there are genital dif-

8. Christine Helliwell, "It's Only a Penis," 805–6.
9. Ibid., 806.

ferences. The circularity comes in as follows: people believe that there are significant differences based on genitals because they are inclined to notice and reify differences based on genitals, and people are inclined to notice and reify such differences because they believe that they exist. In sum, one of the key reasons for success of the system of male domination is its ability to make itself appear as natural—not only in the sense that differences between genitals are natural, but also in the sense that social differences based on differences between genitals appear natural.

This analysis is strongly redolent of MacKinnon. Contrary to Vanessa Munro's analysis of MacKinnon as committed to "essentialism" and to the assumption of sex difference as the "point of departure,"[10] MacKinnon fundamentally rejects the idea that categories of gender are primarily biological, or that gender equality is precluded by biological differences. For MacKinnon, sexuality is the prime site of gender inequality, but this is not the result of any biological imperative.[11] Rather than being a matter of biology—or indeed a matter of morality or psychology—gender is, she argues, a matter of *politics* and a matter of *power*. This analysis of gender in terms of power is, of course, at the heart of feminism. As MacKinnon puts it, "Distinctions of body or mind or behavior are pointed to as cause rather than effect, with no realization that they are so deeply effect rather than cause that pointing to them at all is an effect. Inequality comes first, difference comes after."[12] A side effect of MacKinnon's analysis is that the terms "sex" and "gender" lose their distinctiveness. "Sex" is often taken to refer to the natural, biological differences between men and women, with "gender" reserved for the social differences. However, the foregoing implies that the division is not so clear-cut: any difference is social in the sense that it is a social contingency that the difference is considered significant. As a result, MacKinnon uses the terms "sex" and "gender" interchangeably, as I do in this book.[13]

10. Munro, "On Power and Domination," 83, 86, 95.
11. MacKinnon, *Toward a Feminist Theory of the State*, 109.
12. Ibid., 219. Andrea Dworkin similarly argues that the now-abandoned Chinese practice of footbinding served to create gender difference. As she puts it: "*Footbinding did not emphasize the differences between men and women—it created them*, and they were then perpetuated in the name of morality" (*Woman Hating*, 103; emphasis in the original).
13. MacKinnon, *Toward a Feminist Theory of the State*, xiii. The distinction between sex and gender, with its implication that "sex" differences are natural and objective, is also criticized by Judith Butler in *Gender Trouble* and Moira Gatens in "Power, Bodies and Difference."

Bourdieu shares this aspect of MacKinnon's approach, but his failure to distinguish "sex" and "gender" is criticized by Veronique Mottier as "the most problematic aspect of his gender analysis."[14] Mottier argues that a failure to distinguish the two concepts equates to an analysis of gender solely in terms of sexual difference, without any reference to the role of gender power. However, as the foregoing analysis shows, this criticism is incorrect. The denial of a difference between sex and gender can take either a patriarchal or a feminist form. The patriarchal form is the focus of Bourdieu's criticism: the idea that inequalities of status or power are the natural result of, and therefore justified by, differences in sexual organs. In countering this patriarchal form, feminists can either introduce a sex/gender distinction, as Mottier advocates, or they can argue that sexual differences are themselves imbued with, are in some sense the result of, gender power. As MacKinnon points out, a sex/gender distinction rests on the assumption that there is such a thing as sexual difference that is not imbued with power, and it is precisely this assumption that her radical feminist theory challenges. As she puts it, pointing to sexual difference *at all,* even from a feminist perspective, is an effect of gender power. Bourdieu, far from returning to the patriarchal rejection of the sex/gender distinction, joins MacKinnon in rejecting the distinction from the radical feminist perspective.

Symbolic Violence and Sexuality

If gender is socially constructed, it remains to be seen what form that social construction takes and what its organizing principle is. Bourdieu conceptualizes gender in terms of symbolic violence; for MacKinnon, sexuality is the organizing principle. The two ideas are similar because, for MacKinnon, sexuality is characterized by the eroticization of gender hierarchy, an idea that resonates with symbolic violence and which Bourdieu explicitly endorses.

MacKinnon analyzes gender in terms of the eroticization of male dominance and female submission. This patriarchal form of sexuality imprints itself deep into the bodies, thoughts, and identities of individuals. Moreover, for MacKinnon as well as for Bourdieu, sexuality is deeply hierarchical. For MacKinnon, the eroticization of hierarchy per-

14. Mottier, "Masculine Domination," 350.

vades sexuality within patriarchy and, moreover, defines patriarchy politically.[15] Men's power over women writ large is structured around male sexual power. Power and sexuality are intimately intertwined for MacKinnon, with power structuring sexuality and sexuality reinforcing power.[16] As is the case in Foucauldian analysis, pleasure plays a central role in this process. Sex, and eroticized inequality, are deeply pleasurable for both women and men. Ranging from Pat Califia's fervent defense of sadomasochism, through the rape fantasies of the many women interviewed by Nancy Friday, to the clichés of men sweeping women off their feet in bodice rippers from Mills and Boon to Barbara Cartland,[17] hierarchical sex becomes the source of pleasure and fantasy as well as the source of rape, abuse, and distress. Thus MacKinnon observes that sexuality's "pleasure [is] the experience of power in its gendered form."[18]

Bourdieu agrees with MacKinnon's analysis, stating that sexual relations are "constructed though the fundamental principle of division between the active male and the passive female," a division that "creates, organizes, expresses and directs desire—male desire as the desire for possession, eroticized domination, and female desire as the desire for masculine domination, as eroticized subordination or even, in the limiting case, as the eroticized recognition of domination."[19] For Bourdieu, this phenomenon is understood in terms of symbolic violence, defined as "the *violence which is exercised upon a social agent with his or her complicity.*"[20] Symbolic violence is expressed not physically on the bodies of those it violates, but mentally on thoughts. It causes those who are subject to it to assent to, and thus be complicit with, its dictates. Gender inequality is *symbolic* violence because women (and men) comply willingly, with no need for intentional or forcible coercion, and

15. MacKinnon, *Toward a Feminist Theory of the State*, 241, 137.

16. Ibid., 151.

17. Pat Califia, "Feminism and Sadomasochism"; Nancy Friday, *My Secret Garden*. Recent Mills and Boon titles include *Christmas at His Command, At the Playboy's Pleasure, The Thawing of Mara, A Rich Man's Revenge, Surrender to a Playboy, The Bedroom Surrender, Surrender to the Millionaire,* and *Back in the Boss's Bed.* Similar Cartland titles include *The Cruel Count, The Taming of a Tigress, Kneel for Mercy, The Marquis Wins, Punished With Love, Dangerous Dandy, Complacent Wife, Odious Duke, Poor Governess, Theresa and a Tiger,* and *Royal Punishment.*

18. MacKinnon, *Toward a Feminist Theory of the State*, xiii.

19. Bourdieu, *Masculine Domination*, 21.

20. Pierre Bourdieu and Loïc Wacquant, *An Invitation to Reflexive Sociology*, 167; emphasis in the original.

because its effect is to create symbolic normative images of ideal gendered behavior. Compliance is willing precisely because it never needs to be sought: patriarchy operates significantly through the construction of desires and thoughts, influencing what choices people want to make so that some options are ruled out beforehand. As will be discussed in the next section, Bourdieu conceptualizes this shaping of individuals in terms of "habitus": a durable set of dispositions formed in response to objective social conditions. As a result, patriarchy does not need to rely on the heavy-handed and resistance-prone mechanism of ruling out options after people have decided that they would like to choose them. Instead, compliance is secured more easily by ruling out options before they are considered, so that people never come to choose. In this respect, Bourdieu's approach echoes that of Foucault. Women's compliance is a *prereflexive* compliance: it does not need to be consciously accepted and affirmed because it is always and already the organizing idea of consciousness.[21] The combination of apparent naturalness and symbolic violence renders systems of male domination extremely solid.

Habitus and Field

Bourdieu uses the concept of habitus to explain how social norms become embedded in individuals. An individual's habitus develops, for Bourdieu, in response to the social sphere in which the individual lives and acts: a space Bourdieu terms the "field."[22] A field is a sphere of action that places certain limits on those who act within it, according to their status within the field. That status in turn is determined by the capital, or the collection of resources, the individual has. Different fields prioritize different forms of capital, such as education, money, honor, and beauty.

As Bourdieu points out, the fact that a field imposes certain rules on its members does not in itself explain why those rules are obeyed. Bourdieu offers an explanation for this obedience in terms of habitus. The habitus is the means by which objective social structures are reproduced *in the body,* and thereby influence individuals' actions. The habitus is produced in response to certain external conditions, and itself

---

21. Bourdieu, *Masculine Domination,* 35.
22. Bourdieu and Wacquant, *Invitation to Reflexive Sociology,* 97.

produces certain kinds of actions. The habitus is a durable disposition to act in a certain way, which comes into existence as a result of the objective conditions of existence within a particular society or field. The habitus is both a "structured structure"—the effect of the actions of other people—and a "structuring structure"—it suggests and constrains the individual's actions.[23] The habitus is the result of human interaction. Thus Charles Taylor argues that "following rules is a *social practice*"[24] and describes the habitus as capturing "this level of social understanding."[25]

As people respond to the circumstances within which they live, they become accustomed to those particular responses and, over time, repeat them with little or no conscious awareness or choice—whether or not the conditions that first made the response appropriate actually pertain. Bourdieu's preferred example is "the small, quick steps of some young women wearing trousers and flat heels"[26] which have become habitual because they are required when wearing short skirts and high heels. In this way, the habitus prompts us to act in certain ways without needing to go via the mechanism of conscious thought and rational decision-making. Instead, the habitus operates through the mechanism of embodiment. We understand the norms we obey through acting them out. We do not think consciously about them, and consider on each occasion whether to comply with them. Rather, we comply as a result of prereflexive, habitualized action.[27] Moreover, as MacKinnon argues, what is at stake is not merely whether we will *act* in certain ways. What is at stake is whether we *become* certain sorts of people, how particular discourses construct our identities. Thus MacKinnon quotes a woman coerced into pornography: "You do it, you do it, and you do it; then you become it."[28]

For Bourdieu, an individual's range of possible actions is already suggested by her habitus. If the habitus and field are aligned, what an individual feels inclined to do will match the expectations of the field in which her action takes place. There will be compatibility between action and expectation, and the individual is unlikely to be aware of, or

23. Pierre Bourdieu, *The Logic of Practice*, 53.
24. Taylor, "To Follow a Rule . . . ," 48; emphasis in the original.
25. Ibid., 51.
26. Bourdieu, *Masculine Domination*, 29.
27. Pierre Bourdieu, *Pascalian Meditations*, 170–71.
28. MacKinnon, *Toward a Feminist Theory of the State*, 123.

consciously assess, her actions and dispositions. Individuals are thus very significantly influenced by the surroundings and structures in which they live.[29] As individuals tend to remain in social contexts in which they feel comfortable, their habituses are reinforced and tend to remain constant. It follows, moreover, that the social structures that influence an individual's habitus will be strengthened over time as individuals act in ways that are suggested by, and serve to reinforce, those structures. In other words, in the absence of the kind of dissonance between habitus and field that can lead individuals to become conscious and questioning of their dispositions, systems of disadvantage are unlikely to be disrupted by those who are disadvantaged.

Gender and Field

It is not entirely clear how gender fits into Bourdieu's analysis of habitus and field. It clearly makes sense to think of a gendered habitus, a set of bodily dispositions ordered along gendered lines. The gendered body is a prime example of one ordered by norms, or discipline: women and men hold and use their bodies differently in ways that cannot be explained by biological difference alone. Bourdieu himself provides many such examples of a gendered habitus, such as the effect of clothing.[30]

As a central element of Bourdieu's work is his argument that habitus develops in response to field, it is natural to ask which field is responsible for the development of a gendered habitus. Some feminists have suggested, albeit in other terms, that the *family* is the field in which the habitus is gendered; or the field to which women are confined and in which the female habitus is developed, with the male habitus developing in response to the field of the workplace.[31] Bourdieu explicitly rejects these ideas. The family does operate as a field for Bourdieu, but in the sense that it is the general site of transmission of "economic, cultural and symbolic privileges,"[32] such as those associated with class. The family is not, he argues, the place where masculine

29. Bourdieu and Wacquant, *Invitation to Reflexive Sociology*, 136.
30. Bourdieu's account of the effects of wearing short skirts and high heels has already been described, but see also Bourdieu, *Masculine Domination*, 29.
31. See, for example, Okin, *Justice, Gender and the Family*, and Betty Friedan, *The Feminine Mystique*.
32. Pierre Bourdieu, "On the Family as a Realized Category," 23; see also *Pascalian Meditations*, 167, and *Practical Reason*, 19, 64–67.

domination is principally perpetuated. Instead it is "in agencies such as the school or the state . . . where principles of domination that go on to be exercised within even the most private universe are developed and imposed."[33]

We are left, then with a problem: if the habitus is formed in the context of a specific field but there is no specific field in which the habitus becomes gendered, what is the source of gender difference? Terry Lovell argues that, in the context of Bourdieu's work, gender should be understood in terms of *capital*. Women should be understood simultaneously as "objects—as repositories of capital for someone else" and as "capital-accumulating subjects."[34] But while this interpretation does shed light on many aspects of gendered experience, it does not explain how the suggestive concept of habitus plays a part: how gender becomes embodied. Perhaps the best way to integrate habitus with gender is to conclude that the gendered habitus develops not in response to any one specific field, but rather in response to the gender norms, the symbolic violence, occurring throughout society. Thus, although the family clearly is a site of the perpetuation of gender norms, it is by no means the only such site. We might think of each field as containing (at least) three sets of rules. First, each field is susceptible to some extent to the economic rules of capitalism (or the prevailing economic order). Some fields are more autonomous in this regard than others, but Bourdieu follows Marx in believing that the economic order invades all fields and is partly responsible for their structure.[35] Second, a field contains the rules that pertain to it specifically. Thus the academic field, for example, is influenced by material concerns, but also places value on other forms of capital such as tenure and publications. Third, each field contains and enforces a set of gender rules: norms about the appropriate behavior of the sexes within that field. These gender rules may merely be those that are common to many other fields (general appearance norms, for example), or they may be specific to that field (for example, formal or informal rules concerning which tasks in a factory should be performed by which gender). As with economic rules, some fields may be more autono-

---

33. Bourdieu, *Masculine Domination*, 4.

34. Lovell, "Thinking Feminism," 22.

35. Bourdieu is highly critical of other aspects of Marx's work, such as Marx's failure to separate theoretical classes from actual classes (*Practical Reason*, 11), his focus on consciousness (*Pascalian Meditations*, 172), and his account of ideology (*Pascalian Meditations*, 177).

mous from gender rules than others, but all fields embody some gender rules, and some gender rules apply in all fields. The gendered habitus thus develops in response to all fields, as gender norms are
enforced in comparable if not identical ways across all fields.

Although Bourdieu does not make this argument in the specific
form in which I present it here, I propose that it is the best way to
combine his analysis of gender with his argument that habitus develops in response to field. Moreover, this analysis sits happily with many
feminist accounts, not least because it implies, as Bourdieu points out,
that "a vast field of action is opened up for feminist struggles, which
are thus called upon to take a distinctive and decisive place within
political struggles against *all* forms of domination."[36] In other words,
the possibility of change is introduced.

Change

In Chapter 1, I argued that a Foucauldian perspective on social construction raises problems for the liberal notion that individual autonomy can best be guaranteed by noninterference. However, this point is
made so effectively in parts of Foucault's work that it calls into question
the very possibility of autonomous action, and undermines the
grounds for normative judgment. Bourdieu explicitly attempts to theorize a combination of social influence and individual autonomy, and
thus to avoid the implication of determinism that sometimes limits
Foucault's work. However, although Bourdieu intends to make room
for human agency, his emphasis tends to be on the social constraints
that almost determine individuals, rather than on the opportunities for
resistance, autonomy, or freedom (terms which do not sit easily with
his approach).

Lois McNay suggests that the very value of Bourdieu's work is that it
demonstrates the *difficulty* of change: it "provides a corrective to certain
theories of reflexive transformation which overestimate the extent to
which individuals living in posttraditional order are able to reshape
identity."[37] The concept of habitus draws our attention to the ways in
which norms are imprinted on our bodies, so that it will take more

---

36. Bourdieu, *Masculine Domination*, 4; emphasis in the original.
37. McNay, "Gender, Habitus and the Field," 113.

than a simple act of will or a consciousness-raising class for us to resist or alter them. Change, then, is difficult. The key question for feminists is whether or not Bourdieu's approach in particular, and the idea of social construction in general, gives any chance for change.

In line with McNay's argument, no reader of *Masculine Domination* could get the impression that gender norms can easily be resisted. Indeed, the explicit message is often that such norms cannot be resisted at all. In passages that echo Shulamith Firestone's claim that "no matter how many levels of consciousness one reaches, the problem always goes deeper. It is everywhere,"[38] Bourdieu describes how women are "condemned" to participate in the symbolic violence of gender,[39] and "cannot fail" to adhere to structures and agents of domination.[40] Moreover, the only strategies that women have to overcome male domination are deeply problematic, requiring women to efface themselves and thus confirm "the dominant representation of women as maleficent beings."[41] It seems we must conclude, with Bourdieu, that "*all* the conditions for the *full* exercise of male domination are thus combined."[42]

It is easy to see, then, how the reader could find herself sympathetic to what McNay calls the "common criticism of Bourdieu's work"[43]—namely, its implications of determinism—despite Bourdieu's frequent denials. As Lovell puts it, Bourdieu's work "is at times bleakly pessimistic."[44] Resisting symbolic violence seems almost impossible on Bourdieu's analysis, as its structures of dominance reach so deeply into the understanding. If we can perceive the world only through such structures, where will we find the material from which to construct an alternative consciousness? If women have only the cognitive instruments of patriarchy, how can we theorize feminism?

These determinist implications have some truth: gender norms cannot be overcome by a "simple" act of will alone. For example, knowing that we wear makeup because there are significant pressures on us to do so, and regretting that fact as it renders us objectified, is not enough

38. Shulamith Firestone, "The Dialectic of Sex," 90.
39. Bourdieu, *Masculine Domination*, 30, 32.
40. Ibid., 35; see also Bourdieu, *Pascalian Meditations*, 170.
41. Bourdieu, *Masculine Domination*, 32.
42. Ibid., 33; emphasis added.
43. McNay, "Gender, Habitus and the Field," 100.
44. Lovell, "Thinking Feminism," 27.

to stop us from deriving at least some pleasure from selecting and applying it. However, parts of Bourdieu's analysis also imply that it will be difficult if not impossible for us even to conceptualize radical change, for he asserts that women living under patriarchy lack the cognitive resources to do so.[45] Such a conclusion is problematic for it seems to rule out social change and conflicts with the fact that change does occur, sometimes as the result of radical theorizing, for example, of feminists about and against patriarchy.

Consciousness-Raising and Reflexivity

For MacKinnon, consciousness-raising is fundamental to feminism: it is feminism's method.[46] Precisely because gender and gender hierarchy are socially constructed phenomena, it is necessary for feminists to attempt to deconstruct them, via consciousness-raising. Moreover, the fact that women are themselves partially constituted by the symbolic violence of gender makes consciousness-raising not less effective, as Bourdieu argues, but more effective:

> Feminist method as practiced in consciousness raising, taken as a theory of knowing about social being, pursues another epistemology. Women are presumed able to have access to society and its structure because they live in it and have been formed by it, not in spite of those facts. . . . Feminist epistemology asserts that the social process of being a woman is on some level the same process as that by which woman's consciousness becomes aware of itself as such and of its world. Mind and world, as a matter of social reality, are taken as interpenetrated.[47]

It is not the case, MacKinnon asserts, that the social construction of dominated individuals prevents them from conceptualizing their domination. Whereas Bourdieu's account of symbolic violence casts doubt on the possibility of female emancipation with its idea that women "cannot fail" to adhere to principles of masculine domination since they have "only cognitive instruments that [are] no more than the em-

45. Bourdieu, *Masculine Domination*, 35; Bourdieu, *Pascalian Meditations*, 170.
46. MacKinnon, *Toward a Feminist Theory of the State*, 83.
47. Ibid., 98.

bodied form of the relation of domination,"[48] MacKinnon's account asserts that it is precisely *because* women's consciousnesses are formed by patriarchal social structures that women have access to and can understand the nature of patriarchy. Far from entrenching women's inferiority, consciousness-raising "shows women their situation in a way that affirms they can act to change it."[49]

What MacKinnon's approach shows is that consciousness-raising as a method of change is *particularly* suited to analysis in terms of habitus. Because habitus ties together social structures of domination and the lived experiences, actions, and thoughts of individuals, it follows that individuals can understand those social structures by looking inward, at themselves, as well as outward, at the world. If we start to think about the way we act and the preferences we have, the wider institutions of gender inequality begin to be revealed. As MacKinnon puts it, "Consciousness means a good deal more than a set of ideas. It constitutes a lived knowing of the social reality of being female. . . . [Consciousness-raising] built an experienced sense of how it came to be this way and that it can be changed."[50] Consciousness-raising complements habitus since habitus forges the link between individual experience and social structure that consciousness-raising investigates.

Indeed, feminist consciousness-raising often did inquire into the minutiae of women's lives, the repeated daily activities that form the habitus. As MacKinnon reports, "Extensive attention was paid to small situations and denigrated pursuits that made up the common life of women in terms of energy, time, intensity, and definition—prominently, housework and sexuality."[51] Attention was also paid to the habitualization of appearance and deportment norms, as a 1971 feminist consciousness-raising exercise for men demonstrates. It directs men to "run a short distance, keeping your knees together. You'll find you have to take short, high steps if you run this way. Women have been taught it is unfeminine to run like a man with long, free strides. See how far you get running this way for 30 seconds."[52] Such exercises aimed to make the gendered habitus explicit and thus open to change. Consciousness-raising thus paved the way for Bourdieu's

48. Bourdieu, *Masculine Domination*, 35.
49. MacKinnon, *Toward a Feminist Theory of the State*, 101.
50. Ibid., 90–91.
51. Ibid., 87.
52. Cited in Susan Bordo, "Feminism, Foucault and the Politics of the Body," 186.

assertion that the smallest everyday actions of individuals result from, and thus can give insight into, overarching social rules and patterns.

Despite this apparent harmony between consciousness-raising and analysis in terms of habitus, Bourdieu is ambivalent about consciousness-raising. Indeed, at times, he explicitly rejects it: "The symbolic revolution called for by the feminist movement cannot be reduced to a simple conversion of consciousness and wills . . . the relation of complicity that the victims of symbolic domination grant to the dominant can only be broken through a radical transformation of the social conditions of production of the dispositions that lead the dominated to take on the point of view of the dominant on the dominant and on themselves."[53] Bourdieu's stand on this point echoes his Marxist belief that radical change must be at least institutional and at best economic. This belief cannot be applied to gender without some qualifications, however. Although symbolic violence is perpetuated through social and state institutions, and thus cannot be completely overthrown without institutional change, its symbolic nature isolates it to some degree from the larger economic order. As Nancy Fraser persuasively argues, it would be mistaken to attempt to remedy recognitional disadvantage with (purely) redistributive measures.[54] At times, it seems as though Bourdieu is prey to such confusion.

On the other hand, some of the methods for change Bourdieu does endorse bear a resemblance to consciousness-raising. First, Bourdieu exhorts women to "invent and impose forms of collective organization and action and effective weapons, *especially symbolic ones,* capable of shaking the political and legal institutions which play a part in perpetuating their subordination."[55] This *invention* of new *symbolic* weapons looks very like the consciousness-raising commended in the Manifesto of the Redstockings, the radical feminist group founded by Shulamith Firestone and Ellen Willis in 1969: "Our chief task at present is to develop a female class consciousness through sharing experience and publicly exposing the sexist foundation of all our institutions. Consciousness-raising . . . is the only method by which we can ensure that our program for liberation is based on the concrete realities of our lives."[56] Moreover, Bourdieu's theory of reflexive sociology demands

53. Bourdieu, *Masculine Domination*, 41–42.
54. Nancy Fraser, *Justice Interruptus*.
55. Bourdieu, *Masculine Domination*, ix; emphasis added.
56. Cited in Miriam Schneir, *The Vintage Book of Feminism*, 128.

that sociologists reflect on the social contexts that inform their work, and suggests that such reflection or "reflexivity" can be effective even without institutional change. As Loïc Wacquant argues, reflexivity entails "the systematic exploration of the 'unthought categories of thought which delimit the unthinkable and predetermine the thought.'"[57] Gendered symbolic violence is a paradigmatic example of an unthought category of thought, making reflexivity applicable to gender. If we attempt to identify our habitus, to bring it to consciousness, we can start to resist the social structures to which it corresponds. Bourdieu himself makes this argument when not discussing gender.[58]

Of course, the symbolic transformation entailed by consciousness-raising is not enough. Institutions must also change in order to break the cycle of the development of the gendered habitus. The need for institutional change is a crucial feminist claim. But few feminists have claimed that consciousness-raising will, in itself, subvert the general system of masculine domination. The claim, rather, is that consciousness-raising is an important first step, one which prompts wider institutional change—particularly when it is used to question and challenge public institutions such as media, politics, or the law.[59] Consciousness-raising is the means by which women come to understand both their oppression and the possible remedies for it. Women "know inequality because they have lived it, so they know what removing barriers to equality would be. Many of these barriers are legal; many of them are social; most of them exist at an interface between law and society."[60] In other words, we cannot change our institutions without first theorizing the need for change. Only once theorized can change go beyond consciousness and into institutions.

Lisa Adkins argues, in contrast, that reflexivity has become a normal part of gender, such that its transformative and radical effects are lost. She argues that "for both men and women gender is increasingly taking the form of a self-conscious artifice which can be managed, strategically deployed and performed,"[61] but that this process does not guarantee progressive change. The reason is that the sort of reflexivity that is becoming common is accompanied not by a radical questioning of

---

57. Bourdieu and Wacquant, *Invitation to Reflexive Sociology*, 40.
58. Ibid., 136–37.
59. See Katherine T. Bartlett, "Feminist Legal Methods," 864–65.
60. MacKinnon, *Toward a Feminist Theory of the State*, 241.
61. Adkins, "Reflexivity," 33.

the role of gender, but rather by an increasing understanding of the *proper* roles that men and women must play, an understanding that masculinity and femininity are forms of capital that should be preserved and deployed. Thus Adkins gives the example of a study of female City workers who skillfully plan their appearance, shifting between demure business dress and the "executive bimbo look," depending on the audience.[62] Such manipulation of traditional female roles is not, Adkins suggests, indicative of a progressive transformation of gender but is rather indicative of the entrenchment of traditional gender difference. As a result, Adkins concludes that Bourdieu's reliance on the disembodied, cerebral process of reflexivity represents his failure to apply the basic features of his theory to his account of change.[63]

Feminist accounts of consciousness-raising can help to mitigate some of these criticisms since they entail not merely a reflexive awareness of the configurations of gender, but also a *critical* stance on those configurations. As Pamela Allen writes in her advocacy of consciousness-raising, "We believe that theory and analysis which are not rooted in concrete experience (practice) are useless, but we also maintain that for the concrete, everyday experiences to be understood, they must be subjected to the processes of analysis and abstraction."[64] This critical stance is aided by the facts that consciousness-raising is a group activity—women *share* observations of injustice and ideas for change and encourage others to act radically; that consciousness-raising focuses not only on the thought consciousness but also on the embodied practices of gender; and that consciousness-raising begins from a feminist perspective.[65] Kristin Henry and Marlene Derlet's interviews with members of a consciousness-raising group provide many examples of the importance of the intersubjective elements of that particular form of reflexivity.[66] Group interaction provides the members with new ideas about the injustices of gender and with support for instigating change;

62. Ibid.
63. Ibid., 35.
64. Pamela Allen, "The Small Group Process," 277.
65. Adkins writes, "Why, when it comes to social change, does Bourdieu tend to disembody actors and understand action as a matter of thinking consciousness?" ("Reflexivity," 35). While she is correct to say that Bourdieu does this, it is interesting to note that the reflexivity of the City workers who deploy alternative images of femininity (a reflexivity that Adkins considers insufficiently transformative) is not merely thought but is also embodied.
66. Kristin Henry and Marlene Derlet, *Talking Up a Storm.*

as Allen points out, "The emphasis is on teaching one another through sharing experiences."[67] Similarly, Vivian Gornick cites the testimony of a member of a consciousness-raising group who also focuses on the importance of interaction:

> None of them have been through what I've been through if you look at our experience superficially. But when you look a little *deeper*—the way we've been doing at these meetings—you see they've *all* been through what I've been through, and they all feel pretty much the way I feel. God, when I saw *that!* When I saw that what I always felt was my own personal hangup was as true for every other woman in that room as it was for me! Well, that's when my consciousness was raised.[68]

Of course, it would be wrong to suggest that group interaction is always transformative. Traditional women's groups foster conformity just as radical groups encourage revolution. Nonetheless, the combination of the group setting with the shared desire to act reflexively can be a potent force for change. As Susan Bruley notes of her own group, "The general feeling really was that CR had changed our lives."[69]

Regulated Liberties

It is important to consider consciousness-raising as a possible strategy for change not least because the strategies for resisting prevailing norms that Bourdieu suggests are problematic. Take, for example, the method Bourdieu calls "regulated liberties." Regulated liberties are actions that arise in the context of the existing social order, but which subvert or resignify it in some way. Bourdieu's regulated liberties occur when the disadvantaged or oppressed subversively apply oppressive or unjust norms, questioning and resisting their dominant meaning. Bourdieu gives the example of the images used to characterize male and female genitals in the Kabyle society which he has studied. Although female genitals are described in derogatory terms, women can exercise a regulated liberty by applying those terms to male genitals:

67. Allen, "Small Group Process," 279.
68. Vivian Gornick, "Consciousness," 289.
69. Sue Bruley, *Women Awake*, 21.

The partial indeterminacy of certain objects authorizes antago-
nistic interpretations, offering the dominated a possibility of
resistance to the effect of symbolic imposition. Thus women
can draw on the dominant schemes of perception (top/bottom,
hard/soft, straight/curved, dry/wet, etc.), which lead them to
form a very negative view of their own genitals, in order to
understand the male sexual attributes by analogy with things
that hang limply, without vigour; . . . and they can even draw
advantage from the diminished state of the male member to
assert the superiority of the female sexual organ, as in the saying: "You, all your tackle (*laâlaleq*) dangles, says the woman to
the man, whereas I am a welded stone."[70]

Even from the oppressed position, therefore, women can use the labels
of their oppression to refer to their oppressors. Alternatively, the oppressed can accept and "reclaim" the labels of their oppression, transforming them into positive descriptions, as when homosexuals reclaim
the previously derogatory word "queer" and use it proudly to describe
themselves.[71]

Bourdieu does not, however, see performativity and other regulatory
liberties as opportunities for genuine emancipation from structures
of domination, for two main reasons. First, the regulated liberties are
performed by individuals, and so lack the cohesive, collective character
required for wide-ranging social change. Thus Bourdieu contrasts the
"*political* mobilization" necessary for collective and thus effective resistance with a Butlerian individualist approach, arguing that the latter is
insufficient.[72]

The second limitation on the emancipatory potential of the regulated
liberties is that they take place within the confines of the overall structures of domination, and do not really subvert those structures. Because a regulated liberty is an act that takes the dominant labels and
applies them subversively, it follows that in doing so the dominant

70. Bourdieu, *Masculine Domination*, 14.
71. Judith Butler also points out that Bourdieu's work allows for the effects of repeated yet
unofficial interpellations on an individual and her habitus, such as when a child is repeatedly
called a "girl" and so takes on "girlishness." This fact, Butler argues, allows alternative interpellations and performatives to have a transformative effect: "The social performative is a
crucial part not only of subject *formation*, but of the ongoing political contestation and reformulation of the subject as well" ("Performativity's Social Magic," 125).
72. Bourdieu, *Masculine Domination*, viii; emphasis in the original.

labels are in some sense affirmed. Bourdieu's example of Kabyle genital labeling demonstrates this affirmation. The women exercising the regulated liberties do not question the division of genitals into two groups of hard versus soft, dry versus wet. For example, they do not argue that male and female genitals are more similar than different, as the Gerai do.[73] Perhaps more important, they do not question the value judgments attached to these characteristics (top, hard, straight, dry = good, powerful, superior; bottom, soft, curved, wet = bad, weak, inferior). In fact, the success of the regulated liberty relies on an affirmation of the dominant value system: labeling male genitals as "soft" has no discursive effect if softness des not imply inferiority. In this way, the regulated liberties might even serve to entrench the dominant structures. The slight shifts in representation and small victories of empowerment that the regulated liberties achieve tend, in the long run, to reinforce structural inequalities.

MacKinnon makes a similar point in relation to sexuality: "The capacity of gender reversals (dominatrixes) and inversions (homosexuality) to stimulate sexual excitement [in pornography] is derived precisely from their mimicry or parody or negation or reversal of the standard arrangement. This affirms rather than undermines or qualifies the standard sexual arrangement as the standard sexual arrangement."[74] Sometimes, as this example suggests, the regulated liberties might be reactionary. A case from the United States, the fathers' movement, subverts both traditional gendered parenting norms, which assert that fathers need play only a limited role in parenting, and modified, feminist-influenced parenting norms, which assert that mothers' rights must be paramount after a divorce or that both parents are equal within the home. The fathers' movement subverts these traditionally dominant conceptions but remains within them, by asserting that families need fathers and that fathers need to dominate.[75] The shift that may result from this regulated liberty is a reactionary one because it reasserts male dominance within the home, and emphasizes different roles for men and women in parenting. Although the fathers' movement uses regulated liberties to bring about social change, this change is

---

73. The Gerai, discussed above, conceptualize the penis and the vagina as the same organ, and differentiate them only according to their placement inside or outside of the body. Similarly, the Gerai think of semen and vaginal fluid as identical (Helliwell, "It's Only a Penis").

74. MacKinnon, *Toward a Feminist Theory of the State*, 144.

75. Cornell, *At the Heart of Freedom*, 133–34.

not progressive. Bourdieu's regulated liberties thus guarantee neither extensive nor emancipatory social change.

Disjunction Between Field and Habitus

Bourdieu suggests an alternative opportunity for change. If an individual's position in a hierarchy is reinforced by the fit between her habitus and the field within which she operates, this reinforcement can be weakened by a disjunction between habitus and field. When people move between fields, or when communities encounter each other and their norms collide, there will be a disjunction between habitus and field. In multicultural societies, the norms of different groups, or the logics of different fields, provide constant cross-challenges. As people are increasingly mobile, interaction between groups increases, and complacency over the dispositions that make up the habitus is lessened. One way of encouraging changes in habitus that open up greater options for people, then, is to encourage interaction between fields, between communities or ways of life, so that individuals become aware of new options.

Such a disjunction between habitus and field is not, Bourdieu emphasizes, a common occurrence. There is usually a fit between field and habitus, as most people remain within compatible fields most of the time. In such circumstances, the habitus is continually reinforced. When the individual encounters circumstances incompatible with her habitus, however, it is gradually weakened. In this way, the habitus can be changed, but more usually is not.[76]

One of the ways in which change in the habitus might occur, McNay suggests, is via the disjunction that occurs when women move into the workforce.[77] The idea is that the gendered habitus will change when women enter spheres that were previously closed to them, such as the factory or the boardroom. However, this process is by no means guaranteed, as Adkins points out.[78] In particular, we can identify two questions. First, what would prompt such a move? Why do women move into nonfeminine spheres? Second, how would such a move alter the gendered nature of the habitus?

First, consider why women move into nonfeminine spheres. If a

---

76. Bourdieu and Wacquant, *Invitation to Reflexive Sociology*, 133.
77. McNay, *Gender and Agency*, 53.
78. Adkins, "Reflexivity," 28–29.

disjunction between habitus and field is to be the explanation or cause of a change in the habitus, it follows that the move itself cannot be the result of a changed habitus, or of action which contradicts the existing habitus. Such an account would be question-begging. For this argument to be coherent, social change must result from changes in habitus that are caused by location in an unfamiliar field. The explanation cannot be that the individual decides, from within the confines of one habitus, to move toward another by entering a currently inappropriate field. Why, then, do women enter previously nonfeminine spheres, such as higher education or the workplace? What explains the change in social norms that makes such movements possible and appealing for individual women? If these movements are explained by the choices and campaigns of women, then those women have already engendered social change prior to the disjunction between habitus and field that is supposed to explain that social change.

One option is that a vanguard, perhaps of feminist theorists, actively promotes new ideas or enters new spheres, with the result that nonvanguard women enter the newly opened fields before their habituses have adapted to fit. If this were the case, the disjunction between habitus and field might explain how social change grows in scope. In other words, theory is necessary but not sufficient: it can explain how an emancipatory movement starts, or why emancipatory change in social institutions is initiated, but it is a disjunction between field and habitus that provides the mechanism for altering the beliefs, preferences, and choices of the majority.

An alternative interpretation is that the impetus for the social mobility that creates a disjunction between habitus and field is not subjective but objective, not agent-directed but structural. If social mobility were caused by objective economic factors, for example, it might take place before change in habitus and thus before wide-reaching change in social norms or symbolic structures. Thus the woman who starts to work in a factory may do so not because she believes that gendered employment norms must be overthrown, but because her family is in need of extra resources. This need results from objective economic conditions, not subjective rebellion. However, even in this case some habitus-conflicting reasoning must have taken place. Even in times of economic necessity, if women are to work in factories then a feeling must have arisen that, contrary to the prevailing norms, such work is conceivable or appropriate. Economic conditions cannot force a change in behavior, with no mediation by normative reasoning. A newly poor woman must decide that it is better for her to work in a factory than to work as a prostitute, to steal, or to remain at home to preserve her religious virtue.[79] Such decisions are likely to be implied by the general system of social norms, minimizing the autonomous decision-making that any individual must undergo. However, she must have decided that the existing taboo on entering the nonfeminine sphere can be broken (even if she feels she has little choice), and this very fact will cause a change in her prior to entering the sphere and experiencing the disjunction between habitus and field that is supposed to be the source of social change. Indeed, the more the movement into a nonfeminine sphere is forced by the prevailing economic conditions and thus runs counter to her habitus, the more the woman about to enter the sphere is likely to think about her move and its implications, to steel herself for unfamiliar practices and to prepare to alter her mode of being. In other words, even mobility between fields caused by economic change prompts changes in consciousness prior to changes caused by disjunction between habitus and field.[80]

This analysis suggests that the most effective form of social change is the combination of an enforced, structural change together with active promotion of a new set of norms. For example, if large numbers of women are to move into the workplace when it has traditionally been a nonfeminine sphere, they may need both structural changes (be they advantageous, such as antidiscrimination legislation, childcare provision, and education, or disadvantageous, such as economic necessity or war) *and* symbolic changes in social reasoning (such as consciousness-raising, the feminist movement campaigning for women's rights, or positive media portrayals of working women).

The second question that arises from the notion that a disjunction between habitus and field can cause social change is how and why

79. Martha Nussbaum gives many examples of countries where women are forbidden to work for religious reasons, even if such women and their families are destitute as a result (*Sex and Social Justice*, 93–94).

80. In *Pascalian Meditations*, Bourdieu argues that our habitus is adjusted to our occupational field even before we enter that field, by processes of socialization and preparation that occur in the family and in school. Thus, for Bourdieu, "when we deliberate on entry into the game, the die is already more or less cast" (*Pascalian Meditations*, 11). Such a process cannot apply to cases such as a woman's economically prompted move into a nonfeminine sphere, however, for the unexpectedness and hitherto inappropriateness of such a move means that there has been no prior familial or educational preparation. The deliberation on entry, then, will be genuinely meaningful for the deliberator.

gender would be affected. As I argued earlier, the gendered habitus is not situated in any particular field for Bourdieu. Instead, gender norms are replicated across all fields, in nonidentical but nevertheless reinforcing ways. It follows that a woman entering a previously nonfeminine sphere may find aspects of her habitus altered, but its genderedness will remain intact.

A good example of the pervasiveness of masculine domination despite social mobility is found in Heather Dryburgh's analysis of women in engineering. Dryburgh studied a group of women entering the male-dominated profession, and followed their progress through college. Although their colleagues were also students, and so were not yet fully indoctrinated into the engineering culture, still that field's gender norms were strongly enforced. The presence of the women students appeared not to question those norms but further to entrench them. Dryburgh argues, "As women progress through their professional training, they are making adjustments and learning to manage the masculine culture into which they are entering. . . . [T]his study shows that the educational phase is a period of early socialization into the masculine workplace culture associated with engineering. Women who do make it through the training process . . . face sexism in the workplace that requires new adaptations and strategies."[81] The implication of Dryburgh's account is that, while female engineering students do experience a disjunction between habitus and field leading to alterations in habitus ("adaptations and strategies"), those alterations do not in any way undermine gender, or masculine domination. Instead, the sexism which they encounter reinforces the salience of gender.[82]

The example of women in engineering supports the claim that if the gendered habitus is reinforced in all fields, it cannot be significantly undermined by mobility across fields. This may explain the peculiarly pessimistic and deterministic tone of *Masculine Domination* as compared to Bourdieu's other work: the gendered habitus is even less susceptible to change than is the habitus more generally (and more specifically), for it survives transition between fields. It follows that, as gender is transmitted throughout society, it must be countered by a coordinated program of change in such institutions and in wider social norms. We need a proactive, and proactively normative, program of

81. Heather Dryburgh, "Work Hard, Play Hard," 665.
82. See also Lovell, "Thinking Feminism," 13.

change, reinforced in the social and state institutions that perpetuate masculine domination.

The Role of the State

Theory and consciousness-raising may be the first step toward emancipatory and egalitarian change, but state action must follow. In Part Two, I develop a proposal for state action to remedy inequality. Here, I use MacKinnon's account of the state to illustrate the ways in which the state can be a tool for feminist action.

At first glance, looking to the state as an emancipator appears unwise or even impossible. After all, if masculine domination and other forms of socially constructed inequalities are transmitted in "agencies such as the school and the state,"[83] the state must be understood as part of the problem rather than part of the solution. Hence the state is sometimes seen, for example in some versions of Marxism, as "a tool of dominance and repression" that must be abandoned by any egalitarian movement.[84] This idea stands in stark contrast to a more optimistic, perhaps liberal view of the state as "potentially principled . . . available as a tool that is not fatally twisted."[85] Between these two extremes, MacKinnon notes, feminism has traditionally been stranded: "Either the state is a primary tool of women's betterment and status transformation, without analysis (hence strategy) of it as male; or women are left to civil society, which for women has more closely resembled a state of nature."[86]

It is beyond the scope of this book to deal with these issues in depth. However, several points are worth noting. The first is that it is possible to advocate the radical transformation and use of the state as a weapon in the feminist struggle while remaining aware of the state's role in perpetuating patriarchy. MacKinnon combines both, as I hope to do here. Starting with the critique of the state, she writes:

> From a feminist perspective, male supremacist jurisprudence erects qualities valued from the male point of view as standards for the proper and actual relation between life and law.

83. Bourdieu, *Masculine Domination*, 4.
84. MacKinnon, *Toward a Feminist Theory of the State*, 160.
85. Ibid.
86. Ibid.

. . . Lines of precedent fully developed before women were permitted to vote, continued while women were not allowed to learn to read and write, sustained under a reign of sexual terror and abasement and silence and misrepresentation continuing to the present day are considered valid bases for defeating "unprecedented" interpretations or initiatives from women's point of view.[87]

MacKinnon's work is full of examples, mostly from U.S. case history, of state perpetuation of gender inequality through the formation and enforcement of law. She does not have a utopian vision of an autonomous, virtuous state standing above society. Awareness of the state's role in maintaining the unequal status quo does not, however, preclude use of the state for emancipatory purposes. Indeed, if the state is one of the structures that maintain inequality, how could an egalitarian movement afford to ignore it? If the state is implicated in the social construction of inequality, it will be impossible to undermine that inequality without addressing the state and developing strategies to change it. It will be essential to use state power in the name of equality rather than patriarchy. The fundamental feminist idea that the personal is political expresses, in part, this understanding. It is because the state already shapes the personal, and gender inequality more widely, that it is appropriate to use the state to tackle gender inequality. Thus feminists reject what MacKinnon calls "the liberal view" of the private, according to which "no act of the state contributes to shaping its internal alignments or distributing its internal forces, so no act of the state should participate in changing it."[88] Instead, since the state already shapes the personal, it is crucial to propose ways of reforming the state to render it compatible with equality. Even a state that is traditionally male-dominated and biased *can* develop laws that promote women's equality.[89] Indeed, since the law *inevitably* has a concrete, substantive effect, one that promotes some interests and groups and disadvantages others, it is crucial for any normative project to engage with the law and consider how it might produce substantive effects that are normatively justifiable. As MacKinnon puts this point, "If it was openly conceded that law qua law is on some level necessarily a substantive

87. Ibid., 238.
88. Ibid., 190.
89. Catharine MacKinnon, *Women's Lives, Men's Laws*, 268.

pursuit, as women's engagement with it shows, not mechanistic or scientific or abstract or finally formal, its functionaries and decision makers could less easily hide and legitimate what they do and its levers of power could be more widely shared."[90]

The first reason why social construction leads us to conceive of the state as a tool for change, then, is that the state is already involved. It cannot be ignored, and so must be reformed. The second reason is that analysis in terms of social construction highlights the fact that formal liberal freedoms embodied in state *non*intervention do not truly emancipate. Formal freedoms do not affect individuals' socially constructed preferences, beliefs, and habituses, and thus do not ensure that individuals have the internal resources to secure their own equality—or even their own freedom; as Taylor argues, "If we think of freedom as including something like the freedom of self-fulfillment, or self-realization according to our own pattern, then we plainly have something which can fail for inner reasons as well as because of external obstacles."[91] Moreover, insisting on nonintervention deprives individuals of the necessary *external* resources for emancipation. This point is familiar to the liberal debate about negative and positive liberty—noninterference leaves some individuals unable to act in accordance with their own life plans since they lack the necessary material resources.[92] MacKinnon's example is of the right to abortion, secured in the United States via the constitutional right to privacy in *Roe v. Wade*. Although the right to an abortion is essential to women's equality, MacKinnon points out that rooting it in the right to privacy has the effect that state institutions consider themselves to be under no obligation to provide the means for women to obtain an abortion. As a result, women without adequate funds or access to doctors who are willing to perform abortions remain unable to exercise their right. This example demonstrates the general point that state action is often necessary to provide genuine equality:

> Freedom from public intervention coexists uneasily with any right that requires social preconditions to be meaningfully delivered. For example, if inequality is socially pervasive and enforced, equality will require intervention, not abdication, to be

90. Ibid., 9.
91. Taylor, "What's Wrong with Negative Liberty," 212.
92. G. A. Cohen, "Capitalism, Freedom and the Proletariat." See also Cass Sunstein, "Neutrality in Constitutional Law," 9.

meaningful. . . . [Without intervention] women are guaranteed by the public no more than what they can get in private. . . . State intervention would have provided a choice women did not have in private, would have contradicted the male-supremacist structure of the private.[93]

This combination of reasons leads Nancy Hirschmann to conclude that state nonintervention can actually be more harmful to those who are subordinated than state intervention. "From the perspective of the powerless," she writes, "the state often intervenes most intrusively and egregiously precisely when it claims to be doing the contrary, such as when, under the rubric of privacy, its failure to arrest and prosecute domestic abusers results in the restriction of women's freedom."[94]

Cass Sunstein persuasively argues that the dominant legal understanding of state neutrality leads to a conceptually and normatively flawed view of the appropriateness of state action. This dominant view begins with a concealed substantive understanding of what it means for the state to act at all: "Decisions that upset existing distributions are treated as 'action'; decisions that do not are thought to stay close to nature and thus to amount to no action at all."[95] In fact, all laws amount to action, and what tends to be understood as neutral and thus permissible state action is in fact simply that which rests on, and perpetuates, the status quo and prevailing social norms. For example, Sunstein argues that the Supreme Court's ruling that Andrea Dworkin and MacKinnon's antipornography ordinances were non-neutral and thus unconstitutional is inconsistent with many permitted regulations of speech, such as state prohibition of truthful cigarette advertisements but not truthful antismoking campaigns.[96] Sunstein concludes that "the prevailing conception of neutrality" and its concurrent hostility to the sorts of state action advocated in this book "often operates as a device for ruling out of bounds, as impermissibly partisan, views that see existing distributions of entitlements, wealth, and preferences as partisan and

93. MacKinnon, *Toward a Feminist Theory of the State*, 191–92. While she agrees with MacKinnon's argument that the right to abortion requires state provision if it is to be meaningful, Jean Cohen argues that it is the liberal paradigm of privacy and not the concept of privacy *per se* that implies state nonintervention. See Jean Cohen, *Regulating Intimacy*, 28–44.
94. Nancy Hirschmann, *The Subject of Liberty*, 235; see also Cohen, *Regulating Intimacy*, 7.
95. Sunstein, "Neutrality in Constitutional Law," 2.
96. Ibid., 28.

a product of law."[97] Instead, we should acknowledge that the state inevitably prioritizes some normative views and ways of life, and must thus theorize which priorities are preferable.

Jean Cohen also recognizes the need to develop an appropriate model of state action in the private or intimate domain, rather than dismiss the state as a purely repressive force. As I do, she criticizes what she terms the liberal paradigm of state action, according to which "the state should limit itself to guaranteeing the negative liberty of each to pursue their particular conception of the good."[98] However, she is equally critical of the alternative welfare paradigm, according to which "positive state action is needed to counter injustice due to inequalities of power and status between social groups."[99] The welfare paradigm is problematic, according to Cohen, because it is "intrusive, substantive, and authoritative."[100] In its place, she supports the reflexive paradigm. In contrast to the restrictiveness of the welfare paradigm, the reflexive paradigm encourages "responsible self-regulation" in which "social actors can strike whatever substantive agreements they wish."[101] However, in order to avoid the sociological naiveté of the liberal paradigm,[102] and since reflexivity in itself can have either good or bad effects,[103] self-regulation must be *constrained* by the state. Thus Cohen claims that "regulating self-regulation to ensure that it is guided by the principles of justice can avoid the dilemmas plaguing the other two legal paradigms."[104]

This paradigm suffers from an internal contradiction that Cohen recognizes but does not adequately resolve. She notes that it is "paradoxical to claim simultaneously that reflexive law fosters self-regulation by leaving outcomes indeterminate and that reflexive law should be better institutionalized so that it rests on clearly defined legislative goals with real sanctions backing them up,"[105] and her solution of distinguishing principles from goals is not adequate. It remains necessary for the state to develop substantive normative principles, to monitor

97. Ibid., 48.
98. Cohen, *Regulating Intimacy*, 143.
99. Ibid.
100. Ibid., 144.
101. Ibid.
102. Ibid., 118ff.
103. Ibid., 146, 164ff.
104. Ibid., 145.
105. Ibid., 177.

the extent to which nonstate institutions embody those principles, and to enforce compliance where necessary.[106] Even if diversity in practical policy solutions is permitted, the state retains a crucial, normatively significant role.

Hirschmann argues, however, that feminists still need to be cautious about state power, for there are many ways in which it is used "against women's freedom."[107] She cites as an example Drucilla Cornell's argument that laws against pornography and prostitution "merely replicate obviously sexist uses of the state, such as regulation of abortion."[108] Similar claims have been made about the antipornography laws advocated by MacKinnon and Dworkin, namely that these ordinances were supported by antifeminist right-wing groups, and that they would have been used to censor feminist work such as that of Dworkin herself. Both claims have been denied by Dworkin and MacKinnon.[109]

These issues combine empirical questions about the particular forms of state power or particular laws with a normative question about coalition. It is not clear whether it is a significant or decisive objection to a policy proposal that it can be supported by people with diverse, even opposing political positions. Many forms of democratic theory—including Rawls's idea of the overlapping consensus, most versions of deliberative democracy, and Sunstein's formula of incompletely theorized agreements—see the possibility of convergence as a strength rather than a weakness.[110] It certainly does not seem obvious that we should dismiss a policy purely because it has surprising supporters, or that we should dismiss an entire mechanism for change (the state) simply because it has been used for ill as well as for good. If we find ourselves advocating a policy that is also supported by those we previously thought were our enemies, it is advisable to consider whether the policy has drawbacks or implications we had not previously thought

106. Ibid., 73, 84, 115, 169, 173, 176.

107. Hirschmann, *Subject of Liberty*, 235.

108. Ibid., 234, referring to Cornell, *At the Heart of Freedom*. See also the discussion of sexual harassment law in Cohen, *Regulating Intimacy*, 137.

109. See the transcripts of the Andrea Dworkin Commemorative Conference, available at http://social-justice.politics.ox.ac.uk/events/dworkin/ and the Andrea Dworkin website Myth Buster, at http://www.andreadworkin.net/.

110. At the Andrea Dworkin Commemorative Conference, radical feminist Sheila Jeffreys reported her surprise and at least partial discomfort at finding that her views on transsexualism cohere with those of Conservative Peer Norman Tebbit. See http://social-justice.politics.ox.ac.uk/events/dworkin/.

of, but then again it is always possible that we might be incorrect in our assumption that there can be no common ground between "us" and "them."[111]

A similar issue arising from the idea of emancipatory state action is the question of how to secure support for such action in the democratic process and how, on a micro level, to shift state institutions onto a different path. This is not an issue with which I am primarily concerned here. I am engaged in ideal theory at the level of state action: I propose paths that the state *ought* to take without specifying how to ensure that those paths are in fact taken. The fact that the state may be an unwilling tool of feminism emphasizes rather than undermines the need to address and utilize it.

A more pressing problem is the question of whether state intervention will actually be effective. An argument to the effect that a practice can legitimately be banned, for example, does not in itself demonstrate that banning will be an effective means of eradicating the practice. Gerry Mackie argues that state responses to female genital mutilation (FGM) should vary depending on the character of the society concerned. While prohibition might be the appropriate measure in liberal states where the practice is not entrenched, premature prohibition in societies where it is widespread can actually be harmful. Possible harms include the fact that the practice will be driven underground and become more dangerous, that people will be unwilling to seek medical help when it is needed, that education programs will be hampered by people's unwillingness to talk candidly about an illegal practice, that voluntary communal declarations to desist will similarly be hampered, and that prohibiting a widespread practice can breed resentment and even entrench support for the practice as a form of resistance. As a result, Mackie argues that state prohibition should take place only after the practice has been rejected by most people in the relevant society,

111. It is often not obvious which position on any given issue really is "feminist," for example. There could be differences in principle, different assumptions about probable consequences, different knowledge of or views about the facts, or some combination of all three. One obvious example is the debate within feminism about whether pornography or prostitution should be outlawed. Other examples include Germaine Greer's arguments in *The Whole Woman* that various things that feminist women's groups have fought for, such as cervical screening and personal attack alarms, actually perpetuate women's fear and subordination, or the issue of whether feminist critiques of enforced housewifery actually contribute to a misogynist devaluing of motherhood and domestic labor.

and that anti-FGM campaigners should focus on bringing about social change rather than new legislation.[112]

Considerations such as Mackie's are of great importance. Whenever state intervention is considered, it is always necessary to consider the particular circumstances of the society in question, and what effects any proposed law is likely to have. A successful strategy in one place and time may not work in a different situation. Moreover, the empirical effects of a policy clearly affect its overall normative justification. If banning FGM would, for the sorts of reasons given, only increase the number of women and girls who would suffer from the practice, then the ban would not be normatively justified *all things considered*. However, this is not to say that the ban would be unjustified *in principle:* we can separate the all-things-considered justification, which includes possible unintended side effects, from the principled justification, which asks only whether the intended effects of a ban are legitimate and whether liberty regarding this issue may permissibly be constrained. This distinction is important. Two people might agree that FGM, for example, is harmful and should be discouraged. They might further agree that it should not be banned if to do so would bring about greater harm; in other words, they agree on whether a ban is justified *all things considered*. However, they might disagree about a situation in which a ban would not increase harm or would even decrease it: the first person might think that a ban should be implemented in such a case, since it is *in principle* justified; the second might reject a ban even in such a case on grounds of individual negative liberty. In this book I am primarily concerned with these sorts of in-principle disagreements, rather than the question of all-things-considered justifications. Where I discuss and reject various objections to state action, the question is almost always one of principled justification. Thus, even where my arguments in favor of state action are successful, the questions of whether, when and how such action should actually occur in any particular context are still to be answered.

Finally, a critic might note that my arguments about social construction directly call into question the use of the state: since social construction is not confined to the state, it is not clear that the state is the best mechanism with which to alter it. One response to this point was made

---

112. Gerry Mackie, "Ending Harmful Conventions."

above: while the state may not be the sole or even the main perpetrator of social construction, it is nevertheless a significant actor. However, it is right to say that the state does not exhaust the possibilities for change. As the discussion of consciousness-raising showed, change can come from individuals without necessarily intersecting with the state. Sometimes, indeed, state action (or certain forms of it) is explicitly undesirable: as Hirschmann notes, "I hardly want the state to intervene if my husband shirks his share of the housework, even though I see the division of household labor as an important example of gender politics; that is a battle I would prefer to wage for myself."[113] Change might come not only from individual or familial action; it might be the result of nonstate social movements. My argument, then, is not for state intervention as the only or even the best method of change. I wish to suggest only that the state can be an important instrument of change, and that more state action may be justified in principle than liberals tend to allow. As Jean Cohen argues, although intimate relationships require some forms of privacy if they are to exist as such, this does not render state action redundant: "Individuals need protection within and not only for intimacy."[114]

The Implications of Social Construction

We can now summarize the main implications of social construction for egalitarian political theory in its varied guises.

The Need for Forced Disjunction

First, the idea of social construction emphasizes the fact that there will be circumstances in which the changes that are necessary for justice need to be externally imposed. If change is obstructed by the habitus, and if one method of change is the disruption in habitus that results from a disjunction of habitus and field, one method of bringing about change in habitus is to impose a change in field. Often the state will be best placed to bring about such a change. To put it in liberal terms, the state can ensure that individuals have the resources to become au-

113. Hirschmann, *Subject of Liberty*, 233.
114. Cohen, *Regulating Intimacy*, 41.

tonomous citizens by providing such things as education countering the autonomy-limiting effects of culture and upbringing. What Bourdieu and MacKinnon's theories make clear is that, without such external interference, many individuals will remain within the field that reinforces their habitus, or the cultural context that emphasizes their oppression, and will therefore lack the resources to resist that oppression. As Chapter 4 argues, freedom of exit is not enough, for many individuals will not take advantage of it. Instead, the state needs to provide at least some disjunctions between habitus and field for all, if all are to have a chance at autonomy.

The Need for State Assistance

Second, theories of social construction emphasize that the process of change is often very difficult. Individuals face resistance both from those who have a stake in the prevailing injustice, and from their own prereflexive dispositions. Moreover, as the habitus responds to the objective social conditions, if those conditions are unjust, that injustice will be perpetuated and perpetrated by individual actions. As such, the state needs to take on some of the burdens of ensuring that the social conditions are just. It will not be enough to leave the justice of social practices to individual choice, for once they come to choose, individuals will already be inclined to follow those practices. Instead, the state needs to be proactive in prohibiting those practices or forms of domination which are particularly harmful. The durability of the habitus means that it is unreasonable for liberals to expect individuals to take sole responsibility for altering the conditions which disadvantage them.

The Need for Normative Theory

Foucault, Bourdieu, and MacKinnon all insist that we cannot emancipate individuals by freeing them from social construction, since they assert that social construction is, in a sense, all there is. The problem is not how to free individuals from social construction *tout court* but rather how to free them from *unjust* social construction. As such, it is crucial to develop a normative theory of which sorts of social construction are just and which are not.

In this chapter I have argued that, although theory and consciousness are insufficient for change, they are crucial to it. If change is to be emancipatory rather than reactionary and, sometimes, if it is to occur at all, we need to engage in *theory:* developing normative and philosophical accounts of existing and ideal society and behavior. Despite Bourdieu's skepticism as to the efficacy of philosophy and consciousness-raising, it is fitting to end with an excerpt from *Pascalian Meditations* that has a more optimistic view of normative theory: "The symbolic work needed in order to break out of the silent self-evidence of *doxa* and to state and denounce the arbitrariness that it conceals presupposed instruments of expression and criticism which, like the other forms of capital, are unequally distributed. As a consequence, there is every reason to think that it would not be possible without the intervention of professional practitioners of the work of making explicit."[115] The rest of the book attempts such work.

---

115. Bourdieu, *Pascalian Meditations*, 188.

3

SOCIAL CONSTRUCTION, NORMATIVITY, AND DIFFERENCE

My overall argument is that political theorists in general, and liberal political theorists in particular, should take greater account of social construction. However, I also wish to argue that an awareness of social construction should not lead theorists to retreat to cultural relativism and the abandonment of universal normative principles. In contrast to some communitarian theories that argue that the cultural construction of individuals requires the protection of cultures and the perpetuation of patterns of construction, I claim that an awareness of social construction actually prompts an even *more* questioning attitude toward social or group norms than liberals typically have.

This combination may seem distinctly unpromising. In the previous two chapters I discussed the work of three radical theorists of social construction: Michel Foucault, Pierre Bourdieu, and Catharine Mac-Kinnon. In Chapter 1, I argued that one of the most problematic elements of Foucault's work is his lack of normative resources, and in this chapter I argue that the same problem affects Bourdieu, despite his focus on the normative-sounding "masculine domination." Of the three theorists, only MacKinnon has an approach that sustains rigorous and radical critique; as I suggested in the introduction, feminists are more used to combining an analysis of social construction with a critique of the process. However, even MacKinnon claims that her analysis is "moral or ideal in neither basis nor purpose. It shows that women are a political group—oppressed, subordinated, and unequal—and explores the contours and implications of that reality for theory and politics and law. That reality established, anyone is welcome to defend or contest it."[1] In this chapter I consider some of the problems of contesting the social construction of gender, along with some feminist and other strategies for overcoming those problems.

---

1. MacKinnon, "'The Case' Responds," 710.

Normativity

In the previous chapter I outlined Bourdieu's strategies for change, and highlighted some of their problems. The issue of normativity is problematic in Bourdieu's work more generally, since his analysis leaves open the question of the extent to which any particular habitus is desirable. For Bourdieu, the habitus is inevitable, in that it is a response to objective social conditions. In this sense, it is not open to normative analysis. Individuals have the habitus appropriate to their social condition. However, as liberal egalitarian theory makes clear, we can evaluate the justice of alternative social arrangements. If a society is organized systematically to benefit some people at the expense of others, the resulting habituses will transmit that injustice. We can therefore say that, although the habitus represents an appropriate response to the objective conditions, if the conditions are unjust then the habitus is the embodiment of injustice.

Bourdieu's account itself, however, lacks normative resources. Although Bourdieu uses evocative normative terms, "domination" and "violence," he does not provide the necessary normative framework to render those terms meaningful. As such, his work could be used for either reaction or revolution. A reactionary approach to Bourdieu's account of symbolic violence could begin with the fact that, for Bourdieu, the habitus is an inevitable and in some senses rational response to the conditions that confront it—even if those conditions have the characteristics of symbolic violence. A woman's desire to undergo female genital mutilation (FGM) or to practice it on her daughter, for example, is not the irrational desire of a false consciousness. It is a rational response to the patriarchal society in which she lives, in the sense that it might well be true that a woman is marriageable only if mutilated. Given this fact, the reactionary response might continue, isn't it best to allow individuals to adapt to the norms that govern their lives as best they can? Don't we help women most by letting them practice FGM and reap the rewards? Don't we limit a woman's chances if we prevent her from participating in a practice that, in her society, is the best way to secure advantage? If the habitus is the rational response to the prevailing conditions, why seek to change it?

The second line of argument open to the reactionary follower of Bourdieu is the observation that, under systems of symbolic violence, both women and men are equally compliant. Moreover, Bourdieu explicitly rejects the notion that men exercise influence over women to get them to conform to patriarchal norms. Instead, both men and women accept those norms at an unconscious level.[2] Men, then, are not the evil perpetrators of patriarchy. They too accept its dictates as obvious and natural. In other words, they too are subject to the symbolic violence. If patriarchal norms are imposed on and accepted by both women and men, in what sense can they be described as unjust? This reactionary thought is often expressed by the assertion that men also suffer under patriarchy: they must endure the responsibilities of breadwinning; maintaining a healthy, strong physique; daily shaving; not surrendering to the urge to cry in times of distress; and so on. The fact that there are different norms for different genders does not mean that men are free and women constrained. Instead, as Bourdieu himself asserts, "Men are also prisoners, and insidiously victims, of the dominant representation."[3]

Bourdieu's theory has limited resources for condemning some configurations of habitus as worse than others, as normatively undesirable in terms of justice. His use of the terms "domination" and "violence" certainly implies that he does not view the habitus as a neutral way of being but rather wants to condemn certain social arrangements and the identities that result from them as in some way unjust or oppressive. However, his use of those terms is ambiguous. If symbolic violence is gentle, imperceptible, and ubiquitous, there may not be much wrong with it. "Violence" for Bourdieu looks more like "influence" in the lay sense, and influence can be benign. Bourdieu does insist "I never talk of influence"—rather, for him, people's minds are *"constructed according to cognitive structures that are issued out of the very structures of the world."*[4] But this account exacerbates the problem. If symbolic violence does not destroy or harm a preexisting consciousness but *constructs* that consciousness, it is even harder to criticize. Symbolic violence does not harm us, or damage us; the gendered habitus does not control us, or dominate us; rather, symbolic violence and the gendered habitus constitute us, *are* us. We might wish we had been differently constituted, but why should we? What, from within a gendered habitus, is objectionable about it? If social space *"commands the repre-*

2. Bourdieu and Wacquant, *Invitation to Reflexive Sociology*, 168.
3. Bourdieu, *Masculine Domination*, 49.
4. Bourdieu and Wacquant, *Invitation to Reflexive Sociology*, 168; emphasis in the original.

sentations that the social agents can have of it,"[5] from where do agents derive the means to criticize that space or those representations?

Perhaps the problem for Bourdieu is that we are *dominated*. But the term "domination" is not much more fruitful as a normative signifier. Iris Marion Young gives two reasons why domination is unjust: first, it deprives people of a kind of control over their lives which they ought to have; and second, by implication it deprives some people of this control more than others.[6] Young's approach is all about the ways in which some people dominate others, such that there is an inequality of power. If we start with the liberal presumption that inequality is bad, then we have two reasons to dislike domination.

However, a liberal critique of domination such as Young's will not work for Bourdieu, since he does not believe that anyone can determine their actions, much less the conditions of their actions. Although he does believe that the habitus can change, we have seen that the opportunities for change are limited. His discussion of symbolic violence, in particular, plays down the options open to people. Domination cannot be problematic, then, because it is a special case in which individuals cannot determine their actions or their conditions, as the condition of humans is ever thus.

Moreover, Bourdieu agrees with the second reactionary response outlined above: that all are subject to structures of patriarchy. Not only are men subject to patriarchal norms, for Bourdieu, they are "victims" of them. In other words, men neither benefit from patriarchy nor play a part in influencing women to submit to it. In what sense, then, do men or masculinity *dominate*? Indeed, although it is clear that, for Bourdieu, women are the dominated and men (by inference) are the dominant,[7] in *Practical Reason* he implies that the term "masculine domination" is not meant to refer to domination of or by men, but rather to a general system of domination which applies to everybody but which is structured in terms of norms of masculinity.[8] Men, though they are the dominant actors in masculine domination, are nonetheless dominated by it, in the sense that they too must endure its restrictions. But if the normative sense of "domination" in systems of masculine domination refers merely to the domination of social

5. Bourdieu, *Practical Reason*, 13; emphasis added.
6. Iris Marion Young, *Justice and the Politics of Difference*, 31.
7. Bourdieu and Wacquant, *Invitation to Reflexive Sociology*, 171.
8. Bourdieu, *Practical Reason*, 34.

norms and structures, and not to a power imbalance or inequality between those individuals who are subjected to the structures, we have
little reason to work to overcome systems of domination. For any subsequent set of social norms would also be a system of domination, as
it too would place constraints on social actors. Bourdieu's account is
insufficient as it stands to give us any normative reason to limit domination or the "inferior" status of women. Liberal and feminist concepts
of justice and equality are invaluable in this regard.

Judith Butler highlights the problems that we must face if we wish
to combine a strong account of social construction with normative feminist critique. Like Bourdieu, Butler argues that "power pervades the
very conceptual apparatus that seeks to negotiate its terms, including
the subject position of the critic."[9] This does not mean, for Butler, that
there can be no criticism. Rather, it means that criticism must take as
its starting point its position within the social and political context it
criticizes, and must not portray its own foundations as given, unques-
tionable, or universal. In making this argument, Butler asks a question
that strikes at the heart of many variants of liberalism. She asks, "Are
these 'foundations,' that is, those premises that function as authorizing
grounds, are they themselves not constituted through exclusions
which, taken into account, expose the foundational premise as a contingent and contestable presumption?"[10] The target of this challenge
could be political liberalism, with its exclusion of "unreasonable" people and "indecent" cultures from deliberation about the supposedly
common, consensual good. Liberal political institutions are supposed
to be justified by the fact that they are universally assented to. Consensus is, for the political liberal, one of "the premises which function as
authorizing grounds." But, as Butler insists and as I argued in the
introduction, the consensus is constructed by excluding those who
would disagree if they were included. It is very easy to reach consensus
if you exclude beforehand all those who would disagree.

Political liberalism falls foul of this problem because, in its attempt
to cast itself as an unimposed, tolerant doctrine that can be the product
of an overlapping consensus, it obscures the extent to which its own
foundations are substantive and particular. Butler's critique suggests
that liberalism might do better to embrace its particularism than to try

9. Judith Butler, "Contingent Foundations," 39.
10. Ibid., 39–40; see also Judith Butler, "Restaging the Universal," 11.

to disguise it, for, Butler argues, the universalist feminism of theorists such as Martha Nussbaum and Susan Moller Okin "does not understand the parochial character of its own norms, and does not consider the way in which feminism works in full complicity with US colonial aims."[11] But if liberals embrace their particularism, and if critics accept the situated nature of their criticism, what force can their normative claims have over those who disagree?

It is on this question that Butler's position is weak. On the one hand, she makes forceful claims for the completeness of the critic's entrapment within her existing context, claims that call into question the very possibility of genuinely critical argument or normative theory that can have any application beyond the subject who produces it.[12] On the other hand, Butler wants to avoid the criticism that her approach leaves feminists with no normative resources. As such, she insists that, despite the problems she has outlined, normative principles are required. She even allows that the concept of the "universal," though deeply problematic, is crucial to normative theory. However, we are left with what Butler describes as the "paradox" of the need to construct a universal category that can only ever be culturally specific[13]—a paradox which Butler sometimes suggests can never be answered.[14]

Seyla Benhabib also engages with the question of how to reconcile an account of social construction with normative feminist arguments. She suggests that social construction, or what she calls the "Death of Man," can take either a strong or a weak form, with only the weak form aiding feminism. In its strong sense, which impedes feminism, it declares the death of the subject conceived of as an autonomous agent. According to the strong sense, there can be no autonomy because there is no position immune from social influence, and no individual who has not been shaped by social norms. This strong sense is redolent of Foucault's early work, in which individuals are represented as docile bodies, unable to resist the violent force of their surroundings. It is clear why feminists must reject this thesis: if individuals can never be autonomous, there can never be an emancipatory feminist project.[15] Instead, feminists can accept the thesis of the Death of Man only in

---

11. Butler, "Restaging the Universal," 35.
12. Butler, "Contingent Foundations," 42.
13. Ibid., 129.
14. Butler, "Restaging the Universal," 39.
15. Seyla Benhabib, "Feminism and Postmodernism," 21.

its weak form: the subject is radically situated in various contexts and discourses from which autonomy is possible but difficult. As Benhabib argues, individuals may be strongly constrained by their social circumstances, but the fact of that constraint makes liberation more, not less, necessary from a normative point of view. However, the goal behind a project of emancipation is not to free individuals from all social influence (for that would be impossible and undesirable), but rather to free individuals from *unjust* social influence, or at least the most pernicious forms of it.

Hirschmann on Social Construction

Nancy Hirschmann's account is useful at this stage because it combines a systematic analysis of the general phenomenon of social construction with an explicit feminist normative focus. Hirschmann explains social construction by dividing it into three "levels." She names the first level "the ideological misrepresentation of reality."[16] According to this level, social construction is the artificial creation of social norms and the false representation of the way things are, of their nature. This level of social construction has clear Marxist features, echoing Marx's critique of capitalist ideology. It is also found in feminist analysis of the way in which patriarchy "fools" women into aspiring to standards of beauty that can only be reached by airbrushed supermodels.

Hirschmann highlights two problems with the ideological misrepresentation of reality thesis. First, such an approach appears to require "second-guessing" of people's interests and preferences.[17] If a woman says she enjoys making herself look beautiful, like the models she sees in magazines, the first level of social construction implies that we can say that she is misguided, and that we can—and perhaps should—liberate her by forcibly preventing her from performing her beauty rituals. Hirschmann maintains that such an approach is problematic since it fails to notice that participating in such practices can sometimes contribute to freedom. She argues that although beauty pageants, for example, are generally considered to embody sexist beauty norms, nevertheless "a woman who has entered beauty pageants, endured the rigors of competition, and as a result won scholarships, a degree of

16. Hirschmann, *Subject of Liberty*, 77.
17. Ibid., 78.

fame and wealth, and/or a springboard start to a career in the performing arts would have to be considered autonomous," where autonomy
is understood as "critical competence in rational reflection."[18] As such,
we cannot straightforwardly condemn the ideals of beauty endorsed in
beauty pageants as ideological misrepresentations of reality that constrain women's freedom.

Hirschmann is correct to point out that participating in beauty pageants can increase women's autonomy, in the sense of bringing participants opportunities and success that they would not otherwise enjoy.
It may also be true to say that, if a woman assessed the various options
available to her, she might rationally decide that beauty pageants offer
the best chances of success. In other words, an individual can be affected by social construction without suffering from "false consciousness" or a failure to realize where her rational self-interest lies. However, this observation does not undermine the thesis of the ideological
misrepresentation of reality: that the beauty standards imposed on
women and perfected in the beauty pageant are patriarchal, oppressive,
and imposed on all women despite being unrealizable by the vast majority.[19] The fact that success in emulating such beauty standards can
bring a woman great success in obtaining other social goods in no way
entails that the beauty standards are accurate reflections of womanhood. Moreover, feminists might want to question why it is that a good
path to success for the woman in Hirschmann's example should be a
beauty pageant. Why should it be the case that a good way for the
woman to achieve scholarships, wealth, and a career in the performing
arts is by smiling inanely in a swimming costume and high heels?
Indeed, why should smiling inanely in a swimming costume and high
heels be the path to any social goods at all?[20]

18. Ibid., 79. The concept of autonomy is critically assessed in Part Two.

19. Beauty pageants are different from other competitions that most people could not
hope to win, such as the Olympic games or Mastermind. While these competitions do promote attributes that are seen as generally desirable (fitness and knowledge), they do not set
standards for all people to the extent that beauty pageants set standards for all women. The
difference is a matter of both scope and extent. All women, regardless of their other achievements, are expected to go to fairly lengthy measures to (try to) make themselves beautiful.
All women are expected to make up, dress up, slim down, moisturize, exercise, accessorize,
tan, wax, bleach, clip, color, and style just to go to work; almost no one has to throw a javelin
or know the number of goals made by Manchester United in 1990 just to get through the
day.

20. Kimberley Yuracko puts this point as follows: "Women's choices to sexually objectify
themselves probably look problematic and pressured to some feminists because they feel
women should not be presented with the choice of whether to turn themselves into decora-

In fact, although it may be the case that individual women do autonomously choose to enter beauty pageants, and that winning a beauty pageant may indeed increase a woman's autonomy, there remain considerable grounds for criticizing beauty pageants and beauty norms as ideological misrepresentations of reality. This is not to say that any woman who chooses to participate in them is fundamentally nonautonomous, but it is to say that women's equality would be better realized if the power of sexist beauty norms were lessened.[21]

The second criticism that Hirschmann makes of the first level of social construction is that it implies that there could be a true representation of reality. In other words, the misrepresentation thesis makes "an implicit assumption that if patriarchy would just leave women alone, women would be okay. Beneath that is a further assumption that women could *not* be socially constructed at all, that there is some true identity and set of interests that women have as women—an essentialist or naturalist thesis which, ironically, most feminists would consciously claim to reject."[22] Instead, Hirschmann maintains, social construction goes all the way down. If social construction did not enshrine one set of beauty standards, it would enshrine another. This point is closely connected to the accounts of Foucault and Bourdieu that we have considered so far. However, if we are seeking an account of social construction that can sustain normative feminist argument, we need to elaborate it somewhat.

First, it is possible to reject the idea of an essentialist female nature while at the same time arguing that some beauty norms are more realistic, more "true" than others. Womanhood may not have a conceptual, all-encompassing "truth," but women are concretely embodied, and the nature of women's bodies can be more or less truthfully represented. At the most basic, an idea of female beauty that admits women who range from skinny to plump is clearly more realistic, more in line with the realities of women's bodies, than one that admits only women who are extremely thin. Similarly, a society that finds only youthful

---

tive gift objects for men's gratification in order to achieve their highest possible social status" (*Perfectionism and Contemporary Feminist Values*, 70).

21. For further feminist critiques of feminist beauty norms, see works such as Wolf, *Beauty Myth*; Sheila Jeffreys, *Beauty and Misogyny*; and Bordo, *Unbearable Weight*.

22. Hirschmann, *Subject of Liberty*, 79; emphasis in the original. One example of an explicit feminist rejection of a "true" female identity is MacKinnon, "'The Case' Responds," 710.

faces beautiful requires women to engage in ideological misrepresenta-tion of themselves if they wish to continue to appear beautiful through-out their lives, whereas a society that sees beauty in all ages allows women's self-representations to be more truthful. The fact that social construction does itself work on bodies does not undermine the fact that bodies do have a concrete form which can be more or less con-torted and falsified. Cosmetic surgery represents the falsification of the body, and the misrepresentation of the individual whose body it is, *par excellence*—for its results cannot be achieved by the natural processes of the transformed body (as occurs with diet or exercise) but are con-sciously constructed by the surgeon in line with particular norms of beauty. Moreover, cosmetic surgery often entails reconstructing the body from alien substances, such as silicone or saline implants or colla-gen injections.

Second, even if there is no "truth" to women's nature, there are still grounds to discriminate between alternative norms, such as standards of beauty, on the grounds that some are more compatible with wom-en's equality and well-being than others. In other words, we can make a normative distinction between alternative norms, even if we cannot make a distinction in terms of truth and falsity. Hirschmann actually argues strongly in favor of this point. As she puts it, "Some contexts are better than others at providing women with genuine alternatives from which they can choose."[23] So, even if we are wary of identifying ideological misrepresentations of *reality*, we should not be wary of iden-tifying ideological misrepresentations of equality or autonomy. A soci-ety in which women's autonomy is increased by entering beauty pageants is one in which women's autonomy is ideologically misrepre-sented.[24]

This criticism connects with Hirschmann's second level of social construction: what she calls "materialization." Materialization occurs when social norms construct people's *identities*, not just their behavior. As Hirschmann puts it, "The construction of social behaviors and rules takes on a life of its own, and becomes constitutive not only of what women are allowed to *do*, but of what they are allowed to *be*."[25] The materialization thesis demonstrates one problem with separating so-

23. Hirschmann, *Subject of Liberty*, ix.
24. Diana Meyers similarly argues, in *Gender in the Mirror*, that we should replace patriar-chal "figurations of womanhood" with feminist ones.
25. Hirschmann, *Subject of Liberty*, 79; emphasis in the original.

cial construction into levels, for perhaps the clearest example of materialization is the way that female beauty norms concretely create the female body, an aspect of social construction that Hirschmann uses to illustrate the first level. Women who wish to follow beauty norms will alter the physical shape and form of their bodies, perhaps becoming thin through dieting, gaining larger breasts or smaller noses through cosmetic surgery, or losing wrinkles through botox injections and anti-aging creams.

It is clear, then, that the second level of social construction, the materialization thesis, has a complex relationship with the ideological misrepresentation of reality thesis. On the one hand, materialization is the direct result of ideological misrepresentation: women's bodies take on a different material form in response to the norms enshrined by ideological misrepresentation. On the other hand, once a norm has materialized, it is no longer true to say that it is a misrepresentation of reality. Instead, the norm has become reality. After dieting, breast implants, and botox injections, women's bodies really are thin, large-breasted, and wrinkle-free, and this standard is potentially realizable by all women. It is no longer true to say that such standards of beauty are unrealistic or impossible. In Hirschmann's words, "On this level, social construction is not at odds with material reality; it actually produces it."[26]

It is difficult, then, to see how the first two levels of social construction can be both distinct and part of the same concept. Hirschmann does not want to abandon the first level altogether: she states that while it is "flawed and limited," it remains "important to feminism,"[27] and frequently uses it to explain the issues of battered women, welfare, and veiling that inform her book.[28] But if materialization means that a social norm becomes reality, and if there is no "truth" or reality beyond a social norm, how can a social norm be an ideological misrepresentation of reality? Something will have to give: either social norms are always incompletely realized, or there must be some alternative, in some sense universal or objective, reality that stands outside the social norm. It is my contention that the alternative universal "reality" should

26. Ibid., 80.
27. Ibid., 79.
28. For example, Hirschmann claims that, in the case of domestic violence, "The first level . . .—social construction as domination and ideological misrepresentation—is the most evident" (ibid., 114).

be understood not as an objective feature of humanity, or of woman- or manhood, but as the *normative* principles of equality and autonomy. Materialized social norms can be criticized as ideological misrepresentations only from a standpoint of universal normative principles that do not depend on social norms for their validity.

Normative principles such as freedom and equality should not be understood as objective facts about the essential nature of human beings. Describing someone as free, or as equal with others, can be understood in two ways: as a description of how that person is actually treated in the context in question, or as a claim about how that person *ought* to be treated. For example, describing a black slave in colonial America as free and equal is either an incorrect statement of fact (on the first understanding) or a normative statement that slavery should be abolished (on the second). It is not particularly helpful to understand the claim that the slave is free and equal as referring to some objective fact about the essential nature of humanity, that humans are naturally, metaphysically, or unavoidably free and equal. Not only is it unclear what such a statement would mean, its substantive implications are in any case that people *ought to be treated* as free and equal. Normative principles can be universal without being essentialist: describing how people ought to be treated, rather than how they inevitably or essentially are.

Finally, Hirschmann outlines the third level of social construction: "the discursive construction of social meaning." It is this level which, according to Hirschmann, invokes "postmodern" thought, particularly that of Foucault.[29] "At this level," Hirschmann writes, "construction of reality takes root in our very language, where it establishes the parameters for understanding, defining, and communicating about reality, about who women are, what we are doing, what we desire."[30] In other words, social construction affects our ability to communicate and conceptualize by affecting language. Without language, Hirschmann maintains, we cannot have ideas, and cannot be subjects: "We can only be the kinds of persons that our context and language allow."[31] This level of social construction is needed, Hirschmann suggests, to avoid

---

29. Hirschmann cites thinkers such as Foucault, Derrida, Lyotard, Spivak, and Butler in *The Subject of Liberty* (see page 81). It is Foucault, though, who receives her most detailed analysis.

30. Ibid., 80.

31. Ibid., 81.

the implication of the first two levels that "men are the constructors, women the constructed, just as, for Marx, capitalists are the constructors, the proletariat are the constructed."[32]

As we have seen, Bourdieu in particular explicitly emphasizes that his account of domination does not imply such a crude social analysis of hierarchy, and so Hirschmann's desire to avoid such an implication is well founded. However, it is not clear that such an implication either is entailed by the first two levels, or would be countered by the social construction of language. If a powerful group wishes consciously to dominate a powerless group, and construct it as inferior, it can use the social construction of language as a tool, inventing and using derogatory terms for the members of the powerless group—or, indeed, flattering terms for members of that group who display desired characteristics. Similarly, the powerless group can consciously and intentionally attempt to resignify that same language. Thus, the term "queer" was consciously used and entrenched for a long time as a tool of homophobia. However, it has been consciously "reclaimed" by some members of the homosexual community as a means to fight its oppression, so that "queer politics" now indicates a radical endorsement of homosexual equality. Socially constructed language, then, can be a tool for either top-down oppression or more diffuse, capillary forms of power and resistance.

While Hirschmann's discussion does highlight the key elements of social construction, and helps us to think through the concept in the context of gender, I suggest a return to the basic idea behind Hirschmann's account: that social construction has effects on both the *options* that are available to be chosen, and on the *preferences and beliefs* that lead an individual to choose one option rather than another.[33] In other words, we can ask what it is that an individual is able to choose, and we can ask whether and in what sense she actually, actively makes an autonomous choice.

Liberalism and Universalism

How, then, can liberals respond to the charge that their attempts at developing universal principles are rendered invalid by the social con-

---

32. Ibid.
33. Hirschmann terms these two effects "the external structures of patriarchy and the inner selves of women" (ibid., ix).

struction I am asking them to acknowledge? As we have seen, some liberals attempt to escape this problem by stepping back from claims to universality. Political liberals such as John Rawls, for example, claim that their liberal principles need not be universal since they need not apply to all aspects of people's lives (or to the lives of people who do not live in liberal societies). Rather, liberal principles apply to political life only, and moreover, they can be accepted as appropriate political principles by all reasonable people within a liberal society. If this overlapping consensus pertains, there is no need for controversial claims about universality. Hence Rawls is keen in both *Political Liberalism* and *The Law of Peoples* to distance himself from any claims that liberalism might be a universal doctrine. In *Political Liberalism* the distancing occurs when liberalism is relegated to the political sphere and not the comprehensive; in *The Law of Peoples* liberalism is further restricted to societies that are already liberal.

I suggested earlier that, rather than escaping the problem of universality, the strategy of political liberalism is actually particularly vulnerable to criticisms such as Butler's. Because it attempts to portray itself as a doctrine based on no comprehensive conception of the good, a doctrine to which all can agree without being coerced or accepting power-laden discourse on substantive nonpolitical values, it is particularly vulnerable to accounts of social construction that question the possibility of such neutral universality. However, Rawls's strategy of restricting liberalism to already liberal societies undermines its normative force. Indeed, this strategy conflicts with what Brian Barry sees as liberalism's very purpose. As he puts it, "The point of liberalism is that it is universalistic. . . . The liberal position is clear. Nobody, anywhere in the world, should be denied liberal protections against injustice and oppression."[34]

There is something of a tension, then, between the claim that liberalism needs to recognize its own particularity and the liberal desire to make universal egalitarian claims. Rawls recognizes that comprehensive liberalism is not universal, but even political liberalism rests on substantive premises. Not everyone does, can, or will agree with those premises or with the liberal conclusions, and finding liberal arguments persuasive may have much (though not everything) to do with being brought up within a liberal society. Political liberalism may appear to

34. Brian Barry, *Culture and Equality*, 138.

be universal in origin (since it is derived from an overlapping consensus) and (nearly) universal in application ("nearly" in that the exclusion of unreasonable groups from the domain of deliberation may mean that they are excluded from the domain of liberal freedom and equality). In fact, political liberalism is particular in origin and particular in application, even within politically liberal societies. It is particular in origin because not everyone has or will or can agree with liberal values. As Will Kymlicka argues, "Non-liberal minorities . . . want internal restrictions that take precedence over individual rights. Rawls's political liberalism is as hostile to that demand as Mill's comprehensive liberalism. The fact that Rawls's theory is less comprehensive does not make his theory more sympathetic to the demands of non-liberal minorities."[35] Similarly, Charles Taylor claims, "Liberalism is not a possible meeting ground for all cultures, but is the political expression of one range of cultures, and quite incompatible with other ranges. . . . [L]iberalism can't and shouldn't clam complete cultural neutrality. Liberalism is also a fighting creed. The hospitable variant I espouse, as well as the most rigid forms, has to draw the line."[36] Liberalism must be particular in origin. It does not start from universal premises, or from a position outside social influence. It cannot be derived from every alternative conception of the good. It is not the real meaning behind all other, apparently illiberal, texts, religions, or cultures. Liberalism is a substantive, power-laden, non-neutral, situated doctrine that clashes, fundamentally and sometimes irreconcilably, with other doctrines.

Moreover, *political* liberalism at least is particular in application. As Okin argues, even those groups which are deemed reasonable are allowed to engage in illiberal practices outside the political sphere. As such, some individuals within those groups (often women) do not adequately benefit from liberal freedom and equality. Such groups may claim liberal acceptance, since they comply with liberal justice in public. However, this public compliance allows them to reject those selfsame values in the private sphere—the sphere that most undermines the equality of the most vulnerable individuals.[37]

If we reject political liberalism, two main options remain for restor-

---

35. Kymlicka, *Multicultural Citizenship*, 164.
36. Taylor, "The Politics of Recognition," 63.
37. Okin, "Is Multiculturalism Bad for Women?"

ing consistency between universalism and particularism. The first is to accept that liberalism is a particular doctrine and, as a result, to restrict its application to liberal societies—or more precisely, to culturally homogenous liberal societies. Liberalism becomes openly particular in both origin and application. This option constructs liberalism as a substantive theory of the good like any other, and relegates its ethical status to that of moral relativism, an outcome that is problematic on several levels. At the most simple and practical level, there are very few homogenous liberal societies, and so very few places for such a liberalism to apply. Few liberals would be content to limit their horizons so drastically. Moreover, a political doctrine such as liberalism must be compatible with some account of political obligation. That is to say, it must be able to give a reason why those who do not agree with liberal laws or institutions must nevertheless obey them, and cannot claim the sovereignty of self-interest. Furthermore, as a normative theory, liberalism needs to be able to claim that some positions are flawed, and to have some grounds for making such judgments.

An alternative option is for liberals to recognize that their doctrine can be particular in origin without renouncing all claims to be universal in application. Liberalism can appear caught in a series of paradoxical dilemmas concerning the scope of its fundamental principles and the contradictions of universality and pluralism. These dilemmas take the form of the question "Should we apply X to those who reject X?" Thus we may ask, "Should we tolerate doctrines that preach intolerance?" or "Do we treat people equally if we allow them to treat themselves and each other unequally?" or "Do we violate people's right to choose their own way of life if we argue that a chosen life is better than an unchosen one?" John Gray argues that liberalism has "two faces," with one face answering "no" to these sorts of questions and the other answering "yes."[38] Similarly, William Galston identifies two versions of liberalism and defends the version that would answer "yes" (so that, for example, liberals should tolerate intolerance).[39] In Part Two I discuss similar questions that arise when considering whether the liberal concern for choice and autonomy imply that people should be able to choose nonautonomous lives. In general, I answer "no" to these sorts of questions. It seems to me to be a peculiar denial of the liberal point

38. John Gray, *Two Faces of Liberalism.*
39. William Galston, "Two Concepts of Liberalism."

of view to answer "yes" to them, almost to say that being liberal requires one to be ashamed of liberalism and to attempt to suppress its values.[40] Liberalism seems to entail letting nonliberals win—or, as the old joke goes, a liberal is someone who can't take her own side in an argument.[41]

In defense of my position it is worth reflecting on the relationship between equality and universalism. It is in the nature of liberal equality that it cannot be denied to people on the basis of characteristics such as gender, race, or culture. Equality is not equality if it allows women to be rendered systematically inferior, if it does not recognize the equal moral worth of those in other countries, or if it fails to treat members of some cultures and religions as individuals worthy of autonomy, for example, by failing to protect the rights of women. Indeed, the concepts of equality and universality are strongly linked. It is *possible* to have nonuniversal conceptions of equality.[42] For example, the Declaration of Independence of the United States stated in 1776 that "all men are created equal" but, at the time, that equality applied only to white males. Thus nonuniversal equality applies only to a particular group of people, between whom conditions are equal. However, the more a conception of equality is nonuniversal—that is, the smaller and more specific is the group—the more it is a description of one level of a hierarchy, rather than a statement of equality. "All white men are equal (and not black people or women)" is another way of saying "society is stratified along lines of gender and race." In other words, society is characterized by inequality. Nonuniversal equality is hierarchy. It follows, then, that a strong commitment to equality is *pro tanto* a commitment to universalism.

40. Susan Mendus poses a similar question in her *Impartiality in Moral and Political Philosophy:* she asks whether the liberal ideas of skepticism and reasonable pluralism are self-undermining since they imply their own uncertainty or contingency. See especially 18–22.

41. This point, that the alternative view of liberalism seems to entail letting nonliberals win, echoes what Susan Mendus describes as the paradox of toleration, "which involves explaining how the tolerator might think it good to tolerate that which is morally wrong." Mendus believes that the paradox can be solved by pointing to the liberal belief in autonomy: "We ought to tolerate what is morally wrong because it is part of being an autonomous agent that one should be allowed to do what is morally wrong." However, the paradox remains if the "morally wrong" thing that we are allowing the agent to do in the name of autonomy is to follow a nonautonomous life (*Toleration and the Limits of Liberalism*, 20, 161).

42. It is also possible to have a nonegalitarian conception of universality, if one's conception of universality were something like "everyone should adhere to the rules of this particular hierarchical system."

Joseph Raz considers the concept of universality. He shows, through a variety of examples, that no set of formal conditions can encapsulate the intuitive meaning of the concept, for any proposed conditions have counterintuitive results. As such, he concludes, "The view that values are universal, as a commonly expressed view, seems to me to be a *substantive moral view.* . . . It is a product of the moral struggle for the rejection of certain false value distinctions: the rejection of the special privileges of the aristocracy, and the evaluative beliefs which underpinned them in pre-enlightenment Europe, the rejection of racism and sexism, and the like."[43] This statement echoes Butler's position: any suggested definition of the universal contains within it substantive moral claims about the kinds of people who should count within it, and the kinds of attributes which are normatively relevant. Raz is correct to make such a statement. However, his conclusion that liberals should settle for a minimal, formal understanding of the concept of the universal is unsatisfactory, as his counterexamples show.[44] Rather, liberals should recognize the connection between the concepts of equality and universality: insofar as liberalism is a theory of equality and not hierarchy, it should be universally applied. Paradigmatically, liberal equality denies the moral relevance of ascriptive characteristics such as gender and race, and asserts that the individual is the correct unit of moral analysis. As such, liberal values of freedom, autonomy, and equal worth should be accorded to individuals regardless of their ascriptive characteristics, and regardless of their position within a group hierar-

---

43. Joseph Raz, *Value, Respect and Attachment,* 58.

44. Raz suggests four possible criteria for a value to be universal. The first is that "the conditions for [the value's] application can be stated without use of singular references, that is, without any reference to place or time, or to any named individual, etc." The second adds the requirement that "in principle, [the value] can be instantiated in any place and at any time" (*Value, Respect and Attachment,* 54). Neither of these definitions of universality is sufficient, according to Raz, since they would allow gendered values, such as feminine virtues, to count as universal. The third is that "a value is universal only if, if at least some people can display it, then it is in principle possible for every individual person to display it" (56). Raz dismisses this one as well, since everyone could in principle have a sex change, again rendering gendered values universal. Finally, Raz suggests a definition according to which "only rights which everyone enjoys, not merely ones which everyone can in principle enjoy, are universal." He rejects this suggestion as well, although his reason for doing so is odd: "Not everyone is funny or amusing, but we are, I assume, happy to regard this as a universal evaluative property" (58). It is not quite clear in what way humor is a universal property—on the contrary, people seem to have very different ideas of what constitutes humor or amusement. That problem aside, the point of relevance here is that Raz is correct to dismiss at least the first two definitions, and possibly the third as well, as insufficiently substantive conceptions of universality.

chy. The substantive normative principles that underlie the liberal commitment to equality also suggest a commitment to universality.

Richard Rorty suggests that liberalism has an inherent tendency to universalize, but claims that this tendency need not rest on a commitment to universal origins or to neutral or objective premises. His approach of "ironism" is a version of social construction, according to which we must recognize that our beliefs are "caused by nothing deeper than contingent historical circumstance,"[45] and that our own "final vocabularies," or the sets of words we use to justify our basic beliefs, cannot themselves be given any noncircular justification. Moreover, an ironist feels that there is no sense in which her own final vocabulary is more objective or true than the final vocabulary of others, since she finds admirable qualities in alternative final vocabularies, and since she rejects the very idea that a final vocabulary could ever be "true" or "objective."[46] This combination of views leads liberal ironists such as Rorty to conclude: "We cannot look back behind the processes of socialization which convinced us twentieth-century liberals of the validity of [liberal values] and appeal to something which is more "real" or less ephemeral than the historical contingencies which brought those processes into existence. *We* have to start from where *we* are."[47]

Despite this radical rejection of objective foundations for liberalism, Rorty retains a commitment to universality. I suggested earlier that a commitment to equality entails a corresponding commitment to universality. Rorty does not engage with the concept of equality as such; for him, it is the avoidance of cruelty that defines liberalism. However, he also maintains that liberalism contains within itself the tendency to universalize, a tendency that in no way conflicts with its particular origins but rather flows from it. This is because what might be thought of as the "ethnocentrism" of a liberalism that can only be particular "is the ethnocentrism of a 'we' ('we liberals') which is dedicated to enlarging itself, to creating an ever larger and more variegated *ethnos*. It is the 'we' of the people who have been brought up to distrust ethnocentrism."[48] In other words, even a commitment to liberal values that is self-consciously contingent can be compatible with the wish to univer-

45. Richard Rorty, *Contingency, Irony, and Solidarity*, 189.
46. Ibid., 73.
47. Ibid., 198.
48. Ibid.

salize those values. Indeed, on Rorty's account one can scarcely be a liberal without this desire.[49]

If liberals wish to universalize their values of freedom and equality, it is natural to ask why that wish should be respected. In other words, are there any grounds for liberalism? Rorty fundamentally rejects any answer that claims to be "basic" or to rest on some sort of objective reason; for him, there simply cannot be any noncircular reason other than that liberal values form part of our final vocabulary.[50] While it may be true that there can be no neutral or objective answer about ultimate ends, there nevertheless can be arguments that are more or less likely to convince. In other words, there can be good—even if not decisive— arguments for using liberalism as the standard for judging other regimes. Many such arguments are based on extolling the considerable virtues of liberal autonomy and equality per se: their contribution to human flourishing, to rationality and progress, and so on. But beyond these arguments lies a more general justification for liberalism: even a comprehensive, nonpolitical liberalism is the best way to accommodate difference. Universal liberalism actually allows individuals to make their own choices about their way of life, as free as possible from coercion and injustice. These choices are no longer used as legitimators of unjust outcomes or social structures, and so the paradox of using socially constructed choices to legitimate that which constructed them disappears. Instead, choice is used as a way for individuals to determine what sort of life they wish to lead, from an array of options that do not compromise their equality or well-being. A liberal state that forces a cultural group, for example, to allow its members to be fully autonomous and equal allows for more value-pluralism at the level of the individual than does a state that allows cultural groups to impose themselves on individuals within the group. And, as Nussbaum rightly argues: "The central question of politics should not be, How is the organic whole doing? but rather, How are X and Y and Z and Q doing?"[51] As such, those liberals who are wary of asserting the universal applicability of liberalism out of deference to freedom of choice and diversity are misguided. For to allow other groups to act illiberally by

---

49. Michael Bacon argues that Rorty is as much a liberal universalist as Brian Barry, discussed in Chapter 4. See Bacon, "Liberal Universalism."

50. Rorty, *Contingency, Irony, and Solidarity,* xv, 51, 197.

51. Martha Nussbaum, *Sex and Social Justice,* 62.

imposing their norms is precisely to allow those groups to prevent the freedom of choice and diversity of their members.

Difference

This conclusion brings us to a further major issue arising from an attempt to use accounts of social construction to illuminate feminism and liberalism: difference. The idea of social construction lends support to the claim of "cultural" feminists that there is a tendency in normative theory to privilege the perspective of the powerful. In feminism, this tendency is evident when white, middle-class, heterosexual Western women claim to speak for women as a whole, ignoring the different perspectives and oppressions of poor or lesbian women, and women from ethnic minorities or other cultures. According to cultural feminists, feminists (and normative theorists more generally) must pay more attention, and make more concessions, to difference if they are to avoid this form of cultural imperialism. The question of how to do so is a complex and involved one, and I devote much of Part Two to discussing different liberal approaches to difference. In the rest of this chapter I outline two feminist approaches, each of which attempts to combine feminist normative claims with an awareness of social construction.

Young and the Politics of Difference

Iris Marion Young is a prominent advocate of the moral relevance of difference, and of a combination of liberal normative concerns with ideas of social construction. Young sees her approach as following "the spirit of critical theory," and as drawing on ideas from liberalism, feminism, and communitarianism (among others) while also criticizing aspects of those approaches.[52] In liberal spirit she argues that there are two universal values that must be realized for the good life, values which presuppose that humans have equal moral worth. These values are, first, "developing and exercising one's capacities and expressing one's experience" and, second, "participating in determining one's action and the conditions of one's action."[53] Young emphasizes, however,

52. Iris Marion Young, "Reply to Tebble," 282–83.
53. Young, Justice and the Politics of Difference, 37.

that justice consists in securing only the institutional conditions for realization of the good life, not the good life itself.

However, Young is also highly critical of many aspects of liberalism. Her first criticism is that liberalism focuses too much on redistribution of goods, failing to notice that domination and oppression are in fact the main barriers to justice. Domination is defined as "structural or systemic phenomena which exclude people from participating in determining their actions or the conditions of their actions";[54] it is therefore by definition the main threat to Young's second universal value, autonomy. In *Inclusion and Democracy*, Young refers to domination as the opposite of self-determination.[55] Young defines oppression as "systematic institutional processes which prevent some people from learning and using satisfying and expansive skills in socially recognized settings, or institutionalized social processes which inhibit people's ability to play and communicate with others or to express their feelings and perspective on social life in contexts where others can listen."[56] Elsewhere, she defines oppression more concisely as the opposite of self-development.[57] Oppression and domination clearly must be overcome wherever possible. However, in her discussion of the politics of difference, Young draws some problematic conclusions from this basic idea.

Young argues that a just state is one that follows the "politics of difference" rather than the "ideal of assimilation." According to the politics of difference, equality "sometimes requires different treatment for oppressed or disadvantaged groups";[58] following the ideal of assimilation, however, requires "treating everyone according to the same principles, rules and standards"[59] and "the transcendence of group difference."[60] However, *contra* Young, the difference between the politics of difference and the ideal of assimilation is not that clear. We could treat disadvantaged groups differently as a means to transcending group difference, and could even do so in a manner that treated everyone according to the "same principles." For example, affirmative action policies treat applicants from ethnic minorities and applicants from

54. Ibid., 31.
55. Iris Marion Young, *Inclusion and Democracy*, 32.
56. Young, *Justice and the Politics of Difference*, 38.
57. Young, *Inclusion and Democracy*, 31–32.
58. Young, *Justice and the Politics of Difference*, 158.
59. Ibid.
60. Ibid., 157.

the white majority differently. However, the aim is to remove the disadvantages associated with ethnicity and thus to transcend difference; and moreover, all applicants could be said to be treated according to the same principle if that principle were something like "positions should be allocated according to some combination of talent and compensation for past injustice or a deprived background."

The distinguishing feature of the politics of difference, then, is its aim to avoid the transcendence of difference. Young gives two sets of reasons for this aim. The first set of reasons is to do with bias: an ideal of assimilation is likely to represent the position of a privileged group that does not recognize its own particularity. However, Young recognizes that there could be an ideal of assimilation that recognized the risk of bias in attempts to formulate "universal" values and "impartial" institutions, and actively tried to create genuinely fair institutions. This is the aim of my approach: to recognize existing forms of inequality, injustice, and bias (especially gender bias), and to develop a universal approach that minimizes that injustice. Young argues, however, that even this kind of approach, which she calls "transformational assimilationism," pays insufficient attention to difference. Transformational assimilationism, Young states, "denies that group difference can be positive and desirable,"[61] and thus remains inferior to the politics of difference. Young recognizes that universal approaches do not aim to remove all group differences or diversity; but for Young, this is not enough: we need "a politics that asserts the positivity of group difference."[62]

The sort of positive recognition of difference that Young has in mind entails two things that, she argues, transformational assimilationism cannot adequately realize: group autonomy in the political sphere and group affirmation. As regards the first, Young argues that the pluralism that liberalism endorses is insufficient because it is confined to the private sphere. Political liberalism, for example, which provides universal political rights but allows people to follow their own conception of the good outside the political realm, effectively relegates group identities to the private sphere and thus excludes minority groups from the public sphere of discussion and consideration. Instead, Young claims, her approach "acknowledges and affirms the public and political sig-

61. Ibid., 166.
62. Ibid.

nificance of social group differences as a means of ensuring the partici-
pation and inclusion of everyone in social and political institutions."[63]
Only in this way, for Young, can the oppression perpetuated by apparently 'neutral' state action be eliminated.

This claim is, on the face of it, very similar to one of my claims.
Group differences must have public and political significance, and not
be confined to the private sphere, because group identity is an important determinant of individuals' experience and so must be taken into
account when framing political institutions. Gender is a paradigmatic
example of a group difference that affects individuals' access to goods,
status, and other values such as power and autonomy; culture is another. It is therefore crucial to take the effects of group membership
into account, and not to focus on individuals at the expense of noticing
and countering group-based injustice or inequality. As MacKinnon argues, liberalism's focus on the individual means that it tends to miss
"the inherent group basis of equality claims" essential to feminist analysis.[64]

The question, then, is not whether groups make a difference to individuals, or whether some harms suffered by individuals can be understood only by reference to their group membership. The question,
rather, is how to deal with group-based inequalities, and how to deal
with inequalities *within* groups. Young's focus is on inequalities between groups: on the ways in which certain groups are cast as other
than, and thus inferior to, the dominant (white, heterosexual, middle-
class) liberal majority. She concludes, as a result, that group difference
must enter into the public sphere as a means of *strengthening* that difference: group rights are important, Young states, "because they enforce the group's autonomy and protect its interests as an oppressed
minority."[65] This approach is better suited to gender, and other cases
where group members as a whole suffer oppression. We might want
to protect women's interests as an oppressed group by according special rights to women: perhaps affirmative action policies in certain in-
dustries or in politics, or rights that could apply to all but will in prac-

63. Ibid., 168.
64. MacKinnon, "'The Case' Responds," 710. MacKinnon also points out on the same
page that "women who sue one at a time for sex discrimination are suing for harm to them
as women, not for harm to them as individuals: They are suing as members of their group,
for injury to themselves in their capacity as group members, that is, on the basis of sex."
65. Young, *Justice and the Politics of Difference*, 183.

tice most benefit women, such as a wage for caring work or special protections for victims of rape who testify in court.

Protection of the interests of an oppressed group can be compatible with an emancipatory feminist project, then. The notion of "group autonomy," however, is more problematic. Inasmuch as group autonomy is about enabling a group to resist oppression, it is entirely compatible with the transformational assimilationism that Young rejects—for such assimilation is entirely compatible with diversity that does not undermine individual equality and autonomy. If, on the other hand, *group* autonomy is meant to be distinguished from *individual* autonomy, so that Young wants to allow groups to determine their own affairs and the condition of their members immune from liberal state interference, then it runs counter to liberal accounts of equality and justice. This kind of group autonomy applies more naturally to cultural or religious groups; and as I argue throughout, many such groups use that autonomy to limit the rights of their members, and may claim to do so to secure the survival of the group—or more accurately, the survival of certain of the group's norms.[66] Allowing groups to be autonomous in this second sense, then, runs counter to justice. Group autonomy must not override the autonomy of the individuals within the group, and must not contradict the basic liberal rights that the state guarantees. In her later work, Young recognizes this problem and counsels against reducing the "politics of difference" to "identity politics."[67] It is important nonetheless to bear in mind the dangers of "group autonomy," given the fact of internal group difference.

The second element of Young's politics of difference is the affirmation of group difference. We need, Young claims, group-conscious policies that do more than protect a group from oppression. Instead, such policies need to "affirm the solidarity of groups," and to ensure that "their specific experience, culture, and social contributions are publicly affirmed and recognized."[68] In other words, it is the task of the state to entrench group difference and, moreover, actively to praise the ways in which groups are different from each other. But the question of publicly recognizing and affirming group culture and experiences is problematic. First, it conflicts with another aspect of Young's work. Young

66. See also Okin, "Is Multiculturalism Bad for Women?"
67. Young, *Inclusion and Democracy*, 89.
68. Young, *Justice and the Politics of Difference*, 174.

rejects any possibility of state neutrality, arguing that any supposedly neutral state will actually represent and enforce the dominant group's perception. As such, she rejects Okin's interpretation of Rawls's original position as the view from everywhere, a place in which we imagine the position of every individual and, in taking it into account in our deliberations about justice, affirm its worth. This approach fails, for Young, because it is impossible for us to do: the assumption that one can "empathize with the feelings and perspectives of others differently situated . . . denies the difference among subjects. To be sure, subjects are not opaque to one another, their difference is not absolute. But especially when class, race, ethnicity, gender, sexuality, and age define different social locations, one subject cannot fully empathize with another in a different social location, adopt her point of view."[69]

Young is right to point out that it is difficult for us to empathize with others when we are embedded in our particular experiences. However, it is much easier to take on another's point of view for the purposes of designing fair political institutions than it is to affirm and value their different, alien experiences and culture. The former simply requires that we say "imagine if I were a person with way of life X; I would want the state to enable me to pursue X." We can do this no matter our normative view of X: even a repugnant X can be thought through in this way. Thus, barring fanaticism,[70] even someone with a strong religious view that homosexuality is wrong, for example, can see that *if* they were a homosexual person without such a religious belief, *then* they would want the state to allow homosexuality and outlaw discrimination. It would surely be much harder (though not impossible) for such a person to prioritize fairness and conclude that such state action would be desirable, and even more difficult for that person to recognize and affirm the *value* of homosexuality over and above maintaining a tolerant attitude toward it. The empathy that liberal neutrality requires is technical or philosophical, a matter of conducting a thought-experiment; Young's affirmative empathy requires that we place our hearts and minds behind ways of life that we might find at best unfamiliar and at worst repugnant, and is thus much more implausible.[71]

69. Ibid., 105.
70. The canonical discussion of fanaticism is found in R. M. Hare, *Moral Thinking*.
71. Jean Cohen similarly distinguishes between affirming the value of the substance of others' ways of life and respecting the equal basic liberties and equal citizenship status of

Second, it is both impossible and undesirable for us to affirm publicly all group experiences over and above stating that we allow them to persist (the claim of liberal state neutrality). It is impossible because, in order to have any meaning, affirmation must be based on a set of values that are substantive and thus exclusionary. We are not affirming anything if we say "I affirm your experience because I have to," or "I affirm your experience because I affirm all experiences." In order for the affirmation to be meaningful, it must have reasons attached: "I affirm your culture because it produces beautiful art forms," or "because it contributes to the flourishing of its members," or "because you have chosen it and I value your capacity to choose," for example. In providing such reasons, we necessarily imply that we do not value cultures that do not have these valuable attributes, or to the extent that they do not: we will have to be less affirming of those cultures which produce no art, impede their members' flourishing, and impose themselves on their members.[72] Of course, it is also *desirable* that we are less affirmative of such cultures, for human flourishing, choice, and art are of central importance to any society.

As I argued earlier, the fact that a standpoint is not and cannot be neutral does not mean that it has no relevance outside the context of its origin. Any theory of what we should do about the fact of difference must in one sense deny difference, for it must exclude other such theories. Even Young's politics of difference excludes, and thereby fails to affirm, the politics of assimilation, along with the attitude toward difference of such politics as fascism or religious fundamentalism. These theories could be cashed out in the currency of group differences: we could talk about the culture and experiences of comprehensive liberals, Nazis, or the Taliban, all of which the politics of difference fails to affirm. It cannot be a criticism of a theory simply to say that it excludes some alternatives. Thus Young's observation that state neutrality is not neutral but in fact represents a particular standpoint does not in itself suffice to show that all attempts to combine universal values with a concern for fairness must necessarily fail. Instead, we need to recognize the political and public significance of group difference while

---

others. As I do, Cohen argues that the latter and not the former is a requirement of justice (*Regulating Intimacy*, 82).

72. Charles Taylor makes a similar argument in "The Politics of Recognition," 68–70. He concludes: "In this form, the demand for equal recognition is unacceptable" (71).

maintaining a critical standpoint. Not all difference is compatible with justice, and not all cultural experiences can be affirmed.

Fraser and Transformative Group Identities

The question of group difference has not, then, been resolved. On the one hand, it is crucial to recognize that injustice can be group-based, such that a simple focus on individual outcomes is insufficient. On the other hand, it is individuals who must be the unit of ultimate concern, and who must be protected from their groups where necessary.

Nancy Fraser suggests a solution to this dilemma. She criticizes both the purely redistributive concerns of many liberals and the exclusive focus on recognition of many multiculturalist theorists. Fraser points out that injustice can be either socioeconomic (as is suffered by the working class, for example) or cultural/symbolic (as is suffered by homosexuals). Moreover, these forms of injustice can be intertwined, as in the case of gender: women suffer from both socioeconomic disadvantage, often related to women's supposedly greater responsibility for childcare, and symbolic disadvantage, related to the representation of women as inferior in various ways. However, Fraser points out that groups who suffer from both forms of injustice (she terms such groups "bivalent") face serious problems in remedying that injustice: while the solution to socioeconomic injustice is to minimize differences between groups, the solution to cultural/symbolic injustice is to emphasize and affirm those differences.[73]

If we attempt to remedy gender injustice, then, we face a dilemma: do we emphasize that women are just the same as men and so deserve equal socioeconomic rights, or do we stress that women have different qualities from men, qualities that merit respect? The former is problematic because it takes the male as norm and regards as inferior everything that is not male, the latter risks justifying persistent unequal treatment of women in the workplace and elsewhere.

As a solution to this conundrum, Fraser argues that we must distinguish between affirmative and transformative remedies for injustice. Affirmative remedies tackle inequality between groups without undermining the differences between those groups. What Fraser terms "mainstream multiculturalism" is a good example of this approach, as

73. Fraser, Justice Interruptus, 16.

it "proposes to redress disrespect by revaluing unjustly devalued group identities, while leaving intact both the contents of those identities and the group differentiations that underlie them."[74] Transformative remedies, on the other hand, tackle injustice precisely by reconfiguring the group differences that generate the injustice. As such, all group and individual identities are adjusted. Queer politics, for example, aim to destabilize fixed categories of sexuality and replace them with a more fluid, indeterminate notion of sexual desire.

Fraser argues that, for bivalent groups, injustice is best tackled through transformation, as transformation is the method best able to cope with the competing demands of redistribution and recognition. Fraser's work thus directly calls into question the desirability of the affirmation of group differences, even when the relevant groups are not in themselves problematic from a liberal normative point of view (that is, even when groups do not threaten the equality and autonomy of their members). Fraser points out that, if groups are to achieve both kinds of equality, then it is to their own detriment if they emphasize their difference, for this emphasis calls into question their socioeconomic equality. To take an example: in Chapter 4, I consider Barry's argument that women might simply choose disproportionately to enter lower-paid jobs and that if they did so, there would be no need to attempt to equalize the salaries of women and men. Fraser's work suggests that this argument could be understood as a claim for recognition undermining a claim for redistribution: if we emphasize women's difference, and thus their tendency systematically to make different choices, it is harder to resist the conclusion that subsequent socioeconomic inequality is just.

Fraser's analysis is helpful because it enables us to deconstruct arguments such as Barry's and to see the limits of attempts to affirm group differences. It also provides a critique of Young, in two ways. First, Fraser points out that "the politics of difference may be less globally applicable than Young thinks"[75]—only groups that suffer from pure injustice of recognition will best be served by it, and there are relatively few such groups (homosexuals are Fraser's paradigmatic example). Second, Fraser shows that Young's account focuses on redistribution much more than Young explicitly admits, so that Young does not in

74. Ibid., 24.
75. Ibid., 200.

fact want to confine her approach to cases of pure recognition, and the politics of difference will fail to achieve the goal it sets itself of rectifying all forms of injustice.

Fraser's account is useful and insightful. It is also suggestive, and has formed the basis for much feminist research, perhaps in part because her own prescriptions are relatively vague.[76] One potential problem is that we have good reasons to suspect that a suitably eclectic and transformational solution to injustice may not work: by its nature, any solution will be complex, radical, unfamiliar, and difficult to put into practice. Fraser is aware of this problem. Thus she states that if the transformation of group identities she advocates is to be "psychologically and politically feasible," then "all people [must] be weaned from their attachment to current cultural constructions of their interests and identities."[77] As Fraser observes in a footnote: "This has always been the problem with socialism. Although cognitively compelling, it is experientially remote."[78] It is indeed difficult to see how we could put Fraser's prescriptions into practice, for they seem to imply that all group identities must be broken down, and all human experience be reconceptualized as a shifting, unstable, unordered collection of performances or experiments. Such a vision has a family resemblance to the notion of universal autonomy, but is much less plausible and possibly desirable than even the Socratic notion of constant and active self-scrutiny of which liberals such as Barry and Nussbaum are suspicious. It is a world away from the notion of autonomy as the genuine ability to choose and assess one's way of life that informs this book.

Another problem with Fraser's approach is that it contains inconsistencies—perhaps unsurprisingly, given that it aims to reconcile competing paradigms. Thus her advocacy of the transformation of identities just described conflicts with her defense of subaltern counterpublics in the context of democratic deliberation. As regards the latter, Fraser argues that stratified multicultural societies best meet the requirements of justice by accommodating competing minority groups. Moreover, these groups must be allowed to form their own spheres of deliberation, "arenas for deliberation among themselves about their needs, objectives, and strategies."[79] Such counterpublics

76. See, for example, Fraser, *Justice Interruptus*, 204, and Fraser, "Pragmatism, Feminism, and the Linguistic Turn," 166–68.

77. Fraser, *Justice Interruptus*, 31.

78. Ibid., 39 n. 46.

79. Ibid., 81.

clearly serve to entrench, not transform, group identity and difference. Moreover, Fraser is not contrasting the use of subaltern counterpublics in cases of recognitional injustice with the use of transformation in cases of combined recognitional/redistributive injustice, for she cites women as an example of both a paradigmatic group facing intertwined injustice and a group that has benefited from the use of the feminist subaltern counterpublic. We are thus left with a contradiction.

Fraser's approach, though useful and insightful, needs a clearer statement of its prescriptive implications. In particular, the question of the appropriate response to difference has not been answered: do we affirm it, attempt to transcend and transform it, or some combination of the two?

Reconciling Differences

I have argued that it is necessary to take into account the contingent and socially formed nature of identity, and to recognize the significance of cultural or religious groups in the public sphere, without at the same time reifying group specificity or succumbing to demands for group (as opposed to individual) autonomy. Does this position mean that I am committed to cultural homogeneity? It might appear that I am, for if there is to be a single set of values imposed universally by the state, and if social conditions are a crucial determinant of individual preferences and perceptions, the result will be a homogenous, unthinking, nonautonomously liberal mob.

There are several answers to this critique, some of which I have already dealt with. The first is to restate the earlier argument that even an imposed liberalism allows more room for autonomy than does any other imposed form of state. It is in the nature of liberalism that, even when it is imposed, there is still great room for diversity.[80] This is not because liberalism ought to confine its values to the political sphere and leave people unprotected from inequality and imposition in the private sphere. Rather, it is because the *substantive* liberal values of equality, freedom, and autonomy are themselves the conditions of diversity. For insofar as individuals' ability to choose their way of life is

80. Will Kymlicka, who criticizes some versions of liberalism for taking inadequate account of multiculturalism, nevertheless argues that liberalism necessarily fosters diversity. Thus he writes that "diversity is the inevitable result of the rights and freedoms guaranteed to liberal citizens" ("Western Political Theory and Ethnic Relations in Eastern Europe," 18).

genuinely guaranteed and not just formally allowed, it is likely that individuals will make different choices. The approach I have outlined, and which is developed throughout this book, prevents both the enforced homogeneity of fundamentalism or communitarianism, and the enforced diversity of a political liberalism that allows groups effectively to imprison their members. It is true that some cultures will have to change in certain ways, and some cultures will die out without enforced membership. These changes, however, are to be welcomed rather than regretted, and are certainly preferable to what could come of an absolute commitment to diversity at any cost.

In any case, under my proposals individuals will still find themselves brought up within distinct cultures, and will still have prereflexive commitments to those cultures. Cultural diversity will not be deprived of this method of transmission. I argue only that, as individuals are inevitably (though not totally) formed by their cultures, and as individuals will find exit from their cultures difficult for many reasons, there are limits to the kind of cultural practices that groups may legitimately engage in. These limits are imposed by justice. A group that contains members who did not enter by autonomous choice (in other words, a group in which children are born and raised) may not impose unjust norms.[81] No group may hinder its members' ongoing autonomy by denying freedom of exit (though freedom of exit is not in itself sufficient to secure autonomy). These limits do not mean that groups may not develop and teach their own beliefs, art forms, social arrangements, cuisine, dress, or worship. Nothing in my approach precludes that which is appealing in Young's evocative utopia of city life, where strangers with different ways of life intermingle and enter each other's territory, savoring the change in atmosphere. A society in which the liberal state regulated all groups according to substantive ideals of justice would still be one in which we could enjoy walking through different ethnic communities, eating different ethnic foods, and engaging with "a different crowd of people."[82] Nothing in my approach, in short, threatens the benefits of city life which Young identifies: social differ-

81. Groups that are composed entirely of adults who entered autonomously, and into which no children are brought, have greater leeway to follow hierarchical practices. However, such groups may not render people unable to leave for any reason over which the group has a degree of control: membership in a group must *remain* autonomous. This issue is discussed at greater length in Part Two.

82. Young, *Justice and the Politics of Difference*, 239.

entiation without exclusion, variety, the eroticism of encountering different cultures, and opportunities for public discussion and disagreement. We do need to respect and value difference, but we need to do so only as a tool for respecting and valuing individuals and their autonomy and equality. We may and should respect individuals' ability to choose and lead very different ways of life, without at the same time refusing to respect them as persons of equal intrinsic worth, whose capacity and need for choice continues.

Conclusions

We are now in a position to see how liberal normative values could be reconciled with insights about the limits of individual autonomy and theories of social construction. First, we need to recognize that individuals are strongly formed and constrained by their social circumstances, and that this constraint increases the need for liberation. Moreover, the difficulty involved in overcoming social influence means that individuals cannot be expected to do so unaided: structural change is necessary, often in the form of state action.

Second, however, the idea of social construction suggests that individuals can never be completely free from social influence: the radical autonomy which Fraser advocates is difficult if not impossible to achieve. As a result of this, and of the need to prevent the state from becoming overbearing, state action must focus on freeing individuals from *unjust* social influence: that which harms or disadvantages them. The overall goal is universal autonomy, but the state has a greater role to play in issues of injustice than it has to play in general influence.

Third, this goal of universal autonomy does not amount to the imposition of one way of life; rather, it precludes the imposition of any particular way of life. As such, it is compatible with diversity, and is likely to foster it. A wariness of grand narratives as counter to autonomy or diversity should not lead to a wariness of the liberal grand narrative, for it is best suited to protection of these values. However, this does not mean, fourth, that there can be no criticism of cultural or individual narratives or ways of life. Normative criticism is an essential tool of justice.

The two problems that social construction might pose for my approach can be answered as follows. The problem of the contradiction between the universal status claimed for liberal values and the fact that liberalism is a particular, situated doctrine was answered with the claim that liberalism is particular in origin and universal in application. Although liberalism does not start from neutral premises or unproblematic consensus, it must apply to everybody, as a matter of consistency and of desirability. The problem of group difference was answered by the claim that, although difference can be and remains valuable, and although no one should be excluded simply for being different, still difference can run counter to justice. It will not always be to the benefit of disadvantaged groups to entrench group differences; and even when it is, respect for group difference should not override respect for individuals.

PART TWO

LIBERALISM, CULTURE, AND AUTONOMY

4

ALL MUST HAVE PRIZES:
THE LIBERAL CASE FOR INTERFERENCE IN CULTURAL PRACTICES

When liberal theory uses consent as if it means freedom—to refer to some
unburdened, open, and unforced selection—it often applies the term in situations
that better demonstrate acquiescence in inequality and acceptance of what one has
little realistic possibility of refusing. Calling inequality freedom promotes inequality.
—CATHARINE MacKINNON, "'The Case' Responds"

If choices are constrained by injustice, their protection need not represent liberty
at all.
—CASS SUNSTEIN, "Neutrality in Constitutional Law"

Liberals like choice. Human flourishing, they believe, is to some degree
dependent on individuals' ability to choose their ends and actions.
More precisely, liberals often place choice at the heart of their conception of *justice*. For John Rawls, a key function of justice is to enable
individuals "to form, to revise and rationally to pursue"[1] their conception of the good. The role of choice thus understood is so crucial to
Rawls's theory of justice that its protective principle—the equal basic
liberty principle—is given lexical priority.[2]

Although liberals are clear that choice is crucial to justice and individual flourishing, they sometimes fail to note that an individual acting
according to her own choices will not always flourish, that she will not
always enjoy the freedom and equality crucial to justice. In this chapter
and throughout Part Two, I build on the account of social construction
developed in Part One and show that even outcomes that result from
the choices of the individuals concerned may be unjust.

In this chapter I develop a specific and fairly narrow approach, in

---

1. John Rawls, *Political Liberalism,* 19.

2. In Rawlsian terms, if principle X is lexically prior to principle Y, then principle Y must
not be implemented in any way that would violate principle X. In other words, the requirements of principle X take absolute precedence.

which there are two conditions under which liberals should not rely on individuals' choices as the determinant of justice. I call these conditions *disadvantage* and *influence*. Together, they express the idea that if an individual is encouraged to make choices that disadvantage her, then the ensuing inequality is unjust—particularly if the disadvantage is significant and enduring, and if the encouragement comes from those who make different choices and so end up better-off. Egalitarian liberals, I argue, should be particularly worried about such outcomes, and should revise and reduce the role of choice in determining what is just.

My argument in this chapter has particular relevance to group-based outcomes. In Chapter 3, I discussed the role that group difference might play in developing a liberal normative theory that is sensitive to social construction. In this chapter I focus much of the discussion on Brian Barry's *Culture and Equality*. In that work Barry defends the universal validity of core liberal values and argues that the demands of cultural or religious groups within wider liberal societies must not take precedence over those values. Barry is one of the few, and certainly the most prominent, critics of multiculturalism in the name of universal egalitarian liberalism. However, he is reluctant to interfere with internal group norms, even when they conflict with liberal principles of freedom and equality, if individuals are free to leave those groups and so could be said to have chosen to abide by those norms. I contend, however, that the fact of social construction means that it will often be misleading to describe adherence to internal group norms that treat members unequally as freely chosen in a way that excuses the outcome. As a result, many unequal internal norms of cultural and religious groups should be restricted by a liberal state. *Contra* Barry, liberals have to be fully committed to the value of autonomy, and so cannot consistently ignore significant and unequal restrictions on individuals' opportunities to realize it. Liberals must prioritize individual autonomy over group autonomy, and so I develop suggestions for an institutional framework, which I call the equality tribunal, to take this prioritization into account. I then consider and ultimately reject Ayelet Shachar's alternative feminist multiculturalist proposals for institutional reform.

The Insufficiency of Free Choice

In *Culture and Equality*, Barry considers group-based outcomes in relation to what he calls the Dodo's Dictum. Barry's discussion of the

Dodo's Dictum is a rare example of Barry not being liberal enough—
that is to say, ceding too much to cultural values and awarding too little
to individual human flourishing. In general Barry is keen, and rightly
so, to reiterate the liberal commitment to protecting individuals' ability
to defend themselves against state and social pressure to conform. In
discussing the Dodo's Dictum, however, he lowers the barriers against
such pressure. The reason, I contend, is his unwillingness to take the
phenomenon of social construction into account.

First, what is the Dodo's Dictum? Barry invokes the words of the
dodo in *Alice in Wonderland,* who declares, "Everybody has won, and
all must have prizes."[3] Barry likens this slogan to the belief of multiculturalists such as Iris Marion Young that, in Barry's words, "different
ways of life pursued by different groups should have no effect on their
collective success."[4] Barry profoundly disagrees with such a proposal.
He cites the example of gender difference and states that while liberals
might regret a situation in which women do not make the same
choices as men once given the same rights, they need not suspect that
any injustice lurks behind such an outcome. As Barry says, "What
must be emphasized is that it is perfectly possible to believe that justice
demands equal rights and opportunities for men and women while at
the same time neither hoping nor expecting that this will result in the
career choices of women tending to become statistically indistinguish-
able from those of men."[5]

It is indeed possible to believe that justice and equality do not require identity of choices or outcomes. However, liberals ought to be
interested in why there should be consistent discrepancies between the
choices made by members of different groups. Consider Barry's example of gendered career choices. He accepts that some such choices
could be the result of discrimination in education or recruitment, and
deplores such discrimination. Liberal action is, however, limited to the
elimination of discrimination. As he puts it: "Suppose . . . that women
were as highly qualified as men but disproportionately chose to devote
their lives to activities incompatible with reaching the top of a large
corporation. An egalitarian liberal could not then complain of injustice
if, as a result, women were underrepresented in 'top corporate jobs.'"[6]
The obvious example of an activity that might prevent women from

3. Lewis Carroll, *Alice's Adventures in Wonderland,* 38.
4. Barry, *Culture and Equality,* 95.
5. Ibid., 92.
6. Ibid., 94.

achieving corporate career success is childcare. Barry is committed to the idea that it might simply be the case that women disproportionately choose to focus on childcare rather than on career success and that if this choice does not result from discrimination in education or employment practices, liberals need not worry about it. The sort of discrimination that should worry liberals is largely a matter of what happens to people once they have chosen to apply for certain jobs. There can be no liberal concern for the nature of that choice. To quote Barry again, there is nothing "necessarily unfair or oppressive going on if one aspect of the importance of 'group based affinities and cultural life' is that members of different groups tend to cluster in different occupations by choice. To the extent that this is the explanation of differential group outcomes, there is no question of 'oppression.'"[7]

Contra Barry, I argue in this chapter that there can be something wrong with different group outcomes based on the choices of the group members if the aforementioned conditions—the disadvantage and influence factors—hold. In general, if they are present, it is not enough for liberals to say of an outcome that it was freely chosen by the relevant individuals and is therefore just. In other words, in these circumstances free choice is not the end of the story.

First, the two factors in brief. The first factor which should make us take seriously the possibility that an outcome is unjust is if the choice in question harms the chooser in relation to those who choose differently. It is a simple condition that may apply to a whole variety of freely chosen outcomes, and is necessary but not sufficient to render free choices unjust, and worthy of state interference.[8] Indeed, this element is not, in itself, sufficient to infer injustice, as will become clear, but it is the first indication that the outcome *may* be unjust. The position is worsened, from the perspective of justice, if the benefit accruing to one group is dependent on the other group choosing that which disadvantages them. I call this the disadvantage factor. The second factor applies if there are identifiable pressures on the choosing group to make that choice—especially if those pressures come from the group who choose differently and thus benefit. I call this the influence factor. Again, it may occur in outcomes that, if there is no inequality, do not justify

---

7. Ibid., 98.
8. An outcome may be unjust and yet not worthy of state interference in cases where state interference would compromise values other than justice. This point is expanded later.

extra resources. Egalitarian liberals should, however, aim to reduce the extent of the influence factor. I return to this point later, but for now, we can take the influence factor as also necessary but not sufficient for egalitarian intervention. The existence of either the influence or the disadvantage factor should serve to alert us to the possible existence of injustice. Together, the disadvantage and influence factors are sufficient for an outcome to merit state intervention, even if it is the result of "free choice."

The Disadvantage Factor

The first factor that should make us suspicious about systematic differences in group-based choices is the simple fact of differences in advantage that the differently choosing groups receive. The greater the difference in disadvantage, and the more enduring and less reversible that disadvantage, the more we should worry.[9] For example, women who choose to become full-time housewives rather than chasing corporate careers will not just suffer the disadvantage of a lower income. They will also be significantly disadvantaged by their financial dependence on others, which will leave them less able to make autonomous choices or to resist future oppression from the person on whom they are dependent. Moreover, women who choose to eschew paid work will find that choice, and the consequent disadvantage, difficult to reverse. It is difficult to return to the workforce after prolonged absence, and almost impossible to reach a level of career success open to those who have

9. I discuss the issue of defining harm, and its relation to disadvantage, in greater detail in Chapters 5 and 6. One issue that arises in this context is that it might be objected that different cultures have different views of harm, so that what liberals identify as disadvantage might not be seen so by other cultures. An extreme version of this objection is made by Sander Gilman, who argues, against Susan Moller Okin's critique of female genital mutilation, that "this is the model followed in the debates about female genital mutilation. Only intact genitalia can give pleasure. But is it possible that the projection of Western, bourgeois notions of pleasure onto other people's bodies is not the best basis for anybody's judgement?" ("'Barbaric' Rituals?" 56). I believe, *contra* Gilman, that there are at least some objective standards of harm and disadvantage, and women with ritually mutilated genitals are unambiguously worse off than those whose genitals are intact. However, I shall not argue for that position in this chapter. This chapter presents a liberal case for state intervention in cultural practices, and so will not persuade those who reject fundamental liberal principles such as liberty, equality, and (as I shall argue) autonomy. The argument, instead, is aimed at those who do share these fundamental principles, and who can agree on a liberal notion of harm and disadvantage. Barry argues along similar lines throughout *Culture and Equality*, and especially on pages 284–91. In Chapters 5 and 6 I relax this restriction and explore further issues about defining harm in different cultural contexts.

not had such an absence. The choice, therefore, causes *enduring* disadvantage.[10]

The most pernicious element of the disadvantage resulting from women's choice to become housewives, however, is that that disadvantage can directly advantage men who choose differently. In these circumstances, it resembles exploitation. All households generate a considerable amount of housework, and if a couple have children, somebody has to look after them. It is usually assumed that men will not sacrifice their careers to meet childcare or domestic needs. In general, then, men are able to enjoy the advantages that come from pursuing paid careers only because others, almost always women, take on the responsibility for housework and looking after children. If it is the man's partner who takes on full responsibility for domestic work, so that he and not she works, the man enjoys several advantages. He will receive the bulk of the household income, and as such will have considerable influence over expenditure. Depending on the earning potential of the woman, household income may be greater without the costs of professional childcare. The demands of the man's work will be better met if they do not have to compete with the demands of the woman's work: he will be able to relocate in response to job offers and work late without having to make childcare arrangements. He will be less likely to worry about the quality of the childcare his children are receiving, and will not have to make special arrangements if his children are ill or during school holidays. In these ways, then, the advantages that accrue to fathers who work full-time are dependent on the disadvantages suffered by their partners who look after the couple's children full-time. The disadvantage of one group is directly related to the advantage of another.[11]

The disadvantage factor is not bolstered by relatedness in the case of, for example, the salaries of management consultants compared to the salaries of teachers. There is a significant inequality of salaries between the two professions, but the high salaries of management con-

10. I do not mean to imply that there are no rewards or advantages resulting from looking after children full-time, or that individuals who choose such a lifestyle have no good reasons for doing so. As will become clear, I aim to enable individuals to make such choices more easily, without suffering the accompanying disadvantages. For more on the issue of work and childcare, see Joan K. Peters, *When Mothers Work;* Joan Williams, *Unbending Gender;* and Sally Dench et al., "Key Indicators of Women's Position in Britain."

11. Again, this is not to deny that men might suffer some disadvantages, such as reduced intimacy with their children, if they do not play a significant role in childcare.

sultants do not depend on the low salaries of teachers. It is not necessary that teachers be paid badly if management consultants are to be
paid well. There is no direct link between the advantage of one group
and the disadvantage of the other. There is such a link, to give another
example, between the disadvantage of a low-paid factory worker and
the advantage of the factory owner. The factory owner is advantaged in
indirect proportion to the factory worker: the less the worker is paid,
the more profit is created for the owner. This element of relatedness to
the disadvantage factor suggests that we ought to look more closely at
the position of the factory worker. We should not simply dismiss her
disadvantage as the unproblematic result of her free choice to work in
a factory rather than start her own business. There is not yet enough
evidence for oppression, but the fact of significant and especially dependent, related inequalities is an important indication of the need to
examine the case further. As the example of the factory worker shows,
liberals are used to conceptualizing state intervention in cases of economic disadvantage. In this chapter, I suggest that liberals should use
the conceptual tools they have developed to cope with economic inequalities and apply them to cultural or social inequalities.

The disadvantage factor is more significant, then, the more extreme
and enduring is the disadvantage, and the more the disadvantage is
crucial to others' corresponding advantage.

The Influence Factor

We should start to suspect that systematically different choices might
conceal injustice if they lead to significant, enduring, and related differences in advantage. We can reveal that injustice if we find the second
factor: identifiable processes by which one group is encouraged to
make a disadvantageous choice.

Of course, the influence factor draws heavily on the idea of social
construction. The influence factor aims to capture the idea that individuals may be encouraged, by their social context, to make choices that
harm them. I have already argued that all choices are importantly social, in several senses. First, a choice is only ever possible between
options that are *available* in any given society. Second, choices are constrained by what is deemed *appropriate* in the relevant social context,
and this judgment of appropriateness may be internalized by the
chooser and not merely imposed from outside. Third, the *meaning* of a

practice chosen by a given individual is not thereby determined by that individual. As I outlined in my discussion of a Foucauldian perspective on female and male genital surgeries, the meaning of practices shift between societies and over time. Moreover, as I suggested regarding Bourdieu's regulated liberties, it is not possible for an individual completely to redefine a practice, since she can control neither how it will be understood by others nor how it makes sense for her.

Given these many ways that choices are subject to social influence, my current stipulation of an "influence factor" may appear odd. For, in a broad interpretation of "influence," it will always be present; whereas a narrow interpretation (perhaps one based on explicit coercion or pressure) seems to ignore the myriad forms of social construction. For my current purposes, however, it is the narrow interpretation we need, for several reasons. The first reason is that I want to develop a set of principles for state action that will sometimes be coercive. Liberals will be keen to avoid Isaiah Berlin's totalitarian menace, and to do so it is necessary first to focus the concept of social construction on specific, identifiable processes of influence.[12] The second reason is that the accounts of social construction previously discussed, particularly that of Foucault, alert us to the fact that social construction is omnipresent and inevitable. Although we can engender change, and even radical change, we cannot escape the social. Thus critique, and state action, must be focused on harmful or oppressive social norms (hence the disadvantage factor) and on those cases where generalized processes of influence crystallize into more solidified interpersonal domination. Finally, my account of social construction is not designed to render redundant the liberal value of autonomy, but rather to place it and its protection into sharper focus. This task is taken up in subsequent chapters, but for now the value of autonomy provides us with reason to focus our attention onto identifiable—and alterable— interpersonal influence.

We thus need a clearly defined concept of influence, and an example will help to illustrate it. As mentioned above, fathers can only pursue the top corporate jobs Barry discusses if someone else looks after the children, and fathers are less likely than mothers to consider childcare as their responsibility. One identifiable pressure on mothers to choose to stay at home, then, is the knowledge that if they do not, then nobody

---

12. Isaiah Berlin, "Two Concepts of Liberty."

else will. This discrepancy does not come from nowhere. There are significant social norms that encourage mothers to stay at home to look after their children which do not constitute discrimination of the sort that Barry recognizes. The media are full of articles about the harm done to children if their mothers go out to work.[13] There are scare stories about the dangers of professional childminders, the educational damage to children who are not looked after by full-time mothers, the importance of early bonding between mother and child, and the deprivation of the latchkey child.[14] Even if the media report a study finding no significant harm to children, the emphasis is always on the effects of working mothers and not on working fathers.[15] As a result, even if they do not believe that working will necessarily harm their children, mothers and not fathers are confronted with the notion that their choice to pursue a career is a problematic and difficult one, whereas fathers hardly have to choose at all. When they *are* worried about possi-

13. Consider the following examples from British broadsheet newspapers in 2000. On April 5, the *Telegraph* reported research showing that "most mothers would prefer to stay at home and look after their children if they could afford to do so." Alongside the research the *Telegraph* ran a profile of a female investment banker earning £51,000 a year who gave up work to look after her children and told the newspaper, "I had to make a decision on what was more important to me, to be a mother and spend time with my child or to be a career woman. I didn't have to think very hard" (Celia Hall, "Mothers 'Prefer to Be at Home with Their Children'"; Sally Pook, "'Giving Up Work Was Best Thing I Did' [sic]"). In December, the *Times* columnist Jessica Davies surveyed the evidence that children are damaged if their mothers work outside the home, and concluded that most mothers would leave paid employment if they could ("Am I Damaging My Children?").

14. In 1997, the high-profile case of Louise Woodward spawned panic about the dangers of childminders. Woodward was a nineteen-year-old British au pair who was found guilty of manslaughter in a Massachusetts court when eight-month-old Matthew Eappen died in her care. To compound parents' anxiety, the *Telegraph* ran several stories in 2003 reporting research that nursery care is even worse than childminder care (e.g., Rebecca Abrams, "Nurseries Are Safe and Secure—But Are They Bad for Your Baby?" and Liz Lightfoot, "Too Long at Day Centres 'Can Disturb Children'"). An extraordinary example of a story reporting that working mothers harm their children's education can be found in the *Telegraph*. Its social affairs correspondent reported that "for every year that a mother works before her child starts school, the prospects of gaining at least one A-level fall by as much as nine percent. The greatest impact is felt when the mother works full-time. But the research shows that even part-time employment during a child's pre-school years is detrimental to its academic prospects" (Martin Bentham, "Working Mothers 'Damage Children's Education'"). Bentham's article is inadequate in many ways. No evidence is given to suggest that the connection between a mother's working pattern and the exams that her child takes at least thirteen years later is causal rather than merely correlative. Moreover, Bentham does not consider whether there is evidence for other correlations (such as between exam results and working fathers, or exam results and poverty).

15. In "If You Go Down to the Gender Ghetto Today," Richard Reeves comments on the "complacent sexism" found in such stories, none of which consider the role of the father.

ble harm to their children, or social condemnation of themselves, it is misleading to describe their choice as fully free and not at all as evidence of injustice. The case for injustice is even stronger when the pressures to choose in a certain way are exerted by the advantaged group, which itself makes different choices. When working fathers take part in the condemnation of working mothers, or when fathers forbid their partners from working or persuade them not to, we have even less justification for dismissing inequality of outcome between mothers and fathers as the unproblematic result of free choice.

The influence factor takes a peculiar form, from the point of view of liberal intervention, if there are mechanisms by which individuals are encouraged to make advantageous choices. For example, the child of middle-class university-educated parents might be encouraged by those parents, and by talk between her friends and relatives, to continue with her education rather than to leave school at sixteen. Indeed, the decision to continue with education may not seem to her like a decision at all. It might well be inconceivable for such a child not to continue to university, without her devoting any considerable thought to the matter. While such pressures may weigh heavily on the children, limiting their autonomy, submission to such pressures will tend to improve the lot of those children in the long run. What, then, are egalitarian liberals to say about these cases?

The liberal desire to facilitate autonomous choice will tell against even beneficial instances of the influence factor. In a liberal society, all individuals should be given the resources to enable them to lead their lives with at least basic autonomy. As such, the liberal state should supply education for all: for children, education should emphasize the variety of opportunities available and equip them with the skills needed to pursue a variety of paths; for adults, lifelong learning should be available to facilitate the development of new skills and changes in career. These are measures the liberal state provides for everyone, whether or not they have been subjected to influence. For example, if an individual wants to stop practicing medicine and retrain as a teacher, the same resources should be available to her whether her original career choice was the result of parental pressure or the result of her continuing desire to perform socially beneficial work. Over and above the resources which the liberal state offers to everyone in the name of autonomy, however, those who are made better-off as a result of the influence factor are not deserving of special resources, for two reasons. The first is practical. Because state resources are limited, it is more important that they be devoted to those who are worse off, once the minimum needed for autonomy has been universally provided. Second, in many cases, the fact of being financially better-off enhances autonomy. If an individual is earning a high wage or is in a position of esteem in society, she will be more able to act autonomously. Her financial security will afford her a safety net, should she decide to pursue a risky career or a period of retraining, and the skills and contacts gained from a professional career will stand her in good stead in many new careers. Thus, while an individual who is encouraged to pursue a path that makes her better-off does suffer from restrictions on autonomy in the first instance, her autonomy will tend to be enhanced in the long run. Besides the basic educational resources offered to all, then, the influence factor is not sufficient to justify special state intervention if it results in advantage.

It ought to be clear that the influence factor does merit special intervention when it is accompanied by the disadvantage factor—such as in the case of a child living in a community where further education is not considered. A child who chooses to leave school at sixteen because her friends are doing so, her parents did so, and because staying on is never really considered will be significantly disadvantaged by her choice. There may be further mechanisms of influence, such as peer pressure or the low expectations of her current school. In such circumstances, the child's choice to leave school, though freely made in the sense that the state provides free further education and the child is not physically compelled to reject it, should not put an end to normative concern. The state should perhaps devote extra resources to encouraging education in that area, or offer special support programs or incentives for children who continue with their education (be it academic or vocational).

Multiculturalism and the Insufficiency of Free Choice

We can now consider the insufficiency of choice in the light of multiculturalism. It is often claimed that theories of social construction *support* multicultural claims and undermine liberal universalism. However, the first thing to recognize is that some cultural and religious groups are worse than liberal societies in emphasizing differently advantageous norms of behavior for different people within the group, often but not always based on gender.[16] And, as Ann Cudd shows, different social institutions and normative backgrounds can systematically disadvantage particular groups within a society, even if members of those groups are able to exercise "free choice."[17]

We also need to recognize that individual members of such groups will find it harder to choose to take advantage of the liberal framework of rights that formally applies to them than Barry implies. The fact that a religious group in a liberal society may, under Barry's scheme, tell its members what to do and read as long as it allows them to leave if they want to gives the group scope to exert enormous pressure on its members both to stay and, while they remain members, to "freely choose" to perform roles that significantly disadvantage them.

This is important because Barry's liberal response to cultural diversity allows groups to implement discriminatory norms and laws if individuals are members of those groups, and so abide by the laws, as a result of their free choice. Feminist liberal Marilyn Friedman similarly argues that "cultural practices that violate women's rights are nevertheless permissible if the women in question accept them."[18] As an exam-

16. This point has been made by many liberals and feminists. For example, see Okin, "Is Multiculturalism Bad for Women?"; Nussbaum, *Sex and Social Justice;* and Barry, *Culture and Equality.*

17. Ann Cudd's argument concerns a counterexample to the Nozickian marriage market, whereby a group of men and women are free to marry each other, or not, as they choose. Cudd shows that, if a custom exists that only the men are allowed to propose (women are allowed to accept or reject proposals, but not make them themselves), then the men will be systematically advantaged over the women—even though the women may freely choose whether or not to marry any particular man (*Analyzing Oppression*, 130).

18. Friedman, *Autonomy, Gender, Politics*, 188. This way of phrasing the argument is interesting. Most—possibly all—cultural practices violate people's rights if they are not accepted by the people concerned. If you shake my hand or put a Christmas tree in my house without my consent, you violate my rights, for you invade my bodily integrity or private property. In order to be saying something more significant, Friedman must mean something else. There are some practices, such as assault and murder, that violate rights even when consented to, in the sense that consent is not counted as an excusing factor. One possibility, then, is that Friedman is denying the possibility of such a category of acts and arguing that no practice can be rights-violating if it is consented to by all concerned. However, Friedman's phrasing does not support this interpretation. She states that rights-violating practices "are nevertheless permissible" if consented to, implying that they remain rights-violating, and yet there is something odd about the idea that consent does the normative work of rendering a practice permissible but not at the same time the normative work of removing any rights violation. Moreover, Friedman does not want to deny the possibility of an act that is consented to but nevertheless rights-violating: domestic violence is given as an example of an act that consent does not justify since it is not a "tradition in the honorific sense of the term" (*Autonomy, Gender, Politics*, 202). I criticize the idea that rights violations perpetrated by cultures are

ple Barry considers Orthodox Jewish and Muslim divorce law, under which women and not men require the consent of their spouse in order to obtain a divorce. Barry argues: "Although [Orthodox Jewish and Muslim divorce law] treats men and women unequally, it is beyond the scope of a liberal state to rewrite it, as long as the only reason for anybody's adhering to it is the wish to remain a member in good standing of a certain religious community."[19] But the wish to remain a member of one's own community should not be dismissed as the "only reason" that individuals abide by discriminatory norms. There will be significant pressures on the harmed individuals both to remain within their group and to adhere to its norms. These pressures should worry us because they are manifestations of the more extreme forms of the disadvantage and influence factors. When Orthodox Jewish and Muslim divorce law seriously disadvantages women, it seriously benefits men, giving them control over the divorce process. This discrepancy ought to make us consider the case further. Jewish and Muslim women experience enormous pressure both to remain in their religious groups and to adhere to the unequal laws set by those groups. They will want to remain within the community in which they have grown up, and may have been brought up to believe that women do not deserve an equal say in divorce proceedings. That impression may well be reinforced, not only by other female members of the group, but also by precisely the men who are advantaged by the unequal ruling. The fact that, under these circumstances, Orthodox Jewish and Muslim women have "freely chosen" to remain in those religious groups and abide by their laws does not make the disadvantage they suffer any less unjust. A liberal state ought to intervene.

State intervention could seek to address the disadvantage factor, the influence factor, or a mixture of both. To return to the case of the housewife, the state could address the disadvantage factor through such policies as providing wages for housework,[20] education and support for women wishing to reenter the workforce after time spent looking after children, and financial assistance for housewives wishing to leave their husbands. The influence factor could be mitigated through

---

normatively different from rights violations perpetrated by other sorts of group later in this chapter.

19. Barry, *Culture and Equality*, 128.

20. For detailed analysis of the demand for wages for housework, see MacKinnon, *Toward a Feminist Theory of the State*, chap. 4.

education or advertising campaigns encouraging women to enter paid work, or men to take responsibility for childcare. In many cases, mitigating the disadvantage will go some way toward lessening the systematic influence on particular groups—if childcare is financially rewarded, then more men will consider it as a viable option. The precise method of state intervention in any one case will depend on practicality and, crucially, the demands of other liberal principles. I address this issue and the precise nature of state intervention at greater length later in this chapter.

I have argued that when unequal outcomes result from different choices and not from clear discrimination, we can still identify injustice if the difference between the outcomes is significant and enduring, and if there are identifiable pressures on certain members of a group to make the disadvantageous choice. In such circumstances, we cannot clearly say that the different outcomes are just. Why have liberals such as Barry been reluctant to recognize injustice in such cases? Throughout *Culture and Equality*, Barry demonstrates his willingness to condemn unjust and oppressive actions, even where those result from particular social norms. "The liberal position is clear," he states. "Nobody, anywhere in the world, should be denied liberal protections against injustice and oppression."[21] Why is Barry unwilling to use liberal protections where oppression results from social norms that affect the choices that individuals make, and not just the things that other people do to them? The answer, I think, stems from liberals' wariness to infer oppression when the oppressed are unprotesting. Liberals are right to think that a state which forces people to do what they don't realize is good for them often does more harm than good. Liberals are wrong, however, to be wary of noticing when individuals' freedom and equality would be better served if their choices were genuinely freer. Liberals should encourage the dissolution of discriminatory practices and norms. Without such norms, individuals could still choose courses of action that disadvantage them, but the systematic and unequal pressure that constitutes oppression would be absent. Without the influence factor, in other words, the disadvantage factor does not necessarily indicate injustice. Liberal institutions ought to ensure that, wherever possible, pressures to make disadvantageous choices should not fall disproportionately on a specific group or groups. Where equalizing

21. Barry, *Culture and Equality*, 138.

such pressures is impossible within the limits of what may be done by liberal institutions, those institutions should ensure that one group is not hugely and enduringly dependent on others, and that the burdens faced by one group do not contrast markedly with the benefits enjoyed by others who do not face the same pressures to connive in their own disadvantage. If all of this means interfering with the discriminatory practices of cultural groups, so be it.

One response to my argument thus far, and the response that Barry favors,[22] concerns the practical implications of intervening in cultural norms of inequality. Because these are essentially private concerns, so this response goes, it would be an intolerable invasion of privacy to intervene in them. We are invited to imagine the "nightmarish" scenario of police raids on rabbinical divorce courts, internal informants, and heavy-handed totalitarian state enforcement. Moreover, such a respondent might continue, because the discriminatory religious divorce laws are not supported by state law, it is not necessary for the state to concern itself with those laws' conclusions. If women are unhappy with their treatment under religious divorce law, they can choose not to remain within the religious group which sanctions those laws. In wider society, such women can gain a legal divorce on equal footing with their husbands. If they prefer to stay within their cultural group rather than to utilize the secular divorce laws of the wider society, then that is their free choice. The liberal state should not interfere, even if the practical problems of such interference could be overcome.

Such a response is convincing only if one accepts a rigid separation of public and private spheres, with state intervention limited to the former. Such a distinction has long been criticized by feminists and rejected by many egalitarian liberals.[23] It is often precisely those oppressions which occur in the private sphere that are the most damaging to the freedom and autonomy of the individuals who suffer them. If

22. Barry made this response at a roundtable discussion of *Culture and Equality*, held at Birkbeck College, University of London, on 17 November 2000. He makes a similar point in *Justice as Impartiality*: "It would not be easy to devise a practical policy that would discriminate against the pursuit of conceptions of the good that had not been autonomously arrived at . . . [E]ven if one could conceive of such a policy being carried out accurately by an ideally conscientious dictator, it would be impossible to frame an institution for implementing a policy that would not be open to abuse, since it would entail handing wide discretion to some body to act on ill-defined criteria" (*Justice as Impartiality*, 132).

23. See, for example, Okin, *Justice, Gender and the Family*, and Elizabeth Frazer and Nicola Lacey, "Politics and the Public in Rawls' Political Liberalism."

private sphere oppressions cannot be rectified by state action, then those oppressions will be peculiarly pervasive, and those who suffer from them will have little recourse. It will often be much harder for an individual to argue, on her own terms and against her own parents or community leaders, against a private sphere practice than it will be for her to enjoy the benefits that a law concerning that sphere confers on her by default. A woman who enjoys the protection of the law against an oppressive cultural practice is not thereby implicated in cultural treachery in the way that she might be if she had no option but to argue on a personal level against cultural norms. Katha Pollitt recounts a story about a woman who changed her view of the French dispute on Muslim girls' wearing of headscarves in schools, in favor of a ban. As Pollitt tells it, "She came across a television debate in which a Muslim girl said she wanted the ban to stay because without it, her family would force her to wear a scarf."[24] If women want to take advantage of the equal freedoms that liberalism offers them, it will be much easier for them to do so if those freedoms are "imposed" on them by the state than it would be for individual women to reject the norms pressed on them by those to whom they are close and on whom they may be dependent.

The Equality Tribunal

The practical implications of intervention with cultural discriminatory norms would not be different in character from current state intervention in employment practices. Barry is very strict about discrimination in employment. He argues that the merits of each individual applicant for a job must be considered: employers may not exclude categories of applicants who are merely statistically unlikely to have a relevant qualification.[25] Women cannot be excluded from a particular job, then, even if most of them lack the ability, perhaps the physical strength, to do it. As long as some women could possibly perform any one job, employers must consider all women applying for it. Moreover, Barry places strict restrictions on what may legitimately constitute an individual's merit. As he puts it:

24. Katha Pollitt, "Whose Culture?" 29–30.
25. Barry, *Culture and Equality*, 55.

Employers cannot cite pure prejudice on the part of fellow workers or customers in justification of a refusal to employ members of certain ascriptive groups. Even if it is true that many customers in some area prefer to be served by white shop assistants, and that some will choose a shop catering to their prejudices over one that does not, permitting firms to base employment criteria on these facts would clearly subvert any notion of equal opportunity. For it would mean that people could be denied a job simply on the basis of ascriptive characteristics. Hence, the notion of a relevant qualification must be construed in terms of relevant behavior, as distinct from identity as such.[26]

Presumably these criteria also apply to practices within an organization once people have been employed. It would not be acceptable for a manager at an investment bank, for example, to promote only men, on the grounds that he and other senior staff trusted only men, or that he liked his senior staff to bond in a bar after work and felt that women would not fit in to that environment. In such cases, the employer could be taken to an industrial tribunal and found guilty of sexual discrimination in employment practices. There would be no police raids on his evenings in the bar, or police observers at his promotion interviews. Instead, women from inside the organization who had been discriminated against would take their case to the tribunal and give evidence. They would argue that their job performance was as good as or better than that of their male colleagues, and that, in consequence, they would have been promoted had they been male. Similarly, under the proposed regime of interference in discriminatory cultural norms, women would be able to take their complaints to court and demon-

26. Ibid., 55–56. It is worth noting that this excerpt directly contradicts the response to my argument that Barry makes in "Second Thoughts," where he states that "all anti-discrimination employment law has built into it the proviso that otherwise illegal stipulations of qualifications for jobs become acceptable if the organization can show that the special qualifications it imposes are necessary to the conduct of the enterprise, whatever it is" (225). This cannot be the case, for it seems that being white *is* a necessary "qualification" for employees for the enterprise of a shop in a white supremacist area, since, in Barry's example, being white is necessary to securing sales, which is the main purpose of the shop. We need to have a more substantive set of criteria for determining which qualifications are legitimate. One suggestion (made by Iris Marion Young in *Justice and the Politics of Difference*) is that qualifications are illegitimate if they result from or perpetuate *oppression;* this criterion would rule out racism in the shop example but would surely also rule out sexism in religious employment.

strate that, had they been male, the religious court would have granted them a divorce, for example. An employment tribunal would compel a discriminatory employer to change his promotion procedures and provide compensation, even if it were true that, for reasons to do with his "culture," the employer really did work better with single men who bonded well in the bar. So too, a religious divorce court could be compelled to change its procedures even if it were true that there were cultural reasons for treating women differently.[27]

There are a number of options for such compulsion, as there are in cases of employment discrimination. British employment tribunals may currently employ three remedies in cases of sex discrimination: compensation, for lost earnings and/or for "damage to feelings"; a simple declaration of the rights of the relevant parties; or a recommendation, calling on the employer to take action remedying the discrimination or face further penalties.[28] A declaration of rights has little concrete effect on its own, and would not be enough to remedy religious sex discrimination. Compensation could be applied fairly simply to the case of religious sex discrimination: the relevant religious body could be compelled to compensate a woman who was unfairly denied a divorce, for example. As with employment cases, compensation awards would discourage the religious body from continuing to discriminate, and so would go some way toward changing the religious laws.

A recommendation (enforced with penalties for noncompliance) that the religion change its rulings and grant an individual woman a religious divorce is the most complex option, and recommendations have rarely been used in employment tribunals. However, the main

27. Barry's response to this part of my argument is to say that religions and companies have different functions: whereas religious "communities exist for the sake of their own members"; "profit-making enterprises['] . . . rationale is ultimately that they satisfy the wants of consumers and clients" ("Second Thoughts," 224). I find both sides of this distinction puzzling. On the side of religious communities, saying that they exist "for the sake of their members" would justify sex discrimination only if women are not counted as being among those members (which would be profoundly inegalitarian) or if it could be argued that being discriminated against actually works in favor of the women members (an argument that would require some serious elaboration that Barry does not provide). On the side of profit-making enterprises, as the name suggests, surely a fundamental part of their rationale is to make a profit for the owners and shareholders, with the satisfaction of consumers and clients being only a means to this goal? Insofar as this is true, we might describe profit-making enterprises also as existing "for the sake of their members." But even if we reject this idea, the customers and clients of the shop in the white supremacist area are satisfied if its employees are white, and yet Barry does not allow these preferences to count (see previous footnote).

28. Simon Deakin and Gillian S. Morris, *Labour Law*, 611–16.

legal problem with making a recommendation in the employment context is *not* that it would interfere with the practices or culture of the firm, or that it would be awkward for the individual concerned to be forcibly reinstated or promoted. Instead, recommendations have been overturned on appeal on the grounds that, in one case, automatically appointing the wronged individual to a particular job would violate the statutory regulations for making appointments to the job in question (a consultant microbiologist) and, in another, that automatic promotion would be "akin to positive or reverse discrimination in favor of a person on racial grounds."[29] Two leading textbooks in British law agree that the latter argument is "peculiar" or not "supportable";[30] in any case, neither consideration applies to religious sex discrimination. Gwyneth Pitt goes so far as to say that, if discrimination is to be remedied, "it is essential that such orders should be able to be made"[31]—despite the fact that such rulings would have significant implications for the internal culture of the employer. There would, of course, be difficulties with requiring religious courts to make particular rulings so that, in practice, imposing a recommendation on the religious group might revert to imposing a financial penalty for noncompliance. But heavy financial penalties will strongly encourage religions and employers to change their internal culture in a way that provides for greater gender equality, and such change will be for the better.

The tribunal approach can be understood, in Albert Hirschmann's terms, as a shift from exit to voice. Hirschmann considers both exit and voice as mechanisms to remedy a deteriorating organization or group, since both alert the leadership of the group to their own failings and provide an impetus for change. He argues that the role of voice must increase as the possibility for exit decreases, and notes that the exit option is "very nearly" unavailable "in such basic social organizations as the family, the state, or the church."[32] Although loyalty, of the sort that people feel for their cultures or religions, tends to activate voice,[33] there is no guarantee that voice will be successful. Hirschmann argues that for voice to be effective, exit must be possible but not *too* easy. If exit is too easy, then members of the relevant group will simply

29. Ibid., 615.
30. Ibid.; Gwyneth Pitt, *Employment Law*, 63.
31. Pitt, *Employment Law*, 63.
32. Albert Hirschmann, *Exit, Voice, and Loyalty*, 33.
33. Ibid., 78.

leave rather than engage in voice; however, if exit is impossible, there is no reason for the leaders of the group to listen to the voice of its members.[34] The problem with cultural groups is that exit is inevitably extremely costly and difficult, and that the difficulty of exit could not really be lessened without undermining the very concept of a cultural or religious group to which people develop strong attachments. Instead, we need a way of enhancing the group's leaders' responsiveness to voice. The equality tribunal is one such method.

The demand-led nature of this method of intervention in cultural practices is crucial. It would be up to individual Jewish and Muslim women, for example, to approach the tribunal and ask for the law of equal treatment to be enforced and a religious divorce granted. The tribunal would not intervene in religious divorce proceedings until it had been asked to do so by those concerned. This approach has a number of benefits. First, it avoids Barry's totalitarian scenario, and thus ensures that fundamental liberal principles of individual liberty and limiting state power are not infringed. Second, it helps to ensure that the liberal intervention is not totally alien to the culture in which the intervention takes place. If Jewish and Muslim women are in complete agreement with their religious courts that women and men should not be granted divorce on equal terms, then they will not take their cases to the tribunal. No one, on this approach, is "forced to be free." Third, and similarly, this approach will often reveal the extent to which practices supposedly integral to a culture are in fact endorsed only by particular dominant groups within that culture. If, as seems likely, there are Jewish and Muslim women who do not see unequal divorce laws as crucial to the practice of their religion, we have reason to believe that the integrity of the religion will not be destroyed if it changes one of its customs.[35]

One disadvantage with the tribunal approach, however, is that it may not be sufficient to undermine the influence factor. If the influence is particularly effective, disadvantaged individuals will not take their cases

---

34. Ibid., 55.

35. This seems likely for the simple reason that every Jewish or Muslim woman petitioning a religious court for divorce presumably feels that she has good grounds to be granted one. If any women are denied a religious divorce, there must therefore be a mismatch between the beliefs of at least some women and the dominant members of the religious communities. In other words, not all members hold the rules of divorce as interpreted by the courts to be an integral part of their religion or culture.

to the tribunal or may avoid seeking divorce. As I argued in Chapter 2, a Bourdieuean analysis of social construction alerts us to the possible need for the impetus for change to come from outside, perhaps through imposed structural changes. For this reason, it is quite proper for the state to engage in advertising or education campaigns informing individuals of their new rights and encouraging use of the tribunal. If the cultural practice is sufficiently principled and universally upheld within the culture, it will withstand such external influence. If there is dissent within the culture, however, then the influence factor will be gradually undermined as more people refuse to accept its discriminatory effects.

A second problem with the tribunal approach is that it will be very difficult for individuals to risk ostracism by complaining about the norms of their cultural or religious groups, especially to outsiders. The tribunal approach will require some individuals to act bravely, perhaps against their own immediate self-interest. Going to tribunal may, for the first who do so, be tantamount to leaving the group.[36] The tribunal approach, however, is preferable to freedom of exit in that it improves the situation for others and weakens the unjust norm. Unlike exit, which reinforces the validity of unequal practices through the expulsion of dissenters, laws against unequal practices provide a clear signal that such practices are unjust. In response, religious courts are likely to change their rulings over time as they are forcibly reversed, or incur fines, on appeal to the equality tribunal. This gradual process of change from within is the method of change most consistent with liberal principles. It would not be acceptable for a liberal state to force reluctant women to seek a divorce when they had grounds for doing so, even if there were good reasons for suspecting that such women were reluctant only as a result of pressure from within their culture. Much as we might regret such a situation, we cannot use state power to enforce our ideal state of affairs. Barry understands this point well. As he argues, "The move from principle to intervention has to be mediated by practical considerations. . . . liberals are not so simple-minded as to imagine that the answer to all violations of liberal rights is to send in the Marines."[37] Barry should not, therefore, suppose that the only way to se-

36. The difficulty of pursuing such a path cannot be an objection for Barry, however, because such an objection entails recognition of the difficulty and thus the insufficiency of freedom of exit.

37. Barry, *Culture and Equality*, 138.

cure equal rights for women within cultural groups is to send in the police.

If we return to Barry's original justification for rejecting state intervention in discriminatory cultural norms, we see that that justification provides an even more compelling argument *against* intervention in employment practices—an argument that liberals do not want to make. As described above, the fundamental condition a culture must meet if it is to be immune from internal state interference is that its members must be able to exit freely. In Barry's words: "The only condition on a group's being able to impose norms on its members is that the sanctions backing these norms must be restricted to ones that are consistent with liberal principles. What this means is primarily that, while membership of the group can be made contingent upon submission to these unequal norms, those who leave or are expelled may not be subjected to gratuitous losses."[38] An employing organization conforms perfectly to this condition. The men-friendly employer could be described as making membership of the group—employment in the bank—contingent on submission to unequal norms—promotion of male drinking companions only. He does not subject those who wish to exit from the group to gratuitous losses, which, for Barry, do not include the loss of the intrinsic benefits of membership such as salary or networking. True, the leaving employee needs some form of subsistence, which the salary originally provides; but particularly in a society which provides a welfare safety net, the employer cannot be held responsible for the lifetime subsistence of all ex-employees. Moreover, the unequal norms to which the members of the investment bank must submit are not backed up in state law—it is quite possible for his employees to avoid the norms by exiting. Why, then, should employers be subjected to antidiscrimination legislation from which cultural groups are exempt? Just as Orthodox Jewish women are free to choose to leave their culture and religion if they do not wish to submit to unequal norms, so too employees are free to choose to leave their employer if they do not wish to submit to his unequal promotion practices.

In fact, the freedom of an employee to leave a discriminatory employer is rather greater than is the freedom to leave of a member of a culture or religious group. In general, what matters to employees is having a job. Within certain restrictions of type of work, salary, and

38. Ibid., 128.

location, it is not of fundamental importance that an individual have
any one particular job. If the salaries and job descriptions are roughly
equivalent, an individual's fundamental interests will not be harmed
by working at one investment bank as opposed to another. While it
may be the case that someone develops a connection to their particular
job, or prefers one company to another, the state does not need to and
should not intervene merely to satisfy these sorts of preferences.[39] If a
female employee at the discriminatory bank really dislikes its sexist
promotion practices, she is free to leave for a job at another bank. For
a member of a religious group, however, what really matters is not
membership in a religious group as such, but membership in one particular religious group. The reasons for this preference are obvious
and compelling. In a religious group, she will have strongly held and
fundamental beliefs in many of the teachings and practices of the religion—even if she rejects some of those practices which are discriminatory.[40] In a cultural group, a member will have a similar affinity with
its practices, some of which—such as ceremony, music, or dance—
may be very difficult to replicate outside the group. The member of
either a religious or cultural group will have very strong ties to others
in the group, ties which are likely to be stronger than those within an
employing organization, since many of them will be based on family
relationships and lifelong friends. It will also be easier for an employee
who leaves one company for another to retain her friends in the first
company, since changing jobs is common and does not imply rejection
of those in the company left behind. When individuals leave cultural
or religious groups, however, those remaining in the groups may feel
deeply hurt and betrayed by the rejection of their values and community. In short, what matters to an Orthodox Jewish woman seeking
equal rights of divorce is membership in the *Jewish* community, not
membership in any (religious) community. Her ability to exit is thus

39. There are some exceptions to this rule of substitutability between jobs. For example, if
there is only one employer in a certain field in one part of a country, then it might matter
very much to the individual that she is employed by that particular employer, if her skills are
nontransferable. However, such an employer would fail to meet the criterion of free exit,
since specialist employees who leave will suffer gratuitous losses. Under Barry's scheme,
then, such an employer would not be able to impose unequal norms.

40. In general, liberalism is not particularly well equipped to deal with conflicting identity
positions. Thus a Muslim woman in a liberal society, for example, might face conflicting
loyalties to her culture, her religion, and the rights and principles endorsed by the wider
liberal community in which she lives. The question of which identity she focuses on with
regards to a particular outcome is not best conceptualized in terms of free choice.

much less real than is the ability of a woman to leave a discriminatory employer.[41]

The conclusion to be drawn from this example, it ought to be clear, is not that egalitarian liberals should abandon laws against sexual discrimination in employment. The conclusion, instead, is that formal freedom of exit is insufficient to excuse a cultural or religious group's imposition of unequal norms. Just as the state properly intervenes in discriminatory employment practices, so too it ought to intervene in discriminatory cultural or religious norms, even where those norms are not enshrined in state law, and even where members are "free" to leave the groups in the sense described by Barry.

One final possible objection should be considered. Barry is keen on the idea that an egalitarian liberal can and ought to allow discrimination for employment within religious groups on grounds of belief—for example, that Christian churches should sometimes be allowed to employ only their coreligionists. As he argues: "It seems uncontroversial that discrimination based on religion should be permitted when it comes to a church's choice of candidates for the priesthood or its equivalent."[42] This position is indeed uncontroversial, and my scheme does not contradict it. One simply cannot be a priest unless one believes. It is clearly part of what is required to do the job. Similarly, it is part of what is necessary to doing many jobs well that one should believe them to be at least minimally worthwhile. A stockbroker would be justified in refusing to employ someone who argued that global capitalism is evil and that share trading ought to be abolished. Commitment to the fundamental ideals of the company is something which all employers expect, and the state does not forbid such an expectation. What a company is not entitled to expect, however, is that an employee subscribe to all its practices and all its ideals, where those ideals are not crucial to the workings of the company and where they are discriminatory. A stockbroker may restrict employment to those who are interested in and committed to the company's profit-maximization, or to the smooth running of global markets, but it cannot legitimately restrict employment to white men, or to those who are also members of a Masonic Lodge or the Republican Party.

---

41. For the similar claim that opportunities are subjective and not objective, see Susan Mendus, "Choice, Chance and Multiculturalism," 33, and David Miller, "Liberalism, Equal Opportunities and Cultural Commitments."

42. Barry, *Culture and Equality*, 168.

Barry accepts this principle as regards employment, but rejects it for religion on the basis of individual choice. For Barry, the Catholic Church cannot be forced to ordain women priests, because some Catholics sincerely believe that the sacraments can be administered only by a man. It therefore becomes part of what is necessary to being a priest that one is a man. Barry argues, then, that "freedom of religious worship for individuals, which is an undeniably liberal value, can be achieved only if people are free to attach themselves to churches with a variety of doctrines. (It should be noted that this is not an argument from the value of diversity but from the value of individual choice)."[43] This argument fails. Ordaining women priests would not force individual Catholics to receive the sacraments from a woman; if there were both male and female priests the choice of individual worshippers, male and female, would be increased. Barry might reply that some individuals want to attach themselves to groups that don't allow other individuals to choose certain things, such as worship with women priests, but such preferences cannot be protected by liberals when they violate such a fundamental value as gender equality, and are hardly best defended by an appeal to "individual choice."

More important, it is misleading to focus on people's freedom to "attach themselves to churches." As we have seen, religions are to a large extent groups into which people are born and of which they find themselves already members. While individual choice might be increased by allowing individuals to choose from whom they receive the sacraments, it is threatened by forbidding those whose identity is prereflexively bound up with a certain group from participating in it fully. A ban on women priests harms the choice of women who wish to become leaders of the religion in which they find themselves. It also threatens other liberal values. Equality is clearly violated, not only by the ban itself, but also by the effects it has on the understandings of children who grow up within the religion: that women are not equal to men in the arena of worship, that women are not fit to lead their fellow worshippers, and that the voice of women does not need to be heard when religious leaders are formulating policy. The lack of female voices within a religion's leadership is also likely to have grave consequences for the basic rights of women members: unequal marriage and divorce laws, female genital mutilation, and the prohibition of con-

43. Ibid., 174. See also Nussbaum, *Sex and Social Justice*, III.

traception—all threats to women's individual choice—are less likely to be reformed if women do not participate in the religion's leadership.[44] While it might sometimes be acceptable, therefore, for an appeal to individual choice to justify allowing groups to endorse unequal norms if adult individuals really do choose whether or not to join (the example of employment shows even this principle to be doubtful), it cannot be acceptable for similar norms to apply to a group into which children are born and to which their attachments are not chosen.

The fact that religious associations gain many of their members through upbringing rather than choice means that arguments phrased in terms of "freedom of association" are misleading. For example, Stuart White correctly argues that freedom of association entails the right to exclude, and proposes that associations should be allowed to exclude categories of people (women, for example) in certain carefully defined circumstances. The most relevant here is White's claim that religious groups have a particular interest in excluding those "who have . . . characteristics which can reasonably be seen as incompatible with sincere profession of their beliefs (which may sometimes include ascriptive characteristics like race or gender)."[45] This interest, White argues, should be "regarded as having a strong presumption of legitimacy" given the fundamental importance of "freedoms of conscience and expression."[46]

While White's analysis may accurately reflect the claims of religious leaders, it is problematic in that it does not easily apply to cases where members of the excluded group find themselves part of the religion by upbringing but are excluded from certain aspects of the religion on adulthood. Religions that exclude women do not usually exclude them from the religion *tout court*, but rather exclude them from bearing certain rights or fulfilling certain functions within the religion once they are members. If the issue really were one of excluding women from religious association, the religion would be akin to a men-only club or society such as the Masons—an organization that women could never enter and, as a result, one in which they would never find themselves.

---

44. Nussbaum argues, rightly, that access to contraception (not to mention freedom from female genital mutilation) is a basic human right (*Sex and Social Justice*, 101–2, 118–29). However, she is reluctant to use state power to force religions to allow women to officiate (111, 197). These issues cannot reasonably be separated.

45. Stuart White, "Freedom of Association and the Right to Exclude," 385.

46. Ibid., 386.

In contrast, religious associations tend to welcome women from birth, encouraging parents to bring their daughters up within the faith. The exclusion comes later, once membership is settled and women are firmly situated in the religious structures. It is then that women are denied access to the priesthood, or to a religious divorce, or to equal rights more generally. These categorical exclusions are not best conceptualized as partners to freedom of association, for association has already taken place prereflexively. Instead, they are partners to the maintenance of inequality and domination.

The fact that individuals tend to inherit rather than choose their religious association also has implications for the internal diversity of religions. If religions were associations of which only adults could be members, on condition of acceptance of prescribed religious tenets, it might well be reasonable to expect enduring internal agreement on those tenets.[47] However, once religions are inherited, diversity and disagreement are likely. For some individuals will find themselves, at some stage in their adult lives, firmly believing in some of the religious tenets they have been taught while rejecting or being skeptical of others. Depending on the relative weight that is placed on the competing tenets by either the individual or others, the individual may feel that either her skepticism *or* her belief dominates. One person brought up as a Christian may reasonably come to think that her belief in the doctrine of "Love Thy Neighbor" is insufficient to maintain her Christianity in the light of her doubt about the existence of Jesus. Another may reasonably conclude that her skepticism as to the biblical or other justification for a ban on women priests in no way undermines her Catholicism, given her firm belief in the New Testament, transubstantiation, and so on. Indeed, one might say that if it really is the case that it is fundamentally impossible to be a Catholic and endorse female priests, then no Catholic women will come forward and apply for the

47. Ruth Abbey pointed out to me that some religions do have ceremonies to mark the transition into both adulthood and full membership in the religion. Thus Jewish Bar and Bat Mitzvahs, Catholic First Communion, and so on might count as occasions for marking voluntary adult entry into the religion. In order for such ceremonies to fulfill the normative role of making religions voluntary associations, however, two conditions would have to be met. First, ceremonies could take place only when individuals were sufficiently mature to make responsible choices—for example, at age eighteen rather than the onset of puberty. Second, it is difficult to categorize religions as voluntary associations as long as children are brought up within one particular religion and encouraged or expected to participate in it in some form long before any adult membership ceremony.

priesthood under new laws enabling them to do so. If some women do come forward, however (as we might expect given that there are many current supporters of allowing women to be priests),[48] the belief that women cannot be priests under Catholicism starts to look like one that is contingent, possibly on the nature of the incumbent power structures within the Church.

Against this claim, two points might be raised. First, it might be argued that individuals' freedom to be Catholics *as such* is threatened by state legislation forbidding a ban on women priests, since Catholicism is a religion based on the authority of the pope.[49] As a result, any state decree that overrides papal authority undermines the fundamental basis of the religion. However, as Cass Sunstein notes, all laws place restrictions on what individuals of any religion may do, whether or not their religious leaders endorse those restrictions, and thus the very concept of law undermines religious authority.[50] If murder were decreed by the leader of a religion or culture based on authority, such as the *fatwa* placed on Salman Rushdie, most liberals would concur with Barry that "anyone who killed Rushdie would deserve to be treated as a common murderer."[51] Thus, the question is not "does legislation against gender discrimination outlaw Catholicism as such?" but rather "is gender equality one of those issues which is of sufficient importance to merit intervention?" I believe that it is.

Second, opponents of Catholic women priests might claim that those women who wish to be priests are not, for that reason, "true" Catholics. It is beyond the scope of this chapter to examine this claim in detail, since it raises the enormously difficult question of how to define which tenets are crucial to, and constitutive of, a religion or other belief system. One option is that it would be appropriate to ask whether the leaders of a religion would be prepared to see the religion die out or shrink significantly rather than give way on the tenet in question.[52] In other words, if there were a shortage of priests so acute that it threatened the survival of Catholicism and could be rectified

---

48. A useful source on this issue is John Wijngaards, *The Ordination of Women Catholic Internet Library*, which argues against the theological justifications for preventing women from being ordained. In particular, the site argues that women *were* ordained as deacons in the third to ninth centuries.

49. I am grateful to Zofia Stemplowska and Patti Lenard for observations on this point.

50. Cass Sunstein, "Should Sex Equality Law Apply to Religious Institutions?"

51. Barry, *Culture and Equality*, 280.

52. I am grateful to Cécile Fabre for this suggestion.

only by ordaining women, would the papal authorities allow the ordination of women? There is currently an active campaign within the United States to allow married men to enter the clergy so as to alleviate the shortage of Catholic priests, which suggests that this question is a live one.[53]

White considers this issue. He writes:

> Even if we are satisfied that a disputed exclusion rule can reasonably be seen as protecting a specific expressive commitment, in evaluating the legitimacy of the exclusion rule we should also consider whether this expressive commitment itself really is central to the association's purposes as these currently stand. Is the exploration and/or propagation of the relevant values or beliefs central to the activity of the typical association member? Do they feature prominently in the motivation of the typical person joining the association, or in the self-understandings of current members? If not, then it is far from clear that the disputed exclusion rule really is serving an important integrity interest.[54]

Although White argues in terms of freedom of association, with the implication that adults choose whether or not to enter the religion rather than inheriting their membership, these questions make sense only if we drop this assumption. For if we follow the assumption, and focus on groups that have rules excluding adults from joining groups in the first place (such as the Masons), it is somewhat question-begging to consider only the views of existing members or "the typical person joining the association" when evaluating those rules. Since the group, as currently defined, has as one of its beliefs the idea that a certain group (women, for example) should be excluded, it follows that it is not currently possible to be a group member while believing that women should be admitted. So long as the criteria for belief and membership are set by *existing* members, there is limited possibility for change in the criteria. Any member changing their mind on the exclusion of women would cease to be a "true" believer. White's questions only have critical force, then, if we abandon the idea that religions are

53. See the 2002–3 edition of United States, Bureau of Labor Statistics, *Occupational Outlook Handbook*.

54. White, "Freedom of Association," 388.

like clubs with lists of rules that must be adhered to in order to gain membership. Instead, religions are groups in which the rules of association are essentially contested and unclear. The idea of a "true" Catholic is thus extremely problematic, and aspects of Catholicism frequently are questioned and sometimes reformed.[55] In a liberal society at least, gender inequality is one issue that most requires reform.

Gender, then, cannot be accepted by liberals as necessarily intrinsic to religious practice, but other factors can. Under state intervention in discriminatory cultural norms, a religion would be able to insist that its divorce rules were religious in character (perhaps allowing divorce on the grounds that one partner refused to attend religious worship or to recognize religious festivals), but would be unable to apply those rules unequally to men and to women (both men and women should be able to divorce their spouses on those grounds). In other words, religious groups should be able to place religious restrictions on the actions of their members, but those restrictions should not fall more heavily on one ascriptive group inside the religion than on another. There will be limits on the kinds of restrictions which are permissible, just as liberalism places limits on individual freedom. However, these limits will not need to be very significant if the restrictions are to apply to all, as powerful group members will have clear disincentives to advocate practices that disadvantage themselves.

Alternative Jurisdictions

Ayelet Shachar makes jurisdictional proposals that differ from but focus on the same problems as the equality tribunal. Shachar directly engages with the issue of how to legislate for both multiculturalism and gender equality. She takes as her starting point the fact that the demands of minority cultural groups are often in conflict with women's equal rights. This forms what she calls "the paradox of multicultural vulnerability," which occurs "whenever state accommodation policies intended to mitigate the power differential between groups end up reinforcing power hierarchies within them."[56] Shachar develops the approach of "joint governance" to solve this paradox without abandoning either multicultural accommodation or equal citizenship.

55. One example of reform in Catholicism is the Second Vatican Council, documents of which can be found at http://vatican.va/archive/index.htm/.
56. Shachar, *Multicultural Jurisdictions*, 17.

Shachar's approach is a great improvement on alternative accounts that pay no attention to the risk of injustice inherent in abandoning women to the particular rulings of minority cultures. She considers the problems of multicultural accommodation and makes many apt criticisms. Many of her criticisms are shared by this book, such as the criticism of unequal Orthodox Jewish divorce law according to which a woman may not divorce without her husband's consent. However, despite her criticisms of many multicultural policies, Shachar does not want to abandon them altogether. The approach that she adopts aims to avoid the "'either/or' types of solutions to the paradox of multicultural vulnerability,"[57] where the choice is between accommodation on the one hand, and universal citizenship regardless of culture on the other. In other words, despite heavily criticizing multicultural accommodation, she ends up endorsing some—problematic—features of it. Shachar's arguments in favor of multicultural accommodation do not stand up to the weight of evidence she offers that it can lead to oppression and inequality.[58] As a result, in some cases of injustice that Shachar considers, she misidentifies the source of the injustice.

For example, Shachar describes the case of Julia Martinez, a member of the Santa Clara Pueblos who married outside the tribe. As a result, according to the kinship rules of the tribe, her children were not deemed to be tribal members. Tribal membership was important for the children, Shachar tells us, since membership would have qualified them for health care given solely to Indians. One child was denied emergency health care when she suffered a stroke, and Martinez filed a lawsuit. In hearing the case, the U.S. Supreme Court practiced multicultural accommodation and upheld the tribal kinship system. Shachar concludes that the case illustrates the problems with multicultural accommodation since the Court "effectively gave legal sanction to the deprivation of benefits and the systematic maltreatment of a particular

57. Ibid., 146.
58. One argument that Shachar briefly deals with, and endorses, is the multiculturalists' claim that "any society, no matter how open and democratic, will always have certain cultural, linguistic, and historical traditions which welcome some of its members more completely than others, because the institutions of that society have largely been shaped in their image" (ibid., 23). I discuss this issue at length elsewhere (Clare Chambers, "Nation-Building, Neutrality and Ethnocultural Justice") and do not have the space to do so here. The thrust of my argument is that if this majority culture is liberal, that very fact renders any particularity unproblematic from the point of view of justice. As a result, I do not take Shachar's recounting of this multicultural claim to be convincing, and certainly not decisively so.

category of group member—some Pueblo mothers (and their children)—so long as it was in accordance with the group's traditions."[59]

The problem, Shachar argues, lies in the Supreme Court's recognition of the patrilineal kinship system, whereas it ought to be the case that children of tribal mothers also have a right to membership. Hence the injustice is suffered by "a particular category of group member." Although it is unjust to discriminate in this way, Shachar's criticism seems to miss the key injustice of the case. The injustice lies in the fact that an extremely ill child was denied emergency health care because of her cultural membership or ethnic background. The injustice would have been equally great if the child had been wholly non-Indian. Turning any child—or indeed any adult—away from emergency health care on the grounds of ethnic or cultural origin must surely be unjust from any egalitarian perspective. The injustice is not suffered solely by some category of group member, but by *anyone* not considered to be a group member. In other words, the major source of injustice is the absence of a state healthcare system such that individuals can obtain health care only through membership of some particular group, whether that group is cultural or, in the case of a private scheme, financial or occupational. The key injustice in either case is that one must be a member of such a group to receive treatment, not merely that the boundaries of the group are drawn incorrectly.

This case is important because it illustrates a general problem with Shachar's approach. Many of the injustices that she identifies are not injustices because women are treated particularly badly within an otherwise acceptable framework of multicultural accommodation. They are injustices that arise from the simple fact of allowing cultural groups to deviate from the general rights and duties of liberal citizenship so as to provide their members with special benefits or encumber them with special restrictions. Securing gender equality within the context of multicultural legislative particularity does not in itself render such particularity just. *If* there is to be legislative particularity, it must—on this I agree with Shachar—be internally gender-equal. But it does not follow that gender equality, or equality more generally, is compatible with such particularity.

Why, then, does Shachar advocate some form of multiculturalism despite its frequent injustices? What are her arguments in favor of

59. Ibid., 19.

multicultural accommodation? To a large extent, these take the form of the rejection of what she calls "the 're-universalized citizenship' position"[60] epitomized by Susan Moller Okin.[61] This position "concludes that if diverse societies wish to achieve greater gender equality, then they should completely abolish minority group practices which do not adhere to the state's legal norms, or else they should require these practices to 'transcend' themselves to such an extent that they practically conform to the norms and perceptions of the majority communities."[62] Since this broad definition could apply to my approach, Shachar's objections to it are relevant to the argument of this book. However, she offers only two categories of criticism, both of which apply to the specifics of Okin's brief (sixteen-page) essay and do not apply to all attempts to (re-)universalize citizenship. First, Shachar charges that Okin's account is based on "sweeping generalizations" about cultural patriarchy that do not take account of the fact of cultural diversity and change.[63] Regardless of whether Okin is guilty as charged, the charge is irrelevant to the theoretical position of reuniversalized citizenship: *to the extent that* cultural practices are patriarchal, they are problematic, and *to the extent that* those practices are not being changed by the culture in question, the state needs to step in.

Second, Shachar criticizes Okin for, in effect, ignoring the fact of social construction. Shachar writes: "[Okin] provides a very unsatisfactory account of why so many women participate in traditions that are to their distinct disadvantage (compared to other group members). . . . [P]erhaps the most crucial consideration Okin ignores is that women will stay in minority groups because they have no real alternatives."[64] Although Shachar does not elaborate on these problems, or discuss the concept of social construction, these two points effectively mirror the two features of social construction that I have discussed in this book: the construction of subjects and their desires, and of social norms and the options that are available.

Shachar concludes that the reuniversalized citizenship approach is untenable because it forces women to choose between their culture and their equal citizenship, denying them the option of both. Such

60. Ibid., 64.
61. Okin, "Is Multiculturalism Bad for Women?"
62. Shachar, *Multicultural Jurisdictions*, 65.
63. Ibid., 65–66.
64. Ibid., 67.

disadvantaged individuals will, she argues, face a "wrenching decision" as to which aspect of their identity they wish to uphold.[65] This criticism is odd coming from Shachar, since her own approach requires individuals to decide whether to submit to the jurisdiction of the state or the group on a particular issue. However, this criticism does not apply to my approach since I do not make universal citizenship available to women if and only if they choose to abandon their culture. Instead, the equality tribunal precisely opens to women the option of having their equality respected while staying within their group, unlike approaches such as Barry's, which rely on freedom of exit and thus do require individuals to make wrenching decisions. As a result, if the culture is to survive at all, it must be in a modified form that enables *all* individuals to participate in it in conditions of equality, rather than requiring some individuals and not others to choose between that equality and their culture. Such a consequence is, moreover, *advocated* by Shachar as a beneficial feature of her own proposals. She writes: "If group leaders fail to act appropriately [by reforming discriminatory practices], not only do they lose some of their power (because of the smaller base of supporters they now have); the collective also stands to lose because of the risk that it no longer controls key identity-defining sub-matters."[66]

Shachar's criticisms of the reuniversalized citizenship approach do not, therefore, affect my approach. Moreover, her criticisms of multicultural accommodation are much stronger than her arguments in favor of its partial adoption. As such, several of her proposals are problematic because they accord too much weight to multicultural particularity, as becomes clear when considering her jurisdictional proposals.

One of the strengths of Shachar's work, in the context of this book, is that it proposes specific legislative and jurisdictional arrangements. As these are different from my own, but share the desire to emancipate women and other vulnerable individuals from the paradox of multicultural vulnerability, they merit consideration. Shachar proceeds through rejection of six alternative models of governance. First, she rejects both "secular absolutism" and "religious particularism"—the extremes of the "either/or" dilemma just discussed. Then she rejects four alternative models of joint governance which, she argues, do overcome the "either/or" dilemma, but each of which is separately problematic.

65. Ibid., 68.
66. Ibid., 141.

These four models are described as different forms of accommodation: "federal-style," "temporal," " consensual," and "contingent." Finally, Shachar advocates her own model of joint governance, which she labels "transformative accommodation."[67]

It is beyond the scope of this discussion to consider Shachar's arguments concerning each of these models of governance in detail. Her rejection of secular absolutism has, in effect, already been dealt with, since she deploys the same criticisms here as against reuniversalized citizenship. I agree with many of her other points—particularly those highlighting the flaws in religious particularism and in the four alternative models of joint governance. In what follows, then, I consider only Shachar's arguments in favor of her own transformative accommodation.

The essence of transformative accommodation is that authority should be divided between the state and the group in such a way that both have jurisdiction over some aspect of a particular area of law, such as family law or criminal law, and neither has jurisdiction over the area in its entirety. Shachar calls these aspects sub-matters. The idea is that all sub-matters need to be addressed if a legal decision is to be reached, but because jurisdiction over the sub-matters is split between the state and the group, any decision must be the result of a compromise between them.[68] In the area of family law, for example, Shachar argues that the group should have jurisdiction over the sub-matter of demarcation—determining the conditions under which couples may marry and divorce, and the conditions of membership of the group—with the state having jurisdiction over the sub-matter of distribution—determining how resources should be distributed on divorce and between families.[69] The aim is to limit the power of both the state and the group, and thereby to minimize conflict. As Shachar puts it: "Even when both jurisdictions can furnish strong arguments for laying exclusive claim to the norms and procedures governing each individual, a single cohesive system of checks and balances guarantees that neither the state nor the group is enabled to govern alone. Both the state and the group are consequently forced to abandon their perfectionist and maximalist jurisdictional aspirations, which are so often the source of

67. Ibid., chaps. 4, 5, and 6.
68. Ibid., 119.
69. Ibid., 132.

conflict."[70] One problem immediately arises. Shachar insists on "the 'no-monopoly' rule," according to which "neither the group nor the state can *ever* acquire exclusive control over a contested social arena that affects individuals both as group members and as citizens,"[71] and gives "family law, education, resource development, immigration, and criminal justice"[72] as examples of such social arenas. She does not explain, however, which will be considered as the relevant group to govern any particular individual. Moreover, Shachar insists that transformative accommodation relies on the key assumption that individuals "represent the intersection of multiple identity-creating affiliations."[73] Given that, on her account, individuals are affiliated to many groups, which one should count legally? Should a Jew by descent who is a believer in Islam be governed by Jewish or Muslim law? What, given the no-monopoly rule, happens to those individuals (atheists, libertarians, comprehensive liberals?) who wish to be bound to no group? Should a Jewish atheist be governed by Jewish jurisdiction, or may she remove herself to the monopolistic rule of the state?

Assume, however, that this problem can be overcome and that, contrary to Shachar's own account, each individual can be unproblematically assigned to the jurisdiction of one and only one group in addition to the state. There remain several serious problems with Shachar's approach. First, it is unclear in what interests or according to which principles the state (as opposed to the group) is supposed to govern, and therefore on what basis individuals owe political obligation to the state. Presumably the state is not supposed to articulate the interests of any particular group, since that would replicate the supposed bias of non-multicultural accounts. According to Shachar, "Both the group and the state have normatively and legally justifiable interests in shaping the rules that govern behavior,"[74] but it is not clear why. The state's jurisdiction cannot purely be based on justice, with political obligation to the state deriving from a natural duty to do justice. For a natural duty account of political obligation accords normative weight to whichever laws are just, regardless of where they originate, and so could give no

70. Ibid., 143.
71. Ibid., 121; emphasis added.
72. Ibid., 121 n. 8.
73. Ibid., 118.
74. Ibid.

grounds for the separate jurisdictional authority of sub-state groups or the deviation of their laws from the justice-embodying state law.[75]

The state cannot, then, be acting in the interests of objective, universal justice, since that would render group particularism at best unnecessary and at worst unjust. On what, then, does the state base its laws? In talking of the state Shachar tends to construe it as a monolithic wielder of power to be tamed, and does not explain why the state is needed at all and what it ought to do. For example, she argues: "At the negotiation stage . . . [s]ince the state is the more powerful entity, the presumption in the negotiations must be in favor of the group."[76] This is to imply that there is no legitimacy to the state's claims. However, if the state is a liberal state charged with implementing justice, there ought to be a presumption in favor of it by definition.

Indeed, it is unclear what the role of justice is in Shachar's account as a whole. Her argument cannot be that the combination of laws offered by the state and the group, considered as an *ensemble,* will bring about justice, since the precise combination of laws to be obeyed differs from person to person and the laws enforced differ from group to group. Moreover, it is problematic from the point of view of egalitarian justice to endorse a system of justice that is unequally binding on individuals.[77] Finally, it appears in parts of Shachar's argument that the state *is* charged with enforcing laws based on considerations of justice, since she looks to the state to provide remedies for individuals who suffer from unjust group laws. But if the state epitomizes justice and the group deviates from justice, why endorse group laws in the first place? If it is unjust for divorce to rely on male consent, for example, why allow any group to implement such a law?

The way in which Shachar's approach deals with unjust group law is by allowing individuals to opt out of their group's jurisdiction and look to the state (and vice versa) in certain circumstances. However, this solution is problematic, not least because it is unclear precisely which circumstances qualify. Shachar explains that, under her proposals, individuals have

75. The sort of theory that I have in mind here is developed in Jeremy Waldron, "Special Ties and Natural Duties," and John Rawls, *A Theory of Justice,* chap. 6.

76. Shachar, *Multicultural Jurisdictions,* 129.

77. Seyla Benhabib makes a similar point, arguing that transformative accommodation undermines equality before the law, in *The Claims of Culture,* 129.

the ultimate power to determine whether to "switch" their jurisdictional loyalty from the original power-holder to the rival power-holder . . . on an issue-by-issue basis. . . . [But t]he purpose is not to fracture group solidarity so that members can opt out at the slightest opportunity. The initial division of authority between group and state must still remain meaningful and presumptively binding on its individual members. "Opting out" is justified only when the relevant power-holder has failed to provide remedies to the plight of the individual; only then can the individual instigate a fair claim against that authority.[78]

As an aside, it is unclear to what extent this provision is compatible with the no-monopoly rule and whether there are limits on the number of issues that an individual may opt out on. More substantively, Shachar gives no clear guidance as to what constitutes acceptable grounds for opting out. The vague concept of failing to provide remedy is repeated several times, sometimes amplified by the term "meaningful remedy."[79] But there is no indication as to how a failure to provide a remedy is defined.

Imagine, for example, a case in which the wife but not the husband wishes to divorce. The jurisdiction of the group (perhaps the group is Orthodox Jewish) states that the husband's consent is required for divorce and thus that no divorce can be granted. The jurisdiction of the state declares that the husband's consent is not required (perhaps after a set period of separation) and that a divorce will be granted. Regardless of which entity, group or state, is deemed to have presumptive jurisdiction over the case, surely each party would have grounds for declaring that one ruling fails to "provide a remedy" for their plight. The husband could claim that the state ruling fails to take account of his (their) group association and its attendant laws, and the wife could claim that the group ruling fails to take account of her equal citizenship. So which ruling should prevail? And why, if the case moves from, say, the group to the state in response to the wife's position, would the husband not have grounds for demanding it be returned to the group's jurisdiction in response to *his* position, as the state fails to provide *him* with meaningful remedy? Allowing individuals to shift from one system of law to

78. Shachar, *Multicultural Jurisdictions*, 123.
79. Ibid., 124.

another in pursuit of their favored remedy ignores the fact that law tends to be invoked only over a *dispute,* so that satisfying one party necessarily fails to satisfy the other. In other words, if individuals may opt out of a group's jurisdiction simply when a ruling goes against them (i.e., when they do not agree with the ruling), there will be a see-saw effect between jurisdictions as each individual rejects the jurisdiction which produces the ruling that disadvantages them. There will be no final solution and no real respect for the laws of either jurisdiction. On the other hand, if individuals may opt out only when a ruling is in some way unjust, for example, because it epitomizes inequality, that raises the question of why the unjust laws of groups are recognized in the first place and why they remain in place for other individuals.

Shachar might answer that the mechanism of *competition* inherent in her approach means that the unjust laws do not, over time, remain in place for other individuals. She states that "it is in the self-professed interest of the group and the state to vie for the support of their constit-uents"[80] and argues that, because groups will not want to lose members who opt out in favor of state jurisdiction, they will have a strong incentive to modify or abandon any unjust or unequal laws.[81] The implication is that groups want to increase or maintain their membership numbers as a top priority, and that group leaders value membership quantity over doctrinal purity. However, and this is a further problem with Shachar's account, such an implication clearly ignores the fact that many groups, particularly the most fundamentalist and oppressive religious groups, value many or all of their practices over and above their membership numbers. Those groups would *not* wish to retain members who did not fully support certain tenets, and certainly would not wish to change those tenets so as to retain such members. Indeed, as Shachar's own examples demonstrate, many groups maintain re-strictive kinship systems explicitly designed to limit the group's mem-bership and safeguard its purity. Thus, while groups clearly do experi-ence some pressure to maintain membership, as was described in the case of Catholicism, this pressure will not always be the sole, or even the most important, consideration, and cannot be relied upon as the source of doctrinal liberalization.

Finally, the idea that the paradox of multicultural vulnerability will

80. Ibid., 118.
81. Ibid., 138–43.

be overcome by individuals opting out of a group's jurisdiction looks very much like a reliance on the liberal safeguard of freedom of exit, and shares the problems of freedom of exit. Requiring an individual to "opt out" of a group in order to access her equal rights subjects her to a "wrenching decision" between her equal status and her way of life; demands that she consciously reason about, and reject strongly, her social conditioning and identity; estranges her from the group and portrays her as a traitor;[82] makes no clear statement about the injustice of the group law; and leaves the unjust law intact for others.

Overall, in contrast with my approach, which gives no legal recognition to group rules, Shachar's approach gives recognition with one hand and takes it away with the other. The result is an unhappy medium. Groups are allowed jurisdiction over certain sub-matters, which they may use to implement unjust or unequal laws. However, they are subject to state interference on an ad hoc basis, in individual cases (rather than on the laws themselves) and on uncertain grounds (justice? democracy? might?).

Choice and Autonomy—Culture and Equality

In this chapter, I have proposed the theory of the insufficiency of free choice. Put simply, the theory states that an unequal state of affairs cannot be justified simply by the observation that it came about as the result of the choices of those who are the least well off. In other words, free choice is insufficient to render a state of affairs normatively unproblematic in many cases. Choice cannot be always be a normative transformer. Instead, I suggested two factors that, if present, provide grounds for concluding that the state of affairs under consideration is unjust, and which ought to prompt state action to alleviate the inequality and thus the injustice. These two factors, which vary in extent and thus in injustice from case to case, are disadvantage and influence. When either of them is present, we should be on the alert for possible injustice. When both are present, we should infer actual injustice. A liberal state ought to intervene to ameliorate the effects of either or both factors, inasmuch as is compatible with core liberal values.

---

82. Shachar criticizes an alternative approach for leaving individuals susceptible to being labeled traitors. See ibid., 85.

Liberals should be concerned about cases where the disadvantage and influence factors are present because they illustrate the limitations of individuals' ability to escape contexts that limit, rather than enhance, their choices. Many of these limiting contexts are cultural. In particular, some cultures seek to limit the opportunities open to their members along unequal lines, so that some are denied opportunities that are open to others. In such cases, a liberal state ought to intervene to attempt to reduce the inequality. The appropriate form of intervention may involve addressing either the disadvantage or the influence or both, according to the particularities of the case. Sometimes, an approach similar to that of the employment tribunal will be appropriate, so that individuals can apply to have the rulings of their cultural authorities overturned. If there is no support from within the culture for such change, there will be no need for state action once the tribunal has been set up until such time as a case is brought before it. However, in order to counteract the effects of the influence factor as much as possible, a program of education or advertising will often be appropriate. Without such state intervention, the autonomy and fair equality of opportunity that liberals prize cannot be realized. And, for egalitarian liberals, *all* must have prizes.

5

TWO ORDERS OF AUTONOMY AND POLITICAL LIBERALISM:
BREAST IMPLANTS VERSUS FEMALE GENITAL MUTILATION

Most of the women who seek breast enlargement or augmentation are truly small-breasted. They suffer embarrassment about their size, especially when dressed in summer wear and bathing suits (which are particularly difficult for small-breasted women to find in the right size) as well as during intimate situations. On the whole, small-breasted women don't want to be large-breasted sex bombs, they just want to look "normal" and to be able to buy clothing easily. A smaller number seek breast enlargement after a large weight loss or when they're through breast feeding, after which it's common for breasts to lose volume and look droopy. . . . It's rare that a woman isn't a good candidate for augmentation.
—RANDOLPH H. GUTHRIE, *The Truth about Breast Implants*

A 1998 study showed 34% of American women were dissatisfied with their breasts.
—MARTHA GRIGG ET AL., *Information for Women about the Safety of Silicone Breast Implants*

A woman's chest, much more than a man's, is *in question* in this society, up for judgment, and whatever the verdict, she has not escaped the condition of being problematic.
—IRIS MARION YOUNG, "Breasted Experience"

So far I have argued that a truly liberal project must take account of the two aspects of social construction: the ways in which *individuals* and their *preferences* are formed by social forces, and the fact that individuals' *options* are constrained by social norms—some of which are harmful or epitomize inequality. As such, liberals must recognize that a simple formal framework of freedoms and resources is insufficient to secure genuine autonomy. In this chapter, I focus on the social construction of options and consider whether it is possible to be critically aware of this process while at the same time prioritizing autonomy. I extend my argument through analysis of the recent work of Martha Nussbaum. Nussbaum's approach combines a commitment to political liberalism with a critique of harmful social norms and an awareness of social construction, thus improving on the more standard Rawlsian approach.

Nussbaum improves on Barry's approach and on Rawlsian political liberalism not only with her awareness of social construction, but also with her greater awareness and intolerance of gender inequality. As such, she argues that there are many reasons why individuals' choices may not be the best route to justice, and recognizes that women all over the world suffer from injustice as the result of cultural or religious tradition with which they, in one sense, willingly comply. She is a firm believer in (some sorts of) autonomy and, like Barry, in the universal applicability of many liberal values, and thus advocates that the opportunity for autonomy should be extended to all individuals regardless of their cultural membership. Nussbaum's work thus appears at first glance to answer many questions concerning the compatibility of liberalism, autonomy, and social construction. However, as I shall show, Nussbaum's political liberalism prevents her from making good the promise of her work on social construction and the injustice of social norms. Much of what is valuable about the latter aspect of her work, moreover, undermines or directly contradicts her insistence on political liberalism. In general, political liberalism is peculiarly ill-equipped to deal with injustices resulting from culture and choice because it abandons significant areas of justice to determination by individual choice. Political liberalism is thus a problematic approach for feminists, and substantive egalitarians more generally. Instead, I suggest an alternative framework for dealing with culturally embedded injustices.

I start by distinguishing two forms of autonomy: call them first-order and second-order autonomy.[1] First-order autonomy concerns the attitude one has to the rules and norms that are a part of life. A person is first-order autonomous if she critically examines rules and norms and follows only those that she endorses. Second-order autonomy concerns the way that one comes to lead a particular way of life *writ large,*

---

1. My distinction between first- and second-order autonomy is not the same as Gerald Dworkin's distinction between first- and second-order reflection. Dworkin argues that autonomy is "a second-order capacity of persons to reflect critically upon their first-order preferences, desires, wishes, and so forth and the capacity to accept or attempt to change these in the light of higher-order preferences and values" (*The Theory and Practice of Autonomy,* 20). He therefore integrates various distinct phenomena into one unified concept, missing the ways in which an individual's autonomy is nuanced and multifaceted.

My distinction also differs from Marilyn Friedman's account of content-neutral autonomy versus substantive autonomy. See Chapter 7 for a discussion of Friedman's approach.

what Rawls calls a comprehensive conception of the good. A person is second-order autonomous if she chooses or endorses the overall conception of the good that she follows. I contend that political liberals such as Nussbaum and Rawls believe that only second-order autonomy should be the concern of the liberal state. I challenge that prioritization of second-order autonomy on two grounds. First, I argue that Nussbaum herself provides good reasons to be suspicious of the prioritization of second-order autonomy in her work on social construction—or as she calls it, the social formation of preferences.[2] Indeed, she suggests in this part of her work that opportunities for second-order autonomy are limited. However, there is a tension between Nussbaum's commitment to political liberalism and her concern to improve upon it: her political liberalism leads her to be wary of state intervention, and thus to prioritize individuals' ability to adhere to even those preferences which she has shown to be socially constructed and thus imperfect guides to justice.

Second, I argue that some ways of life or specific choices within a life are sufficiently problematic, even when chosen autonomously, as to merit state intervention. I show that Nussbaum agrees with this position in the case of female genital mutilation (FGM), and that this agreement causes problems: either she must extend that judgment to many other cases and reject her politically liberal prioritization of second-order autonomy or, in maintaining her political liberalism, she must surrender her feminist critique of FGM and endorse a conservative state neutrality. Overall, I propose an alternative approach for conceptualizing and responding to chosen yet harmful practices.

Two Orders of Autonomy

In order to make my argument I must first investigate the concept of autonomy in more detail. "Autonomy" has been used in a great many different ways by different philosophers,[3] and some distinctions are needed. For my purposes, it will be necessary to distinguish three concepts: negative freedom, and first- and second-order autonomy. The first concept, negative freedom, is familiar though contested. Its nu-

2. For example, see Martha Nussbaum *Sex and Social Justice*, especially chap. 10, and Nussbaum, *Women and Human Development*.
3. See Dworkin, *Theory and Practice of Autonomy*, 5–6, for some examples.

ances are not crucial in this context; the basic idea of negative freedom is a lack of interference from others or, to be more specific, a lack of coercion.[4] The second and third concepts are the two orders of autonomy. Second-order autonomy applies to the manner in which an individual comes to have a particular way of life or comprehensive conception of the good. One is second-order autonomous if one actively and willingly chooses one's way of life free from compulsion or influence that would obscure that choice.[5] Thus Rawls's defense of individuals' moral power "to have . . . and rationally to pursue a conception of the good"[6] can be thought of as a defense of second-order autonomy: individuals must be able to lead the way of life that they choose for themselves. First-order autonomy applies to one's attitude to the rules and norms that are part of a way of life. One is first-order autonomous if one leads a daily life in which one questions rules and norms and actively chooses how to respond to them. One may be first-order autonomous and follow rules, but only if one considers the rule and decides that it is a good rule to follow. One is first-order autonomous if one is governed by rules that one sets for oneself or endorses for oneself. In part, this idea is expressed in Rawls's claim that individuals must also be able to "revise" their conception of the good.[7] This conception of autonomy has many followers, as Gerald Dworkin points out: "As a moral notion—shared by philosophers as divergent as Kant, Kierkegaard, Nietzsche, Royce, Hare, and Popper—the argument is about the necessity or desirability of individuals choosing or willing or accepting their own moral code. We are all responsible for developing and criticizing our moral principles, and individual conscience must take precedence over authority and tradition."[8] The distinction between first-order autonomy and negative liberty, though necessary for analytical clarity, can introduce confusion. Consider the question, for example, of whether life in a convent or the army is autonomous. Clearly, if it is chosen, army or convent life is compatible with second-order auton-

4. See, for example, Berlin, "Two Concepts of Liberty," and Hayek, *The Constitution of Liberty.*

5. Thomas E. Hill Jr. describes autonomy-threatening influence as that which threatens the rationality of a person's choice: "Respecting individuals' autonomy means granting them at least the *opportunity* to make their crucial life-affecting choices in a rational manner" ("The Importance of Autonomy," 134).

6. John Rawls, *Justice as Fairness,* 19.

7. Ibid.

8. Dworkin, *Theory and Practice of Autonomy,* 10–11.

omy. Equally clearly, such lives entail great constraints on negative liberty. The position regarding first-order autonomy, however, is ambiguous. Depending on the nun or soldier's attitude to the rules of the institution, first-order autonomy may or may not be present. If she endorses all the rules following critical reflection on their value, then she will obey them with first-order autonomy, even though her liberty is constrained. However, on the reasonable assumption that the nun or soldier has to obey at least some rules which she finds problematic, both first-order autonomy and negative liberty are limited. This issue is important and will be returned to.[9] For now, though, assume that at least some of the rules of a convent or army are not endorsed by its members, so that the lack of negative freedom about which rules to obey leads to a lack of first-order autonomy.

There are four distinct logically possible ways of combining first- and second-order autonomy. First, a person might autonomously choose to live an autonomous life, therefore having both forms of autonomy. For example, she might be a philosopher who has decided to live a life in which she constantly questions rules and norms.[10] It should be fairly clear that liberals of all persuasions will have no normative problem with such an individual. On the other hand, a person might have neither first- nor second-order autonomy, thereby leading a nonautonomous life that they have not autonomously chosen. An example might be an individual living under a fundamentalist religious dictatorship, such as Afghanistan under the Taliban. Such an individual lacks second-order autonomy since she did not choose and cannot alter the government, its religion, or her residence in the country, and she lacks first-order autonomy since the regime explicitly prevents it. Liberals (again, of all persuasions) usually condemn such situations. However, they may be defended in certain circumstances, such as for justly convicted prisoners.

The more interesting cases are those in which only one order of autonomy is present. The third logically possible scenario is that a person could autonomously choose to live a nonautonomous life, such that she has second-order autonomy but not first. This is the category

9. One issue to be considered in more detail is whether a nun or soldier can have first-order autonomy if she adopts or endorses convent or army rules *without* engaging in prior critical evaluation of their worth.

10. In *Culture and Equality* Barry refers to such a life of constant Socratic questioning as "the ideal of autonomy."

on which I focus in this chapter. It includes freely chosen convent and army life. Finally, a person could live an autonomous life that she has not autonomously chosen, such that she has first-order autonomy but not second. An example of this case might be a child who has not chosen to attend a progressive school but who, once there, is required by the teachers to question rules and norms and to find out answers for herself. To give an adult example, we might think of men who are convicted of domestic violence and who are directed by the courts to attend anger management courses to help them control their behavior.

It is more difficult to know what liberals might say about these two cases, particularly as the cases may be in direct conflict. If a liberal state wishes to prioritize second-order autonomy, it will allow convent life but may be wary of forcing criminals to attend classes (although criminals may be thought to have forfeited any right to second-order autonomy). On the other hand, if the state wishes to prioritize first-order autonomy, it may be very keen to use such classes but may also wish to discourage, regulate, or even prevent certain forms of convent life, or at least certain practices within convents.

Consider the situation that combines second-order autonomy with a lack of first-order autonomy: the situation of the nun. There are several possible ways in which one could respond, normatively and philosophically, to it. The first option is to say that a life as a nun is indeed a nonautonomous life in the first-order sense, but that its lack of autonomy is unproblematic because nonautonomous lives are unproblematic (in certain conditions). This is the line of argument adopted by political liberals such as Martha Nussbaum. Nussbaum contrasts her political liberalism with the comprehensive liberalism of John Stuart Mill and Joseph Raz, arguing that they and not she hold that autonomy is a general good for all humans.[11] Nussbaum argues that her position, in contrast, allows people to live nonautonomous lives, for autonomy may be counter to their conception of the good, particularly if that conception is religious. Nussbaum's argument on this point follows Rawls, who writes:

> Full autonomy is achieved by citizens: it is a political and not an ethical value. By that I mean that it is realized in public life

11. Martha Nussbaum, "A Plea for Difficulty." She argues similarly in Nussbaum, "Sex Equality, Entitlements, and the Capabilities Approach." For the arguments of Mill and Raz, see John Stuart Mill, *On Liberty,* and Joseph Raz, *The Morality of Freedom.*

by affirming the political principles of justice and enjoying the protections of the basic rights and liberties; it is also realized by participating in society's public affairs and sharing in its collective self-determination over time. This full autonomy of political life must be distinguished from the ethical values of autonomy and individuality, which may apply to the whole of life, both social and individual, as expressed by the comprehensive liberalisms of Kant and Mill. Justice as fairness affirms this contrast: it affirms political autonomy for all but leaves the weight of ethical autonomy to be decided by citizens severally in light of their comprehensive doctrines.[12]

Nussbaum agrees that, for political liberals, autonomy is a *political* value only. Second-order autonomy must be protected, but individuals must be free to use their second-order autonomy to alienate their first-order autonomy, for example by joining a convent. Nussbaum expresses this by saying that a political liberal "carefully refrains from asserting that non-autonomous lives are not worth leading, or even that autonomy is a key element in the best comprehensive view of human flourishing across the board; and she carefully protects the spaces within which Calvinists and other non-Milleans [who do not value autonomy] can plan lives according to their own lights."[13] It is important to note that Nussbaum is rejecting the universality of first-order and not second-order autonomy: her emphasis on protecting spaces for people to *plan* their lives according to *their own lights* shows that second-order autonomy remains a crucial universal goal. She stresses the universal value of second-order autonomy again when she states that political liberalism "agrees with comprehensive liberalism that a nonautonomous life should not be thrust upon someone by the luck of birth."[14]

Nussbaum's argument, then, is that political liberalism differs from comprehensive liberalism in preferring second-order autonomy to first-order autonomy when the two conflict, but that it agrees with comprehensive liberalism in disliking cases when a nonautonomous life is thrust on someone by luck of birth and so has not been chosen autonomously. For a political liberal understood in Nussbaum's terms,

12. Rawls, *Political Liberalism*, 77–78; see also Rawls, *Justice as Fairness*, 156.
13. Nussbaum, "Plea for Difficulty," 110.
14. Ibid.

then, the crucial normative issue is not what kind of life a person lives in a first-order sense, but whether it has been chosen autonomously in a second-order sense.[15] If it has, then the absence of first-order autonomy is no cause for (political) concern. If a way of life has not been chosen autonomously, then there is cause for concern. If Nussbaum is correct in her description of the two positions, the debate between comprehensive and political liberals is not a debate about the value of autonomy *per se*, but a debate about the (political) value of first- versus second-order autonomy.[16]

For political liberals, then, the state should provide a basic framework of freedoms. Within that framework, justice is served by giving individuals considerable leeway to construct their own conceptions of the good. Nussbaum captures this principle with what she and Amartya Sen term the "capability approach": justice, and the governmental activity that promotes it, must focus on capabilities rather than on actual functioning. This focus on capabilities is, in turn, justified by an appeal to reason and the ability of individuals to choose their own ways of life. As Nussbaum puts it: "For political purposes it is appropriate for us to shoot for capabilities, and those alone. Citizens must be left free to determine their course after that. The person with plenty of food may always choose to fast, but there is a great difference between fasting and starving, and it is this difference we wish to capture."[17]

So, Nussbaum's commitment to autonomy is expressed through the political sphere. Individuals must be able to engage in practical reason

15. Ironically, in this respect Nussbaum's approach is very similar to that of Raz in *Morality of Freedom* (see, for example, *Morality of Freedom*, 370).

16. Nussbaum argues that comprehensive liberalism is ironic in its treatment of autonomy, but the irony disappears—or at least is shared by political liberalism—if we clarify which kind of autonomy the two are concerned with, as I have done in the following excerpt: "Political liberalism also does better along the dimension of respect for citizens; for—ironically, since [second-order] autonomy is what it is all about—comprehensive liberalism does not show very much respect for the [second-order autonomous] choices citizens may make to live [first-order] nonautonomously, as members of hierarchical religions or corporate bodies" ("Plea for Difficulty," 110). By omitting the qualifying label before the first instance of "autonomy"—the kind that liberalism "is all about"—Nussbaum implies that there is one overarching type of autonomy, so that anyone who rejects that kind of autonomy "ironically" rejects autonomy *per se*. However, comprehensive liberals could play the same trick and state that it is ironic that, since [first-order] autonomy is what it is all about, Nussbaum and political liberals do not show very much respect for people's ability to live [first-order] autonomous lives, as they allow that crucial capability to be alienated through a simple [second-order autonomous] choice.

17. Nussbaum, *Sex and Social Justice*, 44.

about their way of life, choosing which ways of life to pursue and which to reject. Under such conditions, individuals may choose even those ways of life which are of no apparent value, or which do not enable autonomy to flourish.[18] In fact, Nussbaum implies that the very fact of choice imputes some worth to a way of life, by strongly distinguishing fasting and starving. On one level, there is very little difference: both have the same physical effects and are fatal at their extreme. The main difference between them is that one is chosen and the other imposed, and it seems to be this which makes the normative difference for Nussbaum. Choice becomes a normative transformer, rendering an outcome just by its mere presence. Nussbaum does not appeal to the reason for fasting, or imply that the difference lies in the value of some ways of life above others. Thus she makes no distinction between the anorexic, the suffragette on hunger strike, and the "breatharian" who has a spiritual belief in her ability to live on oxygen alone. All have chosen to fast. The state exhausts its duties by ensuring that all have the capability of eating, presumably by ensuring that no one is unable to find or afford food. The fact that we might reasonably judge starving to death as bad for individuals, or as counter to their autonomy, does not justify state intervention. We protect individuals' autonomy by protecting their ability to choose.

If we retain Nussbaum's political liberalism, it becomes crucial to identify the conditions under which an individual comes to lead a way of life. For, even if an individual has first-order autonomy, a political liberal might want to interfere if it could be shown that comprehensive liberal meddling had imposed that first-order autonomy. A political liberal would want to ensure that the individual could choose to alien-

18. Nussbaum sometimes implies that it may be compatible with justice for an individual to live a first-order nonautonomous life that has not been second-order autonomously chosen. As long as the society provides the opportunity for second-order autonomy, it may not matter if the individual does not (cannot?) take advantage of those conditions, because their culture or religion encourages them not to. Thus she states: "A nonautonomous life should not be thrust upon someone by the luck of birth. Nonetheless, [political liberalism] respects such lives, given a background of liberty and opportunity, as lives that reasonable fellow citizens may pursue" ("Plea for Difficulty," 110). It is unclear whether "such lives" that should be respected refers to the second-order nonautonomous lives "thrust upon someone by luck of birth" or the first-order "nonautonomous life." Presumably it is the first-order nonautonomy that must be respected, or Nussbaum's rejection of a life thrust upon someone would make no sense; however, her insistence on a "background" of liberty and opportunity rather than the exercise or use of liberty and opportunity undermines this interpretation and raises the question of what it is for a way of life to be "reasonable" if it has not been chosen second-order autonomously.

ate her own autonomy.[19] On the other hand, and more important, a political liberal will excuse and protect a first-order nonautonomous life *if and only if* that life has been chosen autonomously. In order for Nussbaum's distinction between comprehensive and political liberalism to hold, it must be the second-order autonomy status of a way of life which determines its susceptibility to or immunity from state intervention, and not the substantive first-order content. Thus the political liberal response to convent life is to say that a nun is nonautonomous but that lives lacking in autonomy—to be precise, lacking first-order autonomy—are acceptable. Instead, it is second-order autonomy which is a crucial requirement of justice.

The Social Formation of Preferences: Is Second-Order Autonomy Possible?

For political liberals, individuals' choices go a long way toward defining what is just. Nussbaum is very aware, on the other hand, that people's choices are not immune from social influence. She argues, in a chapter that echoes many of the themes of the theories of social construction of Foucault, Bourdieu, and MacKinnon, that "cultural formations affect not just the theoretical explanation of desire but the very experience of desire, and of oneself as a desiring agent."[20] In other words, social interaction has a crucial role to play in forming our attitudes to the world, and indeed our own opinions of those attitudes. If we live within a gendered society, for example, we will experience the world and our own desires according to gendered norms. As a result, we cannot simply take an individual's preferences as given and fail to notice the effects that they have on her. Instead, we can and should critically evaluate structures of choice and desire.[21]

---

19. It is interesting to note that the absence of second-order autonomy can be more or less pernicious. Second-order autonomy may be coercively denied, as in the case of Afghanistan under the Taliban or, to a lesser extent, the woman who is prevented from becoming a nun (lesser because, as one way of life is proscribed rather than prescribed, the opportunity to choose autonomously from a variety of options remains). Or, second-order autonomy may be absent because it has never been cultivated, as in the case of a woman in a Western society who simply follows trends and norms without thinking about them or questioning them. It would seem that Nussbaum does not wish to eliminate all forms of second-order autonomy, forcing the Western fashion-victim actively to rethink her way of life, but merely to eliminate the forced instances of second-order nonautonomy.

20. Nussbaum, *Sex and Social Justice*, 256.

21. Ibid., 64.

How might we make such an evaluation, according to Nussbaum? Throughout *Sex and Social Justice,* she refers to the work of Andrea Dworkin and Catharine MacKinnon. While she has reservations about their specific policy prescriptions and methods, Nussbaum is generally in agreement with their theoretical approach. In particular, Nussbaum is sympathetic to their thesis that heterosexual desire under conditions of patriarchy is characterized by the eroticization of male dominance and female submission.[22] For both theorists, patriarchy teaches us to find this power inequality arousing through a myriad of images, norms, and experiences. As a result, many women find themselves turned on by fantasies of submission, from rape at one end of the scale to the romantic hero sweeping them off their feet at the other. Even feminist women, or nonfeminist women who do not in any sense approve of or desire rape in the real world, may find themselves aroused by images and fantasies with which they are uncomfortable. For example, in the following quotation "Gail" describes her discomfort with the fact that she sometimes fantasizes about a man who actually attempted to rape her when she was seventeen: "At times, even though I know it's wrong or crazy, I have fantasies that he is trying to rape me—either in his car, my home, his home, or even in his own garage. I become awfully excited at these thoughts. . . . I don't know why I have these sexual fantasies. At other times I envision rape scenes, and actually shudder and become nauseated at the idea or thought. So, at times I enjoy my fantasies, and at other times I become almost sick."[23] Not all our desires, then, withstand normative scrutiny, and not all our desires contribute equally to our flourishing. If society is constructed along sexist lines, we should expect those socially constructed fantasies to have recurring sexist elements.

Nussbaum devotes considerable space to the consideration of preference formation in *Women and Human Development.* She argues that individuals' reports of their own welfare might be problematic for three main reasons. The first is what Nussbaum calls the "Argument from Adaptation," and expresses the idea of adaptive preferences. Adaptive preferences are formed in response to the options available, so that individuals come to want only what they can have, or what it is deemed

---

22. See, for example, ibid., 77–78, which refers to Catharine MacKinnon, *Feminism Unmodified,* and Andrea Dworkin, *Intercourse.*

23. Nancy Friday, *My Secret Garden,* 112–13. See also Sheila Jeffreys, *Anticlimax,* 243.

appropriate for them to have. This argument is comparable to that of Bourdieu, whose concepts of habitus and field highlight the way our embodied behavior adapts itself to the particular social contexts within which we live. Nussbaum's second argument against the sovereignty of preferences is institutional. As she puts it, "People's preferences are in many ways constructed by the laws and institutions under which they live. This being the case, we can hardly use preferences as a bedrock in our deliberation about what laws and institutions we wish to construct."[24] This claim applies even more pertinently, of course, to cultures and religions: since individuals' preferences are, in many ways, constructed by the cultures and religions under which they live, we can hardly use preferences as a bedrock for deciding whether a culture or religion is compatible with justice, *contra* Nussbaum's arguments in "A Plea for Difficulty." This argument is redolent of Foucault's account of the process by which social norms become both internalized and pleasure-endowed, such that we actively want to comply. Third, Nussbaum gives the "Argument from Intrinsic Worth." This argument states that there are some things that are desirable in and of themselves, whether or not a person desires them. Examples include sanitation and nourishment: regardless of individuals' attitudes toward them, they are intrinsically desirable. Someone who has become used to living in conditions of squalor may not express dissatisfaction, and yet we should aim to improve those conditions regardless.[25] Nussbaum's thought here is that we should not take a person's lack of interest in goods such as nutrition as reason to deny them the *capability* for nutrition. Even if a person chooses not to eat (which, as we have seen, may be a choice based on principle or one based on adaptation to unjust circumstances), that choice does not mean that the state has no obligation to ensure that they are able to eat. Nutrition must still be provided, since preferences may be adaptive and since nutrition is intrinsically valuable in the sense of being required for most if not all ways of life (it is a primary good).[26]

The argument from intrinsic worth reveals Nussbaum's commitment to at least some universal values. Indeed, she devotes the first chapter of *Women and Human Development* to their defense. Although

24. Nussbaum, *Women and Human Development*, 142–43.
25. Ibid., 144.
26. Nussbaum, *Sex and Social Justice*, 45, where Nussbaum notes that we must keep functioning "always in view" but that still "we are not pushing individuals into the function."

Nussbaum believes that individuals must be free to follow traditional ways of life, she is unsympathetic to charges that liberalism seeks to impose inappropriate Western ways of life on members of other cultures. Rather, she sees liberal values, properly construed, as the universal standard by which cultures may be judged. As she argues: "Traditional practices . . . are not worth preserving simply because they are there, or because they are old; to make a case for preserving them, we have to assess the contribution they make against the harm they do. And this requires a set of values that gives us a critical purchase on cultural particulars."[27] This means that, for Nussbaum, autonomous individuals are not confined to living out the meanings that social norms give to various roles and practices. In other words, individuals do not realize their second-order autonomy by submitting to the social formation of their preferences. As a result, individuals are not necessarily autonomous individuals before state intervention, and state intervention will not necessarily disrupt that autonomy. Individuals are not blank sheets on which the state simply scribbles, preventing them from filling in the space themselves. They are always already scribbled on. What is scribbled, rather than the simple fact of scribbling, thus becomes crucial.

Once we have noticed that preferences are socially influenced, however, we can no longer maintain a position of political liberal nonintervention in the name of second-order autonomy. If preferences can be socially formed, then autonomy cannot *require* state noninterference on the basis that individuals must be left to make their own choices free from influence. Liberal theories of justice rest on two basic values: freedom or autonomy (understood in either a first- or a second-order sense) and equality. Nussbaum's political liberalism implies that the presence of second-order autonomy suffices to make a choice, or way of life, unproblematic from the standpoint of justice: such autonomy is a sufficient condition for justice. However, the social formation of preferences casts doubt on this position, in two ways. First, it suggests that people may be less autonomous than they appear, since their decisions are profoundly shaped by their social contexts. Second, if autonomy is (always) limited, a choice or outcome cannot be rendered just by the mere fact of having been autonomously chosen. We cannot determine whether a situation or practice is just by asking, "Was it

27. Nussbaum, *Women and Human Development,* 51.

brought about solely by the autonomous choice of the individual concerned?" for the answer will often (a Foucauldian account suggests
always) be "no." Instead, the manner of their formation becomes a
matter of justice. We must ask, "Was the social influence that encouraged the individual to make that choice, and is the choice itself, compatible with justice?" Because Nussbaum denies that first-order autonomy is relevant to justice, we must turn to the second liberal value of
equality. If individuals are subject to influence that threatens their
equality, then it is a requirement of justice that that influence be limited where possible. This intervention will take place not in the name
of autonomy alone but in the name of *justice,* as a combination of autonomy and equality. Autonomy functions as a premise to the argument: given that preferences have already been socially influenced,
then protecting autonomy cannot *simply* be a matter of allowing individuals to follow their preferences, and preferences cannot determine
the justice of a state of affairs. In order to distinguish between influence that does and influence that does not threaten justice, we must
consider whether individuals are encouraged to make choices that
threaten their equality.

Second-Order Autonomy and Harmful Norms

So far, we have seen that Nussbaum, and political liberals in general,
prioritize second-order autonomy over first. Put generally, the political
liberal position is that while a first-order nonautonomous life must not
be thrust upon someone, it may be autonomously chosen. But, as it
stands, this position is too crude. It is too crude because people do not
make choices in a vacuum. Instead, as I have argued throughout this
book, they are influenced, sometimes very strongly, by the people,
structures, and norms around them.

Both aspects of social construction arise here. First, social construction may obscure or even prevent autonomous choice, so that people
are never or rarely second-order autonomous. In Part One I argued
that although social construction has a far deeper impact than most
liberals recognize, it is nevertheless possible for individuals to theorize
the need for change and, with assistance and concrete strategies, overcome oppressive norms.

Second, social construction affects the options that are available. Social norms set out what may be chosen, and place conditions on what must be done in order to receive certain benefits. Moreover, social norms are sometimes harmful. If she is to follow a social norm, an individual may be required to harm herself. The harm may be physical, mental, or material. It may also be social—it may require the individual to lower her status relative to that of others. In other words, a social norm may reflect and perpetuate inequality. In some cases a norm may be both harmful and unequal, in that it may require some people but not others to harm themselves.

This second issue is the focus of the rest of this chapter. It should become clearer if we consider a set of four examples. Instead of an intersection between first- and second-order autonomy, consider an intersection between second-order autonomy and the harmfulness or otherwise of social norms. The following table represents possible answers to two questions. First, if an individual is following a social norm, does she do so with or without second-order autonomy? In other words, is she autonomously choosing to follow the social norm so as to acquire some benefit, or is she simply following the norm because she is coerced or it never occurs to her to do otherwise? Second, is the norm that she is following harmful? So as to simplify the example, assume that the individual in question knows whether or not the norm in question is harmful (this assumption will be interrogated later, particularly in Chapter 6).

	The norm is *not* harmful.	The norm *is* harmful.
The norm *is* part of a way of life chosen second-order autonomously.	1	3
The norm is *not* part of a way of life chosen second-order autonomously.	2	4

1. I am aware that there is a harmless social norm regulating access to some benefit. Because I have autonomously chosen the benefit, I choose to follow the norm. For example, David is a member of an Oxford college. There is a norm operating in the college that

people take tea in the common room at a certain time. Those who attend tea reap the benefits of forming social and professional networks. David considers the norm and, because he wants to further his academic career, decides to follow it by attending tea regularly.[28]

2. I follow a harmless social norm regulating access to some benefit, but have not autonomously chosen to seek that benefit. For example, David's colleague, Ben, also consciously attends tea so as to further his academic career. However, he has not autonomously chosen to be an academic: his career is the result of family pressure, his fear at the thought of leaving Oxford, and the fact that he has never really considered any alternatives.

3. I am aware that there is a harmful social norm regulating access to some benefit. As I have autonomously chosen the benefit, I choose to follow the norm. For example, Rachel has autonomously chosen to seek career success. She works in a nonsmoking office. She does not smoke, but her colleague and their mutual manager do. The colleague and the manager regularly go outside to smoke together, where they discuss business matters. As a result, the manager favors the colleague over Rachel. In order to gain the manager's favor, and despite her dislike of smoking, Rachel decides to start smoking so that she can join the conversations in the smoking area and further her career.[29]

4. I follow a harmful social norm that regulates access to some benefit, but have not autonomously chosen to seek that benefit. For example, in China, footbinding was necessary for a girl to secure a good marriage from the middle of the fourteenth century until the very start of the twentieth century. However, girls and women whose feet had been bound were left "crippled and nearly housebound."[30] Chun had her feet forcibly bound when she was a child. As a result, she was able to secure a good marriage, but suffered from severely limited mobility throughout her life. She made no autonomous choice to seek a life of marriage.

What are we to say about these examples? Which ought a liberal to endorse, and which ought she to criticize, or condemn as unjust? Most

28. This example is named after David Miller, who very helpfully suggested it to me.
29. This example is based on "The One Where Rachel Smokes," episode 115 (1999) of the Warner Brothers sitcom *Friends*, in which the character of Rachel faces this dilemma.
30. Mackie, "Ending Footbinding and Infibulation," 1000.

liberals would condemn case 4, the case of Chun and footbinding. The very similar case of female genital mutilation is discussed at length later in the chapter.[31] Cases 1, 2, and 3 are more problematic, and highlight complexities with the political liberal prioritization of second-order autonomy. If second-order autonomy is crucial to justice for political liberals, we might think that Ben, who has never made a choice to be an academic, is suffering from some sort of injustice. However, political liberals do not tend to be too worried about these sorts of cases because, I suggest, the life that Ben has ended up with allows him considerable first-order autonomy. Ben's position is similar to the case I described in Chapter 4, in which an individual is subjected to the influence factor but advantaged as a result. While we might think that his life would go better if he exercised his second-order autonomy and reevaluated it, Ben does not seem to be a particularly needy victim of injustice worthy of state-provided remedy.[32]

What of cases 1 and 3: David with his tea, and Rachel with her smoking? In both cases, Rachel and David are aware of the options that confront them, weigh up the costs and benefits of (non-)compliance with the norm, and choose to comply. But the costs that the norms impose are very different. Rachel will have to cultivate a taste for smoking, which she knows will harm her quite considerably. David's tea, on the other hand, is certainly not harmful and has indeed been shown to have various health benefits. Does this difference, in and of itself, make a difference to the justice of the case?

In the remainder of the chapter, I argue that it does. Specifically, I argue that, in certain circumstances, individuals who submit to harmful norms to reach some higher, second-order goal are suffering from

31. One complexity of the case, however, is whether Chun might be said to have second-order autonomy if, on reaching adulthood, she decides that she does want to be married. It is clear that this decision would not mean that footbinding served her first-order autonomy, for even if she does not regret the necessity of footbinding, she did not in fact choose to submit to the practice at the time. However, some theorists would argue that footbinding would serve her second-order autonomy if she subsequently adopts the goal of marriage. This is the basis of George Sher's perfectionist refutation of the argument that "when governments try to induce citizens to choose valuable activities, the resulting choices never *are* autonomous." On the contrary, Sher argues: "Precisely *by* living the life he was nonrationally caused to prefer, C may become increasingly aware of the value-based reasons for living that way. He may come to appreciate W's (potential) value 'from the inside'" (*Beyond Neutrality*, 61; 63; emphasis in the original. See also Friedman, *Autonomy, Gender, Politics*, 25).

32. If state intervention were advocated, it might be in the area of adult education provision. For a discussion of whether funding for adult education is required by justice, see Alexander Brown, "Access to Educational Opportunities—One-off or Lifelong?"

an injustice. Moreover, the liberal state ought to attempt to rectify that injustice.

Perpetuating Inequality: Female Genital Mutilation and Breast Implants

Generally, political liberals want to protect individuals' second-order autonomy, even if it is used to choose things that are harmful to the choosing individual. Mill's harm principle is perhaps the most famous example of such an approach (although Mill is not a political liberal). Sometimes, though, political liberals are willing to ban things for reasons of justice even when the injustice falls largely to those people who choose them. Female genital mutilation (FGM) causes problems for Nussbaum. As a feminist (and a Westerner?)[33] she finds the practice abhorrent and argues that it should be banned. As a political liberal, she lacks the philosophical resources to justify such a ban. Her arguments against FGM are effective arguments against political liberalism's prioritization of second-order autonomy.

Nussbaum's discussion of FGM gives many reasons for eradicating the practice. A consistent politically liberal approach to the issue would imply changing certain features of the practice, but leaving it optional for those adult women who wished to practice it. However, not all of the criticisms that Nussbaum makes of FGM would be eliminated by that approach. In other words, FGM reveals that Nussbaum wants to label some practices as unjust regardless of whether they have been chosen autonomously, undermining her claim that, for a political liberal, second-order autonomy is sufficient for justice. Such practices are unjust, instead, because they threaten either the equality or the well-being of the choosing individual or, by contributing to social norms, they threaten the equality of a wider group of individuals.

---

33. Western bias is often found in condemnations of human rights violations. For example, the UN has produced a fact sheet condemning "harmful traditional practices" performed on women, but discusses only non-Western practices. See Bronwyn Winter et al., "The UN Approach to Harmful Traditional Practices." Germaine Greer argues that Western condemnations of FGM are highly hypocritical in the light of Western practices such as episiotomy, where a woman's vagina is routinely cut in preparation for childbirth, and the fact that "the American Academy of Pediatrics recommends that clitorises of more than three-eighths of a inch in length should be removed from baby girls before they are fifteen months old" (*Whole Woman*, 94).

Nussbaum argues that we should consider FGM as worse than, and more worthy of elimination than, Western beauty practices such as dieting and cosmetic surgery. She gives eight reasons for her view:[34]

1. FGM is carried out by force.
2. FGM is carried out on children below the age of consent.
3. Women who undergo FGM are more likely than Western women to be uneducated and thus to lack the conditions for autonomous choice.
4. FGM is often carried out in conditions that are dangerous to health.
5. FGM is irreversible.
6. FGM causes lifelong health problems.
7. FGM causes the loss of a certain type of sexual functioning that many women (would) value highly.
8. FGM "is unambiguously linked to customs of male domination."[35]

Only the first three objections to FGM are directly linked to the nature of the practice as unchosen. In other words, if second-order autonomy were the key factor in securing justice, FGM could be made acceptable if it were performed only on women above a certain age who gave their consent and who were given information about the risks involved and the particularity of the custom—the kind of information that is available to women who undergo cosmetic surgery in Western countries.[36] We could also eliminate some of the dangers to health (objection 4) by the provision of appropriate clinical equipment and training. These alterations would render the practice unproblematic from a strictly political liberal point of view (one which holds second-order autonomy as sufficient for justice, and which ignores the social formation of preferences). Are they enough? What is the force of the remaining objections?

We are left with objections 5 to 8. If we are political liberals of the kind Nussbaum wants us to be in "A Plea for Difficulty," there seems

34. Nussbaum, *Sex and Social Justice*, 123–24.
35. Ibid., 124.
36. At least, this information *ought* to be available to women in Western countries. The women in Kathy Davis's study of cosmetic surgery were rarely given adequate or accurate information. See Davis, *Reshaping the Female Body*, 130–31.

to be nothing for us to say about these objections that has relevance for action. FGM is irreversible (objection 5), but so are most tattoos, male circumcisions, abortions, precautionary mastectomies or hysterectomies, and many sterilizations. The irreversibility of even a bodily procedure does not in itself suffice as a reason to ban it. FGM causes lifelong health problems (objection 6), but so do smoking, heavy drinking, unhealthy eating, inactive lifestyles, and many other activities against which political liberals such as Nussbaum do not want to legislate. If we remove the forced element, then the loss of sexual functioning (objection 7) is insufficient for a ban—remember, for Nussbaum, the person who has food may always choose to fast, and there seems to be no reason on the face of it why a political liberal should not allow an individual to deny herself something that others want for themselves. A political liberal does not forbid childless women in Western societies to have a hysterectomy to avoid unwanted pregnancy and the inconvenience of contraception and menstruation,[37] even though the capacity to bear children is one which many women value highly.

Perhaps, then, objections 5 to 7 are not supposed to have any political implications—they are reasons to dislike FGM, but nothing more. Nussbaum often does make a distinction between condemning practices and banning them, endorsing the former but not the latter, as long as the practice is autonomously chosen.[38] However, she does not make this distinction with FGM. In *Women and Human Development* Nussbaum argues that even consensual FGM (performed once objections 1 to 4 have been removed) could and should be banned, because it involves the permanent removal of a capability: "It seems plausible for governments to ban female genital mutilation, even when practiced by adults without coercion: for, in addition to long-term health risks, the practice involves the permanent removal of the capability for most sexual pleasure, although individuals should of course be free to choose not to have sexual pleasure if they prefer not to."[39] This focus

37. Women do in fact choose to have hysterectomies for this purpose: "Oregon researcher, Ov Slayden, said: 'A lot of people don't appreciate the impact of menstrual bleeding. It's not just a lifestyle issue: it's pain and discomfort, it's a serious health issue. It is one leading reason for women to have elective hysterectomy'" (James Meek, "Drugs Could Put a Stop to Periods").

38. See, for example, Nussbaum's position on the Catholic church's refusal to ordain women priests, as laid out in her "Plea for Difficulty," 114.

39. Nussbaum, *Women and Human Development*, 94. Nussbaum's position is not unusual. In the United Kingdom, for example, FGM is prohibited under the *Prohibition of Female*

on capabilities is clearly an attempt to avoid the clash between political and comprehensive liberalism: Nussbaum wishes to show that FGM is non-negotiable because it falls within the jurisdiction of the basic *capabilities* on which all are supposed to agree. But, in order to remain a political liberal, Nussbaum frequently allows individuals to alienate themselves from certain of their capabilities. Sterilization is an example. In true political liberal style, Nussbaum advocates state disinterest.[40] Nussbaum's political liberalism commits governments to ensuring that the basic capabilities are an option for all: that all are capable of the capabilities, as it were. However, she does not want to involve governments in forcibly ensuring that all individuals actually possess the relevant capabilities, regardless of their wishes on the matter— except in the case of FGM. Her official, politically liberal position requires only that the conditions of capability are provided by the state. However, in considering FGM, Nussbaum reverts to the position which is best suited by her awareness of the social formation of preferences and the existence of harmful social norms: just because someone wants to do something, that doesn't necessarily mean that justice requires allowing them to do so.

Nussbaum's position on capabilities does not, therefore, provide the philosophical resources to justify a ban on FGM *tout court*. Neither does her prioritization of second-order autonomy. FGM can be thought of as an ingredient of a way of life that women may choose with second-order autonomy. Within cultures that practice it, FGM is often required for marriage. In such cases, we can think of FGM as an ingredient of marriage. More generally, we might think of FGM as a necessary ingredient of life within certain cultural communities: if women wish to maintain their membership, or to participate in the institution of marriage within it, they must undergo FGM. Some women might consent to undergo FGM, even though they might prefer not to, in order to become or remain eligible for community membership or marriage. A powerful objection to FGM is thus that it is an excessively high price to

---

Circumcision Act 1985, regardless of the age, beliefs, or wishes of the woman concerned (Alex Sleator, *The Female Genital Mutilation Bill*, 21–22). The modified bill, introduced by Ann Clywd as Bill 21 of 2002–3, does not seek to change this aspect of the legislation. Similarly, Nicholas Lund-Molfese argues that if any procedure is "properly described as an act of mutilation, then a doctor would be acting unethically to perform the procedure even where the request for the procedure comes from an adult patient" ("What Is Mutilation?" 64).

40. Nussbaum, *Women and Human Development*, 95.

ask women to pay in order to remain within their communities. But, as we have seen, this is not an objection Nussbaum can make if she is to prioritize second-order autonomy. For that prioritization protects first-order nonautonomous lives—namely, those in which women have no choice but to undergo FGM if they wish to remain within their communities—as long as they are chosen second-order autonomously—that is to say, as long as women are free to choose to leave their communities.

It might seem that Nussbaum can still justify a ban on FGM via second-order autonomy, in two ways. First, the option of leaving one's community is an extremely difficult one to take, and this fact undermines the idea that women do indeed undergo FGM as a result of a truly second-order autonomous choice to stay within their communities. Second, it is the case that marriage is the only viable option for women in many cultures that practice FGM, so that women cannot really be said to choose marriage with second-order autonomy either. These points are strong. They point to the necessity of increasing women's second-order autonomy wherever possible, perhaps by trying to provide meaningful options for women other than marriage or community life. A political liberal prioritization of second-order autonomy would demand such measures. It would not, however, demand a ban on FGM, for such a ban would increase the first- and not the second-order autonomy of women.[41]

41. It is worth noting that it does not seem plausible that political liberals could justify a ban on FGM via the political liberal concept of the overlapping consensus either, as Drucilla Cornell attempts to do. Her treatment of FGM is more brazenly self-contradictory. First, she stresses that political liberalism holds even in cases of unjust identity formation, arguing that while "feminists are right to argue that many women have so deeply internalized their own degradation that they have lost the ability to imagine themselves as equal," nevertheless feminist action should not follow: "If a 'right consciousness' is imposed from the outside by feminists who know what women should want, then the degraded status of those upon whom it is imposed is affirmed rather than challenged. This 'corrective' to false consciousness perpetuates the cycle it tries to break and, ironically, reinforces the intractability of women's position in society. The imaginary domain as an ideal poses an inherent challenge to the symbolic intractability of any sexual identity by demanding that all such positions be left open for reinterpretation" (*At the Heart of Freedom*, 169). One page later, however, Cornell renounces this line in favor of feminist transformative action: "I can see no way to reconcile [FGM] with an equivalent evaluation of [women's] sexual difference. But many women argue to the contrary, insisting that as a Western woman, I just don't get it. But I have not changed my mind. And I strongly believe that feminists within the human rights community should continue to achieve an overlapping consensus that female genital mutilation is inconsistent with the equivalent evaluation of our own sexual difference" (170). This exhortation to "achieve" an overlapping consensus is not only odd in the face of the warnings against feminist attempts to undermine internalized degradation, it is also unrealistic. If

A ban on FGM cannot, then, be explained by either the nonalienability of capabilities—for that would require a ban on sterilization—or the prioritization of second-order autonomy—for that would require undermining the centrality of cultural membership and/or marriage. What, then, could explain the particularity of FGM? Objection 8 is one difference. Nussbaum writes:

> Female genital mutilation is unambiguously linked to customs of male domination. Even its official rationales, in terms of purity and propriety, point to aspects of sex hierarchy. . . . Sex relations constructed by the practice are relations in which intercourse becomes a vehicle for one-sided male pleasure rather than for mutuality of pleasure. By contrast, the ideal female body image purveyed in the American media has multiple and complex resonances, including those of male domination, but also including those of physical fitness, independence and boyish nonmaternity.
>
> These differences help explain why there is no serious campaign to make ads for diet programs, or the pictures of emaciated women in *Vogue*, illegal, whereas FGM is illegal in most of the countries in which it occurs.[42]

This is indeed a salient difference between FGM and sterilization. The former, and not the latter, results from and perpetuates forms of male domination. In other words, FGM undermines gender *equality*.

Liberalism is based on two key values: freedom or autonomy, and equality. We have seen so far how Nussbaum incorporates autonomy into her political liberalism. With objection 8 against FGM, she introduces equality, specifically gender equality. However, the role of equality within political liberalism is somewhat ambiguous. Certainly, politi-

---

political liberals want overlapping consensus to do the work that they suggest it does, then they must accept that we are probably stuck with pervasive gender inequality, a system that much of the world does in fact agree on and which certainly underlies almost all known societies. If, on the other hand, a commitment to gender inequality is indecent or unreasonable and so doesn't count, or if we should try to change the minds of those who are committed to inequality, then consensus is nothing more than a convenient way of getting other people to conform to liberal values with minimum fuss. The justification of those liberal values does not come from the fact of consensus, and the implementation of liberal policies does not avoid the claim that liberal values such as gender equality are *better* than alternatives.

42. Nussbaum, *Sex and Social Justice*, 124.

cal liberalism requires that individuals are equal in the political sphere: that men and women have equal citizenship rights. What is unclear in the writings of both Nussbaum and Rawls, however, is the extent to which equality in general and gender equality in particular must pervade other spheres. On the one hand, it is sometimes argued that gender inequality in religions, cultures, and associations is acceptable so long as it is compatible with equal citizenship. Thus Rawls writes that the principles of justice "do not apply directly to the internal life of churches"[43] and other associations (the examples he gives are universities and the family) so that, for example, ecclesiastical positions do not have to be allocated democratically or according to the difference principle. He does not explicitly say whether church and other positions must comply with equality of opportunity; Nussbaum concludes that they must not and that gender discrimination is permitted. Thus she argues that political liberalism asks religions "to accept the political equality of women as citizens," but claims this position is entirely compatible with allowing the Catholic Church to employ only men as priests, for example.[44] Since women are still able to vote, to leave the Church, and to enjoy other rights of citizenship, gender discrimination is permissible in the priesthood. If the role of equality in political liberalism is limited in this way, then what is required to justify a ban on FGM is an argument to the effect that FGM prevents women from enjoying equal citizenship rights. Nussbaum provides no such argument; indeed, it would seem easier to argue in these terms against the male-only priesthood than against consensual FGM, for the former and not the latter has a direct bearing on women's ability to participate in the religious structures that determine the course of their own lives and the interface between those structures and the state.

On the other hand, Rawls is at pains to point out that political liberalism does not abandon women to pervasive gender inequality in the family. He states categorically: "It may be thought that the principles of justice do not apply to the family and that therefore they cannot secure equal justice for women and their children. This is a misconception."[45] It is a misconception because the principles of justice place

43. Rawls, *Justice as Fairness,* 164.

44. Nussbaum, "Plea for Difficulty," 109.

45. Rawls, *Justice as Fairness,* 163. See Nussbaum's similar statement in *Sex and Social Justice,* 10.

significant constraints on associations even though their fundamental focus is political:

> When political liberalism distinguishes between political justice that applies to the basic structure and other conceptions of justice that apply to the various associations within that structure, it does not regard the political and the nonpolitical domains as two separate, disconnected spaces, as it were, each governed solely by its own distinct principles. Even if the basic structure alone is the primary subject of justice, principles of justice still put essential restrictions on the family and all other associations. The adult members of the family are equal citizens first: that is their basic position. No institution or association in which they are involved can violate their rights as citizens.[46]

In other words, no association can perpetuate gender inequality if to do so would prevent gender equality in the political sense. Rawls's argument suggests that since the political and nonpolitical spheres are interconnected rather than disconnected, political liberalism might require rather more extensive gender equality than could be secured by equal formal citizenship rights. Indeed, in a discussion that he seems to recognize is frustratingly brief, Rawls suggests that the goal of gender equality is so important that it might require state action *over and above* the principles of justice:

> Since property-owning democracy aims for full equality of women, it must include arrangements to achieve that. . . . If we say the gender system includes whatever social arrangements adversely affect the equal basic liberties and opportunities of women, as well as of those of their children as future citizens, then surely that system is subject to critique by the principles of justice. The question then becomes whether the fulfillment of these principles suffices to remedy the system's faults. . . . I shall not try to reflect further on the matter here.[47]

46. Rawls, *Justice as Fairness*, 166.
47. Ibid., 167–68.

This excerpt suggests that it is appropriate for a politically liberal state to aim for the "full equality" of women, critiquing "whatever social arrangements" undermine that. If the role of equality within political liberalism is this extensive, then it certainly is open to political liberals to argue for a state ban of FGM. Such a ban, though, would involve the state making judgments of the value of different ways of life in terms of their accordance with gender equality, rather than leaving such judgments up to individuals. In other words, it would be to undermine individuals' second-order autonomy to choose ways of life that might cast them as inferior. Second-order autonomy would give way to equality.

If we do move in this direction, we shall have to depart significantly from second-order autonomy in other areas in which Nussbaum wants to maintain the priority. The same reasoning, that we should intervene in practices which are linked to male domination, applies to the Western beauty norms, which, for the purpose of state action, Nussbaum exonerates. Many Western images of the ideal female body are unambiguous in their portrayal of women as vehicles for male pleasure. Much pornography, including soft porn and the topless "Page 3" models of British tabloid newspapers, emphasizes women's availability and submission to men. Nussbaum herself makes this argument, in a searing passage that is splendidly resonant of radical feminist revolt in its analysis but disappointingly resonant of political liberal indifference in its conclusion:

> What *Playboy* repeatedly says to its reader is, Whoever this woman is and whatever she has achieved, for you she is cunt, all her pretensions vanish before your sexual power. For some she is a tennis player—but you, in your mind, can dominate her and turn her into cunt. For some, Brown students are Brown students. For you, dear reader, they are *Women of the Ivy League* (an issue prepared at regular intervals, and a topic of intense controversy on the campuses where models are sought). No matter who you are, these women will (in masturbatory fantasy) moan with pleasure at your sexual power. This is the great appeal of *Playboy* in fact, for it satisfies the desires of men to feel themselves special and powerful. . . .

> *Playboy*, I conclude, is a bad influence on men. . . . I draw
> no legal implications from this judgment.[48]

The connection between the images in publications such as *Playboy*
and breast implants is evident in plastic surgeon Randolph Guthrie's
book aimed at encouraging and reassuring women who are considering breast implants. Guthrie insists that most of his patients do not
want to look like the "large breasted sex bombs" you might find in the
pages of *Playboy*. Yet this is what Guthrie does when a woman who
wants breast implants so as to look "normal" visits his surgery: "I ask
the patient to go out and buy some Victoria's Secret catalogs or *Playboy*
magazines and find pictures that show breasts that look best to them
and to bring them to the office. . . . I then take the magazine pictures
that they have given me and tape them up around the walls of the
operating room so that the surgical team understands the end result
that we're after."[49] This strategy is astonishing. Guthrie tells the reader
that all good cosmetic surgeons should show prospective patients "before" and "after" photos of previous operations. Those photographs,
one might think, would make ideal source material—as well as depict-
ing a range of actual, non-airbrushed breasts, they are also examples of
what Guthrie can actually achieve with his scalpel. But it is not from
those photographs that he asks women to select their ideal breasts.
Instead, he asks them to look at photographs of underwear models
or at pornography. Many women are uncomfortable with looking at
pornography, and would find it embarrassing at best and humiliating
at worst to be asked to share their favorite pornographic pictures, the
pictures in which they imagine themselves, with an unfamiliar male
authority figure. (In the United States, approximately 85 percent of
plastic surgeons are men, and 90 percent of patients are women;[50]
Guthrie gives an idea of the kind of man one might expect when visit-
ing a cosmetic surgeon when he notes: "As likely as not, the plastic
surgeon your doctor recommends is a golf partner.")[51] Add to this pic-
ture of humiliation the fact that Guthrie's patients feel that their bodies

48. Nussbaum, *Sex and Social Justice*, 235–36.
49. Guthrie, *Truth about Breast Implants*, 38–39.
50. Virginia Blum, *Flesh Wounds*, 87.
51. Guthrie, *Truth about Breast Implants*, 33.

are subnormal, and the fact that they have explicitly rejected the ideal of the "large-breasted sex bomb." Finally, imagine the operating theater. Imagine being sedated to undergo a serious and painful procedure surrounded by *Playboy* pin-ups. From factory floor to hospital floor: it seems that feminists have made less progress in securing unoppressive space for women than we might have hoped.

Should we not, then, combine Nussbaum's critique of *Playboy* with her arguments about FGM and make illegal cosmetic surgery which women undergo so as to qualify for inclusion as a *Playboy* or Page 3 model, or so as to look like such models, or so as to attract men who have been aroused by such models? Remember, Nussbaum believes that objections 5 to 8 against FGM are sufficient for a ban. But all of these objections apply to breast implants.

Breast implants are reversible to an extent (objection 5), but breasts which have had implants removed do not return to their original appearance, as plastic surgeon Andrew Skanderowicz describes: "In my experience, breast implant removal is rare . . . if you've had your implants for a long time, you may find your breasts end up smaller and droopier then they were originally. This is because the implants will have stretched your skin and it's normal for breast tissue to shrink as you get older."[52] John Byrne describes the appearance of one woman who had implants removed: "Where her breasts had been, there were now just slight ridges of folded, discolored skin—like deflated balloons that had held air for a long time. The wrinkled skin supported nothing. . . . Her nipples were inverted, caved into her chest because there was no longer any breast tissue left to support them. . . . She didn't recognize the person in the mirror, the frightened and pitiful woman whose trembling body was forever disfigured."[53] Removing breast implants is much more difficult than inserting them. During implantation, a relatively small incision is needed since the implant can be folded during insertion. This cannot happen during explantation, so there is more bleeding from the deeper and larger cuts.[54] As a result of these complications, many plastic surgeons are simply unwilling to perform operations to remove breast implants without replacing them with new ones, and surgeons who do perform explantations have been ostracized by colleagues.[55]

52. Andrew Skanderowicz's answer to "How Are Breast Implants Removed?" 42.
53. John A. Byrne, *Informed Consent*, 3.
54. Ibid., 158.
55. Ibid., 150–56. In the United Kingdom in 2004, 9,731 women had their first cosmetic

To avoid the disfigurement of removed breast implants, it is not enough simply to leave the implants alone. Implants must be maintained by repeated surgery throughout the woman's life. The British Department of Health advises that "breast implants do not come with a lifetime guarantee. They are likely to need replacing with consequent further surgery and expense. A young woman who has implants may expect to have further operations in her lifetime to maintain the beneficial effects of the implants."[56]

The combination of the limited lifespan of implants, the disfigurement of breasts which have had implants removed, and the likelihood of complications (discussed later) puts many women into a distressing trap, as "Caroline," a victim of failed implants, reports: "You can't just stop in the middle of things and say: 'I'm not going to do this any more.' . . . You can't go back. You can't just say that after an implant has been taken out, 'I'm not going to do this.' Of course, you think about it, but it's impossible because then there you'd be with one big breast and one small one. That would be a real life sentence. So you just have to keep going."[57] Breast implants, then, are neither truly reversible nor a permanent, trouble-free "improvement."

Breast implants also may cause lifelong health problems (objection 6). Opinion on the safety of breast implants is very mixed, and the history of their regulation is turbulent. Silicone implants were invented by the Dow Corning Corporation, and first marketed in 1963. Implants were used on women for decades before any regulation or adequate safety testing, as the following report by the U.S. Institute of Medicine details:

> Until 1976, when the "Medical Devices" law was passed, there was no federal regulation of implants. . . . In 1988, the FDA [Food and Drug Administration] categorized silicone breast implants as requiring stringent safety and effectiveness standards and later required premarket approval applications from manufacturers. On April 10, 1991, the FDA issued a regulation requiring manufacturers of silicone-gel-filled implants to sub-

breast implants and 961 women had replacement implants, but only 36 women had breast implants explanted (i.e., removed and not replaced with new ones) (UK Breast Implant Registry, *Annual Report 2004*).

56. United Kingdom, Department of Health advisory leaflet, *Breast Implants*.

57. Davis, *Reshaping the Female Body*, 147.

mit information on their safety and effectiveness in order for
the devices to continue to be marketed. In 1992, the FDA
banned most uses of silicone-filled implants because the manufacturers had not proved their safety. In 1993, the agency no-
tified saline implant manufacturers that they, too, must submit
safety and effectiveness data, although these implants were allowed to stay on the market. . . . [S]ilicone breast implants were
widely used before there was any requirement for the safety
and effectiveness of medical devices.[58]

Dow Corning did perform a limited study of implants in dogs. However, its implants were used on women before the results of the survey
were known. Even once the study was finished it was far from complete, as Silas Braley, in charge of promoting implants for Dow Corning at the time, describes: "There were no tests for implant materials
either on the material or on the patient, or on the animal. All we could
do was put it in and look and see what happens. There were no standards. There were no protocols. There was nothing."[59] In the United
Kingdom, only silicone gel and saline-filled implants are permitted,
and in September 2003 the Department of Health reclassified breast
implants to "the highest risk category for medical devices."[60]

Although silicone implants are now used in both the United Kingdom and the United States, many women claim to have suffered serious illness as a result of their implants. Perhaps the most remarkable
example of such a story is that of Colleen Swanson. She had her silicone implants removed in 1991, after seventeen years, and it is her
appearance after removal that Byrne describes above. The reason that
Swanson had her implants removed was not unusual. Like the 410,000
women awarded a $4.23 billion global settlement against silicone im-
plant manufacturer Dow Corning Corporation, she suffered a range
of symptoms, including migraines, numbness of the limbs, a frozen
shoulder, joint pains, loss of appetite, diminished sex drive, body
rashes, and chronic fatigue.[61] What is unusual about Swanson's case is

58. Grigg et al., *Information for Women*, 4.
59. Byrne, *Informed Consent*, 49.
60. United Kingdom, Department of Health, "Health Minister Lord Warner Welcomes
New Safety Measures for Breast Implants."
61. Byrne, *Informed Consent*, 234, 156.

that her husband, John Swanson, was a loyal lifelong employee of Dow Corning, the company which provided her implants. Still more remarkably, he was the only permanent member of Dow Corning's Business Conduct Committee, responsible for the company's ethical and social responsibility policies, and so he was in charge of ensuring that the company behaved responsibly. It is understandable, then, that for years the couple had absolute faith in the company. Only their growing realization, based on Colleen's debilitating illness, that the company had not properly tested the implants and was failing to ensure the safety of the thousands of women who had them finally shook that faith and led John to resign.

While there is controversy about the role of breast implants in the conditions that women such as Colleen Swanson report, there is no doubt that breast implants have side effects. In 1997 the U.S. House of Representatives commissioned the Institute of Medicine (IOM) to undertake an extensive study of the safety of breast implants, surveying medical research, industry reports, and public testimonials. The study was published in 2000. It found that local complications—those that occur in the breast itself—are the "primary safety issue" with implants. Such complications, they report, "can cause discomfort and, in some cases, considerable risk. . . . [They] occur often and may themselves prompt additional medical procedures, including operations. . . . [A]lthough breast surgery has a low risk of death, many complications can occur when implants are removed, revised, or replaced."[62]

Perhaps the most serious and common local complication is capsular contracture. Contracture occurs when the body forms a thick layer of scar tissue around the implant. This tissue then hardens and contracts, like a fist closing around a tennis ball, as the body attempts to isolate and remove the foreign body. The British Department of Health (DH) informs women considering implants that 10 percent of women suffer from contracture, "causing the implant to deform, become hard and, in some cases, painful."[63] The IOM's description of "severe" contracture, in a document aimed at women considering implants, is that "the breast is firm, hard, tender, painful, and cold. Distortion is marked." The IOM finds that this "severe" form of capsular contracture

62. Grigg et al., *Information for Women*, 10–11.
63. United Kingdom, Department of Health, "Breast Implants."

affects not 10 percent of women but *100 percent* of those who have silicone implants for twenty-five years, and that complications "can be serious."[64]

Contracture is not the only predictable side effect. Up to one in twenty women suffer scars that are "red, or highly-coloured, thick, painful and . . . take several years before they improve."[65] All women are likely to have painful nipples for three to six months following surgery, according to the DH. The IOM reports that "a majority of women do experience pain after implant surgery, and this pain may be long-lasting."[66] Ironically, although pain and immobility of the arm are more than twice as common when the implant is placed under rather than over the chest wall muscles, the majority of implants are now submuscular so as to lessen the chances of severe contracture.[67]

Implants may also rupture, cause "creasing, kinking, vertical ripple folds and rippling in the breast," look or feel "unsatisfactory," and bleed or become infected.[68] According to the IOM, rupture may be caused by anything from a car accident or biopsy to a "tight hug" or, ironically again, by medical procedures to break up contracture (essentially involving a surgeon squeezing the already painful breast extremely hard so as to break the scar tissue and, sometimes, the implant itself). Rates of rupture, the IOM reports, are unknown: studies report anything between 0.3 percent and 77 percent of implanted women. Saline implants can also deflate: the IOM found that between 1 and 3 percent would do so in the first year of implantation, and that "this percentage would rise steadily with time."[69]

All implants "interfere with the ability of x-rays to detect the early signs of breast cancer, either by blocking x-rays or by compressing the remaining breast tissue and impairing the ability to view any changes which may indicate breast cancer."[70] Breast implants may remove the capability for certain forms of sexual pleasure (objection 7): one in seven women suffers "permanent loss of nipple sensation."[71]

64. Grigg et al., *Information for Women*, 15.
65. United Kingdom, Department of Health, "Breast Implants."
66. Grigg et al., *Information for Women*, 19.
67. Ibid., 19, 8. See also Guthrie, *Truth about Breast Implants*, 11.
68. United Kingdom, Department of Health, "Breast Implants."
69. Grigg et al., *Information for Women*, 14.
70. United Kingdom, Department of Health, "Breast Implants"; see also Grigg et al., *Information for Women*.
71. United Kingdom, Department of Health, "Breast Implants."

Overall, when reading the literature on breast implants, one gets the distinct impression that they simply do not work very well. This conclusion becomes unsurprising once one reflects on the difficulty of getting the body to accept even useful foreign objects such as transplanted organs, and on the galling lack of safety tests performed before their introduction. Real women have been the guinea pigs, and the results have not been promising.

Breast implants, then, are guilty of all the objections that Nussbaum makes to FGM on consenting adults. We have just seen the evidence for objections 5 to 7, and Nussbaum herself argues that the images which breast implants attempt to replicate are unambiguously linked to gender hierarchy (objection 8).[72] Surely, then, if we were to follow Nussbaum's recommendation to ban FGM even when performed on consenting adult women in sterile, clinical conditions, we should also ban cosmetic surgery of the type described. Surely, a political liberal who prioritizes second-order autonomy would not be able to ban either.

Nussbaum hints at the key to the issue under objection 1 to FGM. She argues that FGM is distinct in being directly forced, but recognizes that the issue is not clear-cut for Western beauty norms: "The choices involved in dieting are often not fully autonomous: They may be the product of misinformation and strong social forces that put pressure on women to make choice[s], sometimes dangerous ones, that they would not make otherwise. We should criticize these pressures and the absence of full autonomy created by them. And yet the distinction between social pressure and physical force should also remain salient, both morally and legally."[73] Here Nussbaum has reached the heart of the matter. We would still be worried about an adult woman who consented to undergo FGM under conditions of relative safety because we would be worried about the context that had led her to want such a thing. We would ask ourselves what pressures she had faced in coming to her decision, what she believed about the world in order to conclude

---

72. Other feminists agree. Sheila Jeffreys criticizes harmful Western practices such as cosmetic surgery, arguing that such practices are advocated for and practiced by "those groups who occupy a despised social status, such as women" ("'Body Art' and Social Status," 410). Alkeline Van Lenning criticizes Jeffreys's account, but agrees that "some examples of body modifications, like almost all cosmetic surgical procedures, are intended to bring the body closer to the dominating beauty ideal" and that, moreover, this beauty ideal "is embedded in a system of male-dominated values and practices" ("The System Made Me Do It?" 551, 547).

73. Nussbaum, *Sex and Social Justice*, 123.

that genital mutilation would be beneficial, and the extent to which she was being forced into a suboptimal practice by the salience of social norms. Put simply, we would ask ourselves what conditions would have to hold for such a decision to make sense. And we would be worried because the answer would include references to the deeply gendered nature of society, and the effects which that gender inequality has on the choices of women within it.

We should ask the same questions, and have the same worries, about the woman who chooses to have breast implants. We should ask ourselves what conditions have to hold for such a choice to be intelligible. In many cases, the conditions will include the widespread belief that women's success depends on their appearance, specifically on an appearance that emphasizes sexual availability. The following extract from *The Guardian*, about the fifteen-year-old British girl Jenna Franklin who wanted breast implants, illustrates both the concept of female success which is embodied in the surgically enhanced figure and the role of example in perpetuating that concept:

> Franklin's motivation for wanting to undergo surgery as soon as possible is nothing if not hopeful. "I want to be famous. And I don't think you can be famous without boobs. When I'm going out and I've got to get dressed up, the world's over for me." Her parents, not uncoincidentally both employed in the cosmetic surgery industry, were happy to shell out the £3,250 required for the operation, but it looks as if their daughter still has a long wait ahead of her.
>
> "I had thought about having my breasts enlarged when I was 12," she says, "but when I was about to turn 15, I saw so many people having it done that I wanted mine bigger as well. Every other person you see on television has had implants. If I want to be successful, I need to have them, too."[74]

We should be concerned about this case not simply because Jenna Franklin is not yet adult.[75] It will have the same tragic resonances

74. Anita Chaudhuri and Crystal Mahey, "The Silicone Generation."

75. Franklin's case is by no means unique. Davis describes several similar women whom she has interviewed about their cosmetic surgery, including "Susan," who had breast implants after feeling unusually flat-chested, learning that her mother and various other relatives have had implants, and being encouraged by her mother (*Reshaping the Female Body*, 124).

when, as seems likely, she has the surgery at a later date. (She may not have long to wait until a surgeon agrees to operate—two thousand girls aged under eighteen had breast implants in Britain in the year 2000.)[76] The choice to have breast implants is relevant to justice because it takes place in the context of profound patriarchal influence.

The quotation from Jenna Franklin illustrates the two problems with the prioritization of second-order autonomy highlighted in the first part of this chapter. Franklin's statement—"When I was about to turn 15, I saw so many people having it done that I wanted mine bigger as well"—suggests that her desire for breast implants is the result not of autonomous choice but of socially formed preferences: the power of example has cultivated in her a desire for conformity. Once the surgery has been performed on Franklin, moreover, it adds to that influence. The more women have breast surgery, the more it is acceptable or even expected that other women have breasts of a certain size and shape, and that those are achieved through surgery if they do not happen naturally.[77]

On the other hand, Franklin's claims—"I want to be famous. And I don't think you can be famous without boobs" and "Every other person you see on television has had implants. If I want to be successful, I need to have them, too"—illustrate the second problem with the prioritization of second-order autonomy: people might autonomously choose to follow harmful norms because they believe they cannot access a desired benefit without complying with the norm. The claim here, then, is not that women who want breast implants must be suffering from "false consciousness." Franklin may be right in thinking that breast implants are crucial for fame, just as the women who practice FGM are right in thinking that mutilated genitals are crucial for marriage. Indeed, the more women have breast implants, the more it actually is the case that they are requirements of success for women like

76. Chaudhuri and Mahey, "Silicone Generation." In the United States in 2005, 3,446 women under eighteen had breast implants, and 434 women under eighteen had "breast lifts." Women under eighteen had 2 percent of all cosmetic procedures and 0.9 percent of all breast implants. Breast implants were the fifth most popular procedure for women under eighteen, after rhinoplasty (nose reshaping), otoplasty (ear reshaping), breast reduction, and liposuction. Note, however, that the statistics for rhinoplasty, otoplasty, and liposuction include both women and men, such that breast implants may rise up the ranking if the statistics were broken down by sex (The American Society for Aesthetic Plastic Surgery, *Cosmetic Surgery National Data Bank Statistics 2005*, 10).

77. This point is also made in Bordo, *Unbearable Weight*, xxv, and Kathryn Morgan, "Women and the Knife," 165, 174–75.

Franklin. This requirement is felt by educated, middle-class women, not just by those who want to be famous: British plastic surgeons report that young women are increasingly having breast implants in preparation for university. For such women, a certain sort of appearance is thought to be "important in society," and cosmetic surgery is seen as "helping them achieve more in their education and careers."[78]

The answer, then, is not to educate women but to alter the social circumstances that justify the harmful practice, and banning the practice is a good way of doing this. Gerry Mackie gives an incisive account of the similarities between FGM and footbinding. Mackie argues that both practices require women and girls to undergo severe physical harm in order to secure the benefit of marriage. It follows, Mackie argues, that it remains rational for each woman or girl to undergo FGM or footbinding as long as the norm remains in place. As long as both men and women prefer marriage to nonmarriage, and as long as women's life chances are dependent on marriage, "they are trapped by the inferior convention. . . . However the custom originated, as soon as women believed that men would not marry an unmutilated woman, and men believed that an unmutilated woman would not be a faithful partner in marriage, and so forth, expectations were mutually concordant and a self-enforcing convention was locked in."[79] In other words, the only way for most individuals to escape a social norm that is a requirement for achieving social status (such as marriage) is in a context of (near-) universal noncompliance so that the norm ceases to function. Otherwise, there will always be an incentive for an individual to follow the norm and thus increase her status. A complete ban would be necessary if the society were to reach the position where no individual had an incentive to harm herself.[80]

At this point, Nussbaum and other political liberals have two options. Nussbaum could recognize that her political liberalism does not allow her to ban consensual FGM; or she could conclude that her arguments about the social formation of preferences and the existence of harmful social norms lead to a more complex conception of justice and

78. Plastic surgeon Professor Kefah Mokbel, quoted in Sarah-Kate Templeton, "Girls Take to Surgery so They Can Face University."

79. Mackie, "Ending Footbinding and Infibulation," 1008.

80. For a similar argument concerning male circumcision, see Sarah E. Waldeck, "Social Norm Theory and Male Circumcision," 57.

autonomy, one which conflicts with a politically liberal state. The first option would require Nussbaum to become like other Rawlsian political liberals who do not share her feminist concerns and her insights into social norms. Following this option might restore the consistency in Nussbaum's account. But her arguments about social preference formation are compelling. In making them, Nussbaum rightly identifies the limits of more minimal forms of political liberalism, which leave a great deal of substantive inequality intact, and do not provide individuals with the resources they need in order to overcome that inequality. Taking this option, then, would mean that Nussbaum's work would lose the substantial benefits it has over alternative accounts of liberalism, and would limit the extent of Nussbaum's feminism.

The second option, then, is for Nussbaum to recognize that if justice is about enabling people to make autonomous choices about their way of life in conditions of equality, then justice does not require a politically liberal neutral state which makes no judgments about the content of a way of life—*even if autonomy is understood only in the second-order sense.* The fact that preferences are socially formed in ways that can perpetuate harm and inequality means that the state must pay attention to the manner of that formation and take more radical action where it is required to secure justice. As an individual's ability to form, revise, and pursue her way of life is constrained by the social formation of her preferences and the need to comply with harmful norms, the goal of state action should be to ensure that these constraints do not perpetuate harm, inequality, or both (unequal harm). Liberals should not use an appeal to autonomy to excuse and justify inequality.

How might such state action be formulated? I propose that two conditions are individually necessary and jointly sufficient for state interference in practices that harm the choosing individual. The first condition is that the practice in question is significantly harmful. In order to have a possible case for state interference, we need to be sure that the harm involved is sufficiently severe to merit state action. The premise here—which most liberals would, I think, accept—is that some degree of state paternalism is justified: that the state should at least regulate very harmful or dangerous activities such as drug-taking or driving. Drawing the line between harm that is not sufficient for state action to be considered and harm that is will not be easy, but states do in fact make such distinctions,[81] and it seems that the harms involved in breast implants are enough at least to make us consider intervention. Having identified a practice as a candidate for intervention, then, we ask whether there are any good reasons for individuals to follow the practice, reasons that outweigh the costs involved. Some practices have costs that individuals may choose to accept in return for a benefit. Thus taking the contraceptive pill, for example, brings with it various health risks, such as an increased risk of thrombosis, which may be fatal; but it also brings the benefit of being able to control one's fertility, along with some beneficial side effects such as a decreased susceptibility to certain forms of cancer or severe period pain. Similarly, pregnancy and childbirth entail health risks and sometimes even cause the death of the pregnant woman; but pregnancy and childbirth also lead to the deeply valuable good of motherhood. In both cases, then, significant risks are accompanied by significant benefits which are not purely social, and so it is appropriate for individuals to decide for themselves whether the benefits outweigh the risks.

Conversely, the state should intervene to prevent the harmful practice if its benefits depend on the acceptance of a social norm— particularly one that is unequal or unjust. Even (indeed, especially) if it is true that breast implants will enhance Franklin's career prospects and her sense of self-worth, or that FGM will enhance a woman's marriage prospects, the only reason for these connections is the concept of female success or desirability endorsed by the relevant society. Because this norm of female success is also endorsed by men, who do not fall within its scope and so do not undergo harmful practices in order to comply with it, the injustice is magnified. Nobody should have to harm themselves to receive benefits that are only contingently related to that harm, and where the contingency is a social one. This is for the simple reason that harm, by definition, is to be avoided where possible; and where it is only a social norm that requires the harm, it is clearly within the scope of social action to limit that harm. Moreover, without a state ban ensuring universal noncompliance, any individual will face pressures to comply with the norm in order to receive the social benefit.

81. For example, Van Lenning argues that it is possible and desirable to distinguish bodily practices according to the extent of the damage they do. Thus she argues that dieting and anorexia can be distinguished for the purposes of normative critique since anorexia but not dieting "can lead to irreparable damage and death," and distinguishes high heels from cosmetic surgery on the grounds that the former and not the latter cause *reversible* harm ("The System Made Me Do It?" 550).

An example can illustrate this point. Smoking is physically harmful. It also has benefits that may lead people to choose to smoke. Some of those benefits are social: the wish to look cool, for example, or Rachel's desire to gain favor with her manager. As a result, the state should try to adjust social norms in this respect by banning or regulating cigarette advertising, or through antismoking campaigns. Perhaps, in Rachel's case, the company ought to instigate alternative rituals for informal discussion and networking, such as the common-room tea-drinking favored by David's Oxford college. Some benefits of smoking, however, are not social: they result from the chemical effects of nicotine in the body, and the pleasurable physical sensation of inhaling smoke. As such, some people might autonomously choose to smoke (leaving addiction aside) even if there were no *social* advantages to doing so. The benefits of smoking, then, are not contingent on a particular social norm, much less an unequal one, and thus do not rest on an injustice, and so it may be proper in such cases to leave individuals to choose whether the harms are worth the benefits to them.[82]

Breast implants, on the other hand, are beneficial only inasmuch as they increase the career options, self-esteem, or sexual status of the woman who has them. As these benefits are norm-dependent,[83] society has a much greater duty of care over individuals who might be persuaded by such norms. Because an inequality is involved, the position becomes even clearer: the benefit is socially contingent; and moreover, only women are socially encouraged to undergo this harmful practice in order to receive the benefit.[84] Specifically, nobody (in this case, women) should have to harm themselves (by undergoing breast surgery or FGM) in order to receive benefits (such as a successful career, a sense of self-worth, or the ability to be married) that, for other members of society (in this case, men) do not carry similarly harmful requirements. Where the harm is so significant that state intervention would not be grossly disproportionate, the state should prohibit such practices.

82. For an analysis of the ethics of smoking that far surpasses the purposely simplistic treatment given here, see Robert Goodin, "The Ethics of Smoking."

83. I argued for the norm-dependence of beauty and sexual behavior in Chapter 1. See also Naomi Wolf, *The Beauty Myth* and *Promiscuities*.

84. The United Nations goes further, stating in a Fact Sheet that "the harmful traditional practices focused on in this Fact Sheet have been performed for male benefit" (*Harmful Traditional Practices Affecting the Health of Women and Children*, 4). The Fact Sheet does refer to FGM but not to cosmetic surgery. Its omission of Western beauty practices is criticized in Winter et al., "UN Approach to Harmful Traditional Practices."

Although this argument refers to harm, it is not the same as the Millian harm principle. The state should prohibit self-regarding practices (those where no harm is done to others in the Millian sense) if, first, those practices are (significantly) harmful to the individual who engages in them *and,* second, if the only benefits of the practice for the individual concerned are the result of acceptance of an (unjust) social norm. Harm to others, then, is not the final justification for state action. Rather, harm to the actor in question is the premise without which the case for state action cannot be made. If there is insufficient harm, then the state cannot get involved through the mechanism of prohibition, even where the action concerned forms part of an unjust social norm. Applying makeup is a good example: although it results from and perpetuates gendered appearance norms that are unjust, it does not cause sufficient harm to the women concerned to justify a ban. The reason for state restraint in such cases is that the liberal state must maintain proportionality between the harm its actions prevent and the harm caused by the fact of prohibition. In some cases, such as makeup, a state ban would not be proportionate (using nonairbrushed photographs of makeup-free women in state media campaigns or leaflets might). In other cases, such as breast implants and FGM, the harm involved is sufficient to justify a ban.

Finally, this approach would not fail to respect individuals as desiring, choosing agents. Political liberalism is often justified as the only method of providing this respect; however, Nussbaum's formulation of this point actually compromises respect for others. Nussbaum writes: "The political conception makes room for . . . inadequate desires and respects them, by protecting spheres of choice and aiming at capability rather than functioning."[85] However, Nussbaum does not take into account the fact that respecting some desires is incompatible with respecting the individual. It is impossible, I contend, to respect such desires while at the same time respecting the desiring person.

Imagine, for example, a woman who is the victim of serious domestic violence, but who wishes not to prosecute her attacker. She might believe that he will not attack her again, or she might be afraid that pressing charges will in fact prompt him to attack again if the charges are not taken seriously, or she might be the victim of "battered woman syndrome," according to which victims of domestic violence "feel in-

85. Nussbaum, *Women and Human Development,* 160–61.

tense shame which may make them reluctant to come forward at all, or even to admit to themselves, let alone anyone else, that they are battered women."[86] Of course, it is crucial that domestic violence is taken seriously by the courts, so that the second fear is unfounded. Once that is the case, though, if we respect such a woman's desire and refrain from prosecuting her attacker, we fail to respect her as a person. By allowing her attacker to escape prosecution, we effectively undermine the importance of her bodily integrity and well-being, and thereby undermine the basis for respecting her. Instead, if we are genuinely to respect the victims of domestic violence, we must insist that perpetrators are prosecuted and dealt with firmly. As Hirschmann points out: "Prosecutors [in the United States] allow battered women more discretion in deciding whether to prosecute than is normally permitted for violent crime, even in jurisdictions with 'no drop' prosecutory policies. While such discretion apparently increases women's control, and respects many women's belief that domestic violence is a private matter, it also makes women more vulnerable to ongoing threats from their attackers."[87] Thus, by focusing on choice and refusing to treat domestic violence with the seriousness that is accorded to other violent crimes, we refuse to respect the women themselves.

We must refuse to respect those desires which themselves undermine respect for the desiring individual.[88] We can say that a woman's desire to have breast implants is not deserving of respect without thereby saying that she is not worthy of respect. Indeed, refusing to respect that desire is a crucial part of our respect for her as a being in her own right, regardless of the size of her breasts, her conformity to beauty norms, or her sexual availability to men. If we say to Jenna Franklin, "Your decision to enlarge your breasts is one which deserves our respect," we are thereby saying to her "it is reasonable to believe that women need large breasts in order to be successful, and that belief and the reality to which it refers is worthy of our respect. Moreover, your feeling that you are inadequate with natural breasts, and your

---

86. Hirschmann, *Subject of Liberty*, 113. See also Friedman, *Autonomy, Gender, Politics*, 151.
87. Hirschmann, *Subject of Liberty*, 116.
88. As Seyla Benhabib argues: "It does not follow that if we respect human beings as culture-creating beings that we must either 'rank or order' their worlds as a *whole* or disrespect them by dismissing their life-worlds altogether. We may disagree with *some* aspect of their moral, ethical, or evaluative practices without dismissing or holding in disrespect their life-worlds *altogether*" (*Claims of Culture*, 40–41; emphasis in the original).

consequent desire to undergo dangerous and unnecessary surgery, are understandable and worthy of respect." What we should be saying to her, in contrast, is "you as an individual are worthy of more respect than is compatible with you undergoing breast surgery in an attempt to become successful, and women in general are worthy of more respect than is compatible with their bodies being shaped in line with male fantasies." As David McCabe argues, "On any plausible view of a liberalism grounded in equal respect, my perspective alone cannot be the final criterion for whether an action respects me. That criterion must be determined at least partly by the force of good reasons."[89] Respect for individuals requires a critical perspective on those desires which undermine individual respect.

The Limitations of Political Liberal Prioritization of Second-Order Autonomy

Overall, then, once a commitment to the universal value of even second-order autonomy is combined with an understanding of social construction—the social formation of preferences and the existence of harmful or unequal social norms—political liberalism as defined by Nussbaum is unsustainable. Nussbaum's work is a considerable improvement on accounts of political liberalism that fail to recognize the social formation of preferences and fail to criticize social norms. As a result, she and other political liberals should not attempt to maintain consistency by refusing to advocate emancipatory and egalitarian state action. On the other hand, Nussbaum should not be condemned to dodging the consequences of her work on preference formation and feminism by making exceptions for practices such as FGM—exceptions that cannot be conceptually justified from within the political liberal paradigm. Instead, work such as Nussbaum's illustrates the limitations of political liberalism as she defines it, and should lead her to abandon it.

In place of politically liberal state restraint, liberals need to recognize that oppression can constitute rather than simply contravene individuals' desires, and that social norms can make it rational for individuals to want things that profoundly threaten their well-being and equality. As a result, the liberal state needs to take a stance against some in-

89. David McCabe, "Knowing about the Good," 326.

stances of desire formation, going against unequal social norms to secure justice. A liberal state should prohibit those practices which cause significant harm to those who choose them, if they are chosen only in response to unjust, unequal norms. Such a state will not be a politically liberal state, but it will be one that best combines individual autonomy with a commitment to liberal equality.

6

PATERNALISM AND AUTONOMY

Paternalism has often been thought of as a paradigmatic enemy of both liberalism and autonomy. However, a critical awareness of social construction undermines such rigid antipaternalism.[1] In this chapter, I consider whether and how my proposals are paternalist, and the sense and extent to which they are nevertheless compatible with autonomy. The discussion is necessarily brief. I cannot hope to do justice to the literature on paternalism and autonomy in this chapter, but aim instead to highlight those features of my account that render it a more acceptable variety of paternalism that does not rule out autonomy.

Paternalism

Although my proposals for the prohibition of breast implants may appear unusual or extreme, most liberals neither advocate the legalization of FGM nor oppose all forms of state paternalism. Most liberals accept the need for some state regulation of dangerous practices, even those which are principally harmful only to the practicing individual. For example, when discussing whether Sikhs ought to be exempt from the law requiring motorcyclists to wear helmets, Brian Barry considers but rejects the argument that the law ought not to exist simply because it is paternalistic.[2] Moreover, liberals (as opposed to libertarians) do not tend to argue in favor of abolishing the requirement to wear seatbelts in cars, or regulations on cigarette smoking and drug use (except perhaps cannabis). Why, then, do proposed laws against breast implants face more criticism than laws in these other areas? One possible reason, discussed briefly earlier, is that FGM is demonized as a non-West-

---

1. This position has been argued for throughout, but see also Sunstein, "Neutrality in Constitutional Law," 2.
2. Barry, *Culture and Equality*, 47–48.

ern practice, whereas Western beauty practices such as breast implants are, by definition, normalized in Western societies. But this cannot explain the general acceptance of other paternalistic laws. More specifically, we might say that breast implants conform to the patriarchal norm that devalues women's natural bodies and portrays them as objects that require modification for male consumption. This argument is an old, familiar one from feminist analysis. But its relevance to the issue of state paternalism is acute, and undertheorized.[3] Take, for example, the so-called "Spanner Case" of 1990, in which several English men were prosecuted for taking part in extreme but consensual sadomasochistic encounters. The men were convicted, and the conviction was upheld through the appeal system, right up to the House of Lords and beyond it to the European Court of Human Rights. Each court considered and rejected the possibility that a conviction would rely on a demonization of homosexual practices as particularly degraded and deviant, and claimed that heterosexuals committing similar activities would also be convicted.[4]

In his discussion of the case, Richard Green implies that the various courts' denials of discrimination were not entirely ingenuous. He compares the Spanner case with preceding case law, and writes: "Was the Spanner ruling heterosexist? Why was a husband branding his initials [with a knife] on his wife's buttocks, with her consent, distinguished from the *Brown* [Spanner] case? Branding was one of the acts of the SM club. How many additional acts would this couple have had to engage in, anatomical constraints notwithstanding, before they fell under the [Offences Against the Person] Act of 1861?"[5] Two things are noteworthy about Green's analysis. The first is that, in labeling the act possibly "heterosexist," he implies that the conviction was particularly *advantageous* to heterosexuals and *disadvantageous* to homosexuals. In other words, he assumes that it is better to have the choice to undergo harmful mutilations than it is to enjoy legal protection from such acts. But while it is possible that one or more of the judges ruling on the case was motivated by repugnance for homosexuality, it is by no means clear that banning a harmful practice epitomizes disgust, rather than *respect,* for the individual whose body is thereby protected.

3. One exception is Sheila Jeffreys's *Beauty and Misogyny,* which argues that beauty practices should be dealt with under the UN framework for responding to harmful cultural practices.

4. Richard Green, "(Serious) Sadomasochism."

5. Ibid., 548.

Instead, banning a harmful practice can actually epitomize respect for the protected individuals, in the sense that the ban can stem from a view about human dignity and the worth of the human body. If this is correct, it is interesting to note that the earlier case law cited by Green fits a pattern whereby consensual harm has been permitted when the harm is perpetrated on a woman by a man and forbidden when it is a man who is harmed.[6] In other words, the Spanner ruling may have been not heterosexist but misogynist, with women's bodies deemed to be less valuable than men's. In this light the otherwise inconsistent case law becomes coherent. The fact that men were acquitted after subjecting their consenting female partners to nipple clamping in one case and branding in another, but convicted after damaging the genitals of other men in the Spanner case and participating in a prearranged fight in another may suggest that, in the eyes of the law, the male body is sanctified and must be protected whereas the female body is fair game, an appropriate surface on which men may etch their fantasies. Without a broader analysis of case law it is not possible to judge how consistently this analysis applies, but it is interesting to note that a similar evaluation is expressed in the disparity with which male and female bodies are treated by obscenity law. Portrayals of the male erection have typically been subject to far greater regulation than the aroused female vulva.[7] The refusal to criminalize heterosexual sado-

6. Green cites three cases in which men were harmed, all of which resulted in conviction: in 1882, prize fighting was held to be unlawful (Green does not give the gender of the fighters, but we may safely assume they were men); in 1980, a man was convicted for causing actual bodily harm to another man in a prearranged fight that they had both agreed on beforehand; and the Spanner case. The cited cases in which women were harmed all resulted in acquittal. In 1992, the judge directed the jury to acquit a military man who used nipple clamps and piercing on a woman in a consensual bondage session; and in 1996 a husband who branded his consenting wife's buttocks with a knife was acquitted. The final case that Green cites in which a woman was harmed is less clear-cut and cannot easily be categorized. In 1934, a man gave a fairly severe beating to a seventeen-year-old woman. The case defies categorization since the woman denied in court that she consented, and since the man was first convicted but then had his conviction overturned. See Green, "(Serious) Sadomasochism," 544.

7. The British Board of Film Classification (BBFC) has become more lenient in issuing R18 certificates (for films which may be sold only in licensed shops) since its refusal to grant certificates to seven pornographic films was overturned by the Video Appeals Committee (VAC) in 1998. Nonetheless, even the VAC's judgment insisting that the films be allowed demonstrates the belief that the erect penis is more significant than the vagina. It states: "The distinctions the [BBFC] makes . . . seem somewhat insignificant. . . . Is an erect penis in the hands of a woman masturbating a man likely to be less upsetting than an erect penis entering a mouth or vagina?" This rhetorical question is clearly meant to be answered in the negative, illustrating that it is the objectification of the penis that may properly be regarded

masochism in the light of the Spanner case may be not heterosexist but misogynist.

Defining Paternalism

The most celebrated formulation of liberal antipaternalism (and the one most responsible for the marriage of liberalism with antipaternalism) is John Stuart Mill's statement: "The only purpose for which power can be rightfully exercised over any member of a civilized community, against his will, is to prevent harm to others. His own good, either physical or moral, is not a sufficient warrant."[8] On the face of it, this definition clearly rules out my proscriptive proposals, which exercise power over an individual for her own good—a good that could be described in physical terms (to prevent the physical harms which can ensue) or in moral terms (to prevent the individual from participating in, and being defined by, norms of male dominance).

However, several recent discussions have proposed alternative definitions of paternalism that are less applicable to my approach. For example, Richard Arneson criticizes those philosophers who dismiss, reject, or hedge Mill's formulation and aims to defend it—yet even he reformulates it, and does so in a way that renders my proposals nonpaternalist. Arneson writes:

> I propose this reformulation of Mill's antipaternalist principle: Paternalistic policies are restrictions on a person's liberty which are justified *exclusively* by consideration for that person's own good or welfare, and which are carried out either against his present will (when his present will is not explicitly overridden by his own prior commitment) or against his prior commitment (when his present will is explicitly overridden by his

---

as "upsetting," regardless of the presence or absence of a vagina (United Kingdom, Video Appeals Committee, *Judgment of Appeals Numbers 15 &16*, 30). In 1999 (new regulations have since been introduced) the BBFC's distinctions included the fact that "'sight of erections'" was restricted to R18 films, and "the 'Mull of Kintyre test,' whereby a film may not be broadcast that contains a shot of a penis that is more erect than the Scottish peninsula appears on a map" (Steve Platt, *Censored*, 15). Similarly, Joel Feinberg notes: "The commercial assumption is that the audiences [of pornography] are primarily *men* who will be titillated by scenes of female homosexuality but repelled or threatened by parallel episodes with men, or even by the unveiling of the masculine sex organ" (*Offense to Others*, 134; emphasis in the original).

8. Mill, *On Liberty*, 78.

own prior commitment). Mill's principle states that paternalistic policies so defined are always wrong.[9]

This formulation renders my proposals nonpaternalist in two ways. First, though it is a consideration, the person's "own good or welfare" is not the only justification for my proscriptions. Also at stake are equality (the concern that people should not be unequally required or encouraged to harm themselves), justice (the idea that it is unjust if society requires people to harm themselves to receive some benefit), and influence (the idea behind social construction that the desire to self-harm, particularly in response to a social norm, is socially mediated and, as a result, an individual self-harmer thereby increases the pressure on others to follow suit). This means that my proposals are also exempt from Gerald Dworkin's definition of paternalism, according to which paternalism is "the interference with a person's liberty of action justified by reasons referring exclusively to the welfare, good, happiness, needs, interests or values of the person being coerced."[10]

The second way in which Arneson's reformulation renders my proposals nonpaternalist is that his definition "excludes from the category of paternalism some types of restriction on liberty ordinarily characterized as paternalistic."[11] The example he gives mirrors my proposals. According to Arneson, proscription of dueling is not paternalistic if it responds to the fact that people would prefer, first, not to have to engage in duels but, failing that, their second preference is to respond appropriately to a challenge to duel. In this case, Arneson contends that prohibition of dueling is not paternalistic since it does not restrict anyone's freedom against their will. It merely enforces existing preferences. To put it another way, the proscription solves a collective action problem—everyone would prefer not to duel, but no one wants to look weak and suffer sanctions by refusing a challenge.[12] Finally, to put it in the language of first- and second-order autonomy, the individuals in Arneson's example have a second-order desire to maintain their dignity and standing in society, and a first-order desire not to duel. They are

9. Richard J. Arneson, "Mill versus Paternalism," 471; emphasis added.
10. Gerald Dworkin, "Paternalism," 62. In a later piece, Dworkin argues that paternalism does not in fact have to involve a restriction of liberty. See Dworkin, *Theory and Practice of Autonomy*, 121.
11. Arneson, "Mill versus Paternalism," 471.
12. Cass Sunstein makes a similar argument in "Preferences and Politics."

willing to use their second-order autonomy to alienate their first-order autonomy when that is necessary, but they would rather it were unnecessary.

Phrasing Arneson's example in this way shows how it mirrors my proposals.[13] First, make the extremely plausible assumption that people would prefer their second-order autonomy not to require them to alienate their first-order autonomy—they would prefer not to harm themselves so as to receive a benefit if they could receive the benefit without harming themselves. For example, assume that women prefer most of all to feel good about themselves (or to become famous, be a model, or attract men) *without* having breast implants[14] but that, if this is not possible, their second preference is to gain those goods *via* breast implants. In these circumstances, the second, also plausible, premise needed to complete the symmetry with the dueling case states that it would be possible for women to achieve their second-order goals in a world without implants. In other words, we need to assume that prohibition of breast implants will not in itself prevent women from becoming famous or feeling good about themselves. As I argued in Chapter 1, there are good reasons to think that female appearance norms are not fixed but rather adapt and shape themselves to different social contexts. There is therefore no reason to think that a norm of breasts that are large relative to waist and hip size should persist indefinitely, or that only large-breasted women would have access to fame, fortune, or self-esteem in a world without implants. In fact, the converse seems true: the availability of cosmetic surgery reinforces the idea that women ought to look a certain way, and that any deviations from the idea are precisely that, "deviations," which can—and should—be "fixed." As one surgeon says in justification of facelifts:

> Now, if you can argue that age twenty-five is maturity and you
> had exactly the right amount of skin coming from the brow

13. Arneson's example also mirrors Gerry Mackie's convention account of FGM, discussed at various places throughout the book. See Mackie, "Ending Footbinding and Infibulation."

14. In order for the comparison with Arneson's dueling example to work, not all women have to have these preferences. Since Arneson's account of paternalism refers to the justification of a law rather than its effect, what matters is whether these sorts of preferences motivate and justify the law, not how widespread those preferences are. Thus, with reference to dueling, Arneson writes: "Of course, in any actual society not everybody will have this pattern of desires, but if it is this pattern of desires that generates reasons for forbidding dueling, then the antidueling law [even if it is unfair or unjust] is nonpaternalistic" ("Mill versus Paternalism," 471–72; phrase in brackets appears thus in the original).

down to the first fold and exactly the right amount of skin coming to the eyelashes . . . and that was normal, then is it normal to allow time to change it, so that the skin begins to slide down over the jaws and the bags begin to show? Well, that's not the way it was when it was twenty-five, any more than when I painted my house it was natural for me to let it gradually deteriorate. I keep it up—repair and maintenance.[15]

Cosmetic surgery responds to some socially inculcated demands for differently shaped bodies, but also creates its own demands by introducing new procedures and adding to the sense that particular physical features are and must be malleable. Undermining cosmetic surgery is one step toward undermining women's sense that they must have a certain appearance if they are to succeed or be happy.

If we make these extremely plausible assumptions about the breast implant case, it mirrors the dueling case. So, following Arneson's definition of paternalism, my proposals are not paternalistic and I do not have to respond to his objections to paternalism.[16]

My proposals do, however, conform to the far more general and moderate definition of paternalism offered by Joel Feinberg, which states, "*It is always a good and relevant (though not necessarily decisive) reason in support of a criminal prohibition that it will prevent harm (physical, psychological or economic) to the actor himself.*"[17] This definition certainly does not exhaustively capture my proposals; among other things, it does not mention the harm that might be caused by making someone unequal to others. However, the definition contains within itself an escape clause: the harm listed does not have to be the decisive reason behind the law in question, but merely one good reason. On this definition, then, my proposals are paternalistic: they are a version of

15. Blum, *Flesh Wounds*, 76.

16. If I were to respond to his objections, I would begin by criticizing the fact that Arneson agrees with Joseph Raz that second-order autonomy entails the first-order autonomous choice of "all the foreseeable consequences to himself that flow from this voluntary choice." I criticize this position at some length in Chapter 7. It is also worth noting that Arneson's position is in tension, not agreement, "with the Rousseauian-Kantian tradition which prescribes (roughly) that to be autonomous a person must, so far as lies within his power, conform his actions to laws or principles that he has chosen for himself," since some of the foreseeable consequences flowing from an individual's voluntary choice are that the individual will have to submit to laws and principles that she has not chosen ("Mill versus Paternalism," 475).

17. Joel Feinberg, *Harm to Self*, 4; emphasis in the original.

what Feinberg calls "mixed" paternalism: that for which the prevention of self-harm is not the sole aim.

One of the great merits of Feinberg's approach is that it offers several ways of categorizing varieties of paternalism. In what follows, I show how my proposals fit in to some other of Feinberg's categories, and attempt thereby to defend them.

Harm

As just mentioned, my proposals take account of more than merely physical, psychological, and economic harm. Social norms, for example, can be characterized not only by the actual physical harm they inflict upon the individual, but also by what I call their "status harm." An individual suffers status harm when she follows a norm that portrays her as inferior. With breast implants, physical harm and status harm coincide: implants are physically damaging to the woman's body, and they also harm her by casting her as an inferior being, as a sexual object that serves male fantasy. Physical harm and status harm need not coincide. It would be possible for a woman to respond to sexually objectifying appearance norms in a way that caused no physical harm but did bring her status harm, perhaps by wearing certain clothes or makeup. To take another example, imagine a man who takes steroids to increase the size of his muscles, so as to conform to a normalized image of male strength. If the steroids are dangerous to his health, then he suffers physical harm but not status harm, since the effect of the steroids and the norm is to portray the man as powerful, strong and superior to others. If the man decides to respond to the same male appearance norm by going to the gym, exercising, and lifting weights, creating muscles naturally and healthily, he suffers neither physical harm nor status harm. In this latter case the man is affected by the influence factor but not the disadvantage factor, and has therefore suffered no injustice.[18]

Which harms, then, are relevant to my proposals? The short answer is that all of them are. With each case, it is a matter of weighing up the harms caused and considering whether they are grave enough to warrant proscription. In some cases, as liberals would accept, status harm

18. This case is conceptually similar to the case discussed in Chapter 4 of the middle-class child who never really considers any alternative to higher education.

alone is sufficient for proscription. We can see this by remembering that even Mill ruled out voluntary self-enslavement, and did not give as a reason the fact that physical harm might accrue to the slave.[19] In other cases, again as many liberals would accept, physical harm alone is sufficient—most liberals endorse regulation of drugs via prescriptions, and many endorse prohibition of drugs such as heroin and crack cocaine. In each individual case, the level of physical harm and status harm must be considered and weighed up together—remembering Feinberg's warning that "wherever a line is draw between permission and prohibition, there will be cases close to the line on both sides of it."[20]

What distinguishes my proposals, perhaps, is that they combine the harm element with the idea that self-harming practices are unjust if they are performed only in response to a social norm, since in such cases society is both culpable for and able to remedy the harm caused. Although my approach is decidedly normative—via its focus on unjust and unequal social norms as well as the notion of status harm—it is not a species of what Feinberg calls "Moralistic Legal Paternalism." He defines this approach as follows: "It is always a good reason in support of a proposed prohibition that it is necessary to prevent *moral harm* (as opposed to physical, psychological, or economic harm) to the actor himself. (Moral harm is 'harm to one's character,' 'becoming a worse person,' as opposed to harm to one's body, psyche, or purse.)"[21] While it might seem possible to describe both status harm and *unequal* physical harm as moral harm, Feinberg's bracketed explanation of the term seems to rule out such a description. What Feinberg has in mind—and what he labels as dubious—is the idea that the individual concerned will be somehow corrupted—the sort of argument that may be levied against obscenity.[22] This is not the idea behind my approach. I do not argue that having breast implants will somehow corrupt or deprave a woman, or compromise her moral character; I do argue that it renders her inferior and subjects her to discourses of inequality. As Catharine MacKinnon puts it: "The concerns of feminism with power and powerlessness are first political, not moral."[23]

19. Mill rules out voluntary slavery out of "consideration for . . . liberty," the fact that one person is under the control of another, not physical harm. See *On Liberty*, 171–72.

20. Feinberg, *Harm to Self*, xv.

21. Ibid., xvii; emphasis in the original.

22. See, for example, Feinberg, *Offense to Others*, 100.

23. MacKinnon, *Toward a Feminist Theory of the State*, 196.

My approach does share some features with Feinberg's "Legal Moralism," which states: "It can be morally legitimate for the state to prohibit certain types of action that cause neither harm nor offense to anyone, on the grounds that such actions constitute or cause evils of other ('free-floating') kinds."[24] The match is by no means exact, since in my approach harm is required. However, I have drawn attention to the fact that, as the result of social construction, one person's actions necessarily affect others. Thus I argued, following Foucault, that practices such as routine secular male circumcision make sense only in a social context, and that general adherence to such practices makes that practice more acceptable or required for others. Unequal practices do cause harm not only to the individuals directly concerned but also to others who are influenced and portrayed according to those practices.[25] My approach is not, then, a species of legal moralism, but it is sympathetic to the basic observation behind it.

Finally in this section, we can briefly revisit the issue of how to define harm, and how to respond to objections that harm is a subjective issue. If harm were subjective, so that one person's harm is another's inconvenience or even benefit, this would be extremely problematic for paternalist proposals based on limiting harm. Marilyn Friedman quotes a study that found that "many Egyptian women . . . expressed no anger whatsoever over having had genital surgery performed on them. These women planned to have it performed on their daughters. They thought that natural adult female genitalia were disgusting and could not imagine that a man would want to marry a woman who had not undergone the surgery,"[26] and accepts that these finding undermine the case against FGM. Similarly, Sander Gilman objects that critiques of practices such as FGM are misguided since they involve "the projection of Western, bourgeois notions of pleasure onto other people's bodies."[27] However, Gerry Mackie reports several studies which show, unsurprisingly, that women who undergo FGM do value their health and sexual pleasure (even if pleasure is defined simply as the absence of pain) just as Western women do. Women who practice FGM

24. Feinberg, *Harm to Self*, xvii.
25. Another example is what Feinberg refers to as the defamation argument against pornography: "It spreads an image of women as mindless playthings or 'objects,' inferior beings fit only to be used and abused for the pleasure of men" (*Offense to Others*, 147).
26. Friedman, *Autonomy, Gender, Politics*, 188.
27. Gilman, "'Barbaric' Rituals?" 56.

do so not because they have a different concept of harm but because they often do not realize that FGM is responsible for the harm which they know has befallen them, or because they do not realize that their bodily functions are *abnormally* difficult.

As an example of the first phenomenon, Mackie cites a study of fifty women in Sierra Leone who underwent FGM after they had been sexually active: "All reported decreased sexual satisfaction after the operation, but they were unaware of the causal relationship until informed by the interviewer. Ironically, some of these women had become promiscuous in their search for lost satisfaction."[28] Similarly, while communities which practice FGM are clearly aware of, and suffer from, the serious illness and death which befalls some mutilated girls and women, they may not realize that FGM is to blame. This lack of knowledge can be attributed to several factors: a lack of basic health education, the fact that FGM tends to be practiced universally within any given community so there is no basis of comparison, and the fact that some practicing communities exacerbate the "universal human reticence about discussing matters related to human sexuality" by "powerful norms of secrecy," such as the idea that women who discuss the practice will be cursed by evil spirits.[29] Once these problems are overcome, there is little if any doubt among practitioners that FGM is harmful. Mackie describes his experiences with a village in Senegal that abandoned FGM (which he terms FGC, or Female Genital Cutting) after some of its female members participated in a wide-ranging education program, and recounts an interview with Lala Baldé, president of a local women's association:

> She told me that the women never suspected a causal relationship between FGC and complications. When girls died, bled, or got infected at cutting, they attributed it to evil spirits; they did not know, for example, that heavy blood loss might retard child development, and gynaecological complications were considered the lot of women.
>
> On hearing of the causal relationship from a source they considered credible, Baldé told me, it took them 30 minutes of discussion to decide that the causal claim was correct. They

---

28. Mackie, "Ending Footbinding and Infibulation," 1009. The cited study is Olayinka Koso-Thomas, *The Circumcision of Women.*

29. Gerry Mackie, "Female Genital Cutting: A Harmless Practice?" 147–49.

reviewed local history and suddenly realized that incidents of death, haemorrhaging, and infection were immediately associated with FGC, and they broke down and wept.[30]

This is clearly a case in which the people involved recognize and deeply regret that harm has been done. They practiced FGM not because they have a different concept of harm, but because they did not realize what causes the harm.

The second phenomenon, that women may not realize that they have been harmed, is more complex. Consider the following:

> Lightfoot-Klein's initial interviews with Sudanese women elicited the response, for example, that urination was "normal." She then switched to more descriptive questions such as "How long does it take you to urinate?" The answer then was "Normal—about 15 minutes."
>
> The painful surgery, prolonged urination and menstruation, traumatic penetration, and unbearable childbirth accompanying infibulation are all accepted as normal. Because it is inflicted on all girls before puberty they have no basis of comparison.[31]

In these cases, women do not realize that they have been harmed by FGM. However, this is *not* to say that they have a different conception of harm, or that the harms, once revealed, are immaterial to them. They accept their lot because they have no reason to think that it can be changed. Once women do realize that they have been harmed by FGM, they are keen to put in place the village-wide declarations that are necessary to abandon the practice, as Mackie's fieldwork demonstrates. As he aptly puts it: "If one cannot escape the tragic circumstances of having to suffer a harm in order to obtain a greater benefit, that does not mean that one believes there is no harm."[32]

To conclude, then, it is by no means clear that different cultures or individuals have different concepts of harm. What is the case is that

30. Ibid., 147. See also Gerry Mackie, "Female Genital Cutting: The Beginning of the End," 260.

31. Mackie, "Ending Footbinding and Infibulation," 1009. The cited study is Hanny Lightfoot-Klein, *Prisoners of Ritual*, 22, 59.

32. Mackie, "Female Genital Cutting: A Harmless Practice?" 150.

cultures and individuals differ in what they see as an acceptable trade-off between harm and benefit, or between harms to some people and benefit to others. Liberal justice precludes most instances of the latter kind of trade-off, in which some people are required to make significant sacrifices for the benefit of others, and ought to limit the cases where an individual's access to social benefit is contingent on her willingness to harm herself.[33]

These points notwithstanding, we are still left with the difficulty of how to deal with individuals who genuinely want to submit themselves to practices that "we," but not "they," may see as harmful. Examples might include extreme sadomasochism, extensive tattoos, and the like. While my proposals do not directly impinge on such practices as long as they do not regulate access to social benefits, it is important to show how they fit into my general arguments. The next section suggests a further relevant consideration.

Single-Party versus Two-Party Paternalism

An extremely useful distinction outlined by Feinberg is between single-party and two-party paternalism.[34] In essence, single-party cases are those in which an individual harms herself without assistance from another. Single-party paternalism would therefore proscribe or regulate what an individual could do to herself in this most literal sense. Examples include suicide, drug-taking (although not drug-procurement), and self-mutilation in the most literal sense, such as cutting one's own arms.

Two-party cases are those in which a second person harms the first with her consent—voluntary euthanasia, sadomasochism, or cosmetic surgery, for example.[35] Many of the cases that I have discussed in this

33. The most obvious example of a case in which liberal states do require certain individuals to make enormous sacrifices for the benefit of others is war, particularly wars fought by conscripted soldiers.

34. Feinberg also refers to the distinction as direct versus indirect paternalism. Dworkin refers to it as pure versus impure paternalism. See Dworkin, "Paternalism," 65–66.

35. Feinberg notes that the word "harm" has a different meaning in the contexts of the Millian harm principle and the two-party case. The other-regarding harm proscribed by the Millian harm principle refers to "'wrongful injury'"—i.e., injury that contravenes the will of the harmed individual—whereas the harm proscribed by two-party paternalism is "the sense of simple setback to interest, whether 'wrongful' or not" (Harm to Self, 11). Thus, as Dworkin also notes, paternalism in the two-party case is not equivalent to the Millian prohibition of other-regarding actions ("Paternalism," 66).

book are of the two-party variety. Moreover, the example of drug-taking demonstrates that many single-party cases rely on prior assistance from a second party (in this case, to procure the drugs). This fact suggests a useful principle for my proscriptive proposals: wherever possible, penalties for noncompliance should be imposed on the second party rather than on the harmed individual. So, the penalty should be imposed on the plastic surgeon and not the woman being operated on—or, in cases of extreme sadomasochism, on the sadists and not the masochists.[36]

This approach has one main advantage which helps to mitigate liberal antipaternalist concerns. The proscribed act is no longer harming oneself, but harming another person (albeit with their consent). This approach declares: "It is wrong to harm another person. Even if that person asks you to, or tells you that she does not mind, you should not do it." To the cosmetic surgeon: "Even if a woman comes to you asking you to put her health at risk by performing an operation that serves no medical purpose, it would be wrong of you to do it and you should refuse." To the man who branded his wife's buttocks with a knife: "Even if your wife asks you to carve your initials into her flesh, it remains wrong of you to injure and objectify her in such a way. She may be within her rights to cut herself with a knife; it is not within your rights, under any circumstances, to perform the cuts, and it is not within her rights to expect that her request that you do so would be granted." Put this way, the proscriptions lose some of their paternalistic flavor. They become not a way to patronize individuals and undermine their autonomy, but a way of preventing one individual from harming another.[37] Such laws do not interfere with an individual's

36. Other examples might include prosecuting the pimp and the john rather than the prostitute and the manufacturer of steroids rather than the user. (I say "might" because I have not discussed whether the specific cases of prostitution and steroid use merit proscription.) Similarly, the Committee on Obscenity and Film Censorship, chaired by Bernard Williams, argued that it should not be a criminal offense for someone under the age of eighteen to attempt to view a film with an "18" certificate, and that the offense should rest with the cinema licensee (*Obscenity and Film Censorship*, 158). Finally, it is illegal to perform FGM on a girl or woman in the United Kingdom, but it is not an offense for a woman to mutilate her own genitals (Sleator, *Female Genital Mutilation Bill*, 32).

37. Phrased this way, the paternalistic proposals become very similar to the idea, enshrined in many liberal legal systems, that consent does not justify murder or physical assault. Arneson argues that such laws are "nonpaternalistically justifiable" on the grounds that "the perpetrators of assault have the means to coerce their victims into 'consent' (to avert a threatened worse consequence)"—grounds that bear at least some resemblance to the idea that social norms may require individuals to alienate their first-order autonomy so as to avoid

right to act as she wishes as regards her own body, but interfere instead with an individual's right to have *others* interfere with her body. Such two-party cases do not involve properly self-regarding harm. They are cases in which one person knowingly and willfully harms another. It is wrong for one person to harm another in the sorts of cases covered by my approach, and right that the law ought to intervene in such cases.

Feinberg, however, finds two party-cases more "complicated" than single-party cases, since paternalist legislation against two-party paternalism interferes with the liberty of two people rather than one. Imagine that breast implants are prohibited, and that cosmetic surgeons are prosecuted instead of patients. For Feinberg, this invades the patient's liberty, since she can no longer get breast implants, and her autonomy, since her voluntary consent to the surgery is no longer effective. If the surgeon is the only one who is prosecuted then, Feinberg states, "[the surgeon] is treated even worse than [the patient], for while both . . . are prevented from doing what they intended to do, it is only [the surgeon] who is punished."[38] By saying that the surgeon is treated "even worse" than the patient, Feinberg suggests that the surgeon also loses liberty and autonomy, but to a greater degree than the patient. The implication of Feinberg's claim is that paternalist legislation is actually worse in two-party cases than in single-party cases, not better as I have suggested.

A good example of this problem concerns those people who are unusually unable to carry out their wishes alone. By "unusually unable" I mean those who are physically or mentally disabled, for example, or perhaps those who are unusually poor. There are many self-regarding actions that all people, even if able-bodied, cannot perform alone. Any woman who wants breast implants is unable to achieve that goal alone: she needs a surgeon, an anesthetist, and so on to perform the operation on her, not to mention a company to manufacture the implants. However, those who are mentally or physically disabled will be unusually unable to perform certain self-regarding actions alone. For example, most people are able to commit suicide without outside help. Unlike breast implants, any materials that are needed are not provided solely

the threatened worse consequence of failing to achieve their second-order goals ("Mill versus Paternalism," 472).

38. Feinberg, *Harm to Self*, 172.

for that purpose, and so their manufacturers and retailers are not complicit in the act. So, if there is a paternalistic prohibition of suicide in two-party cases only, able-bodied people will be able to commit suicide without falling foul of the law. On the other hand, someone who is seriously disabled—perhaps she is paralyzed from the neck down and so can communicate her wishes but not carry them out—is unable to commit suicide without assistance. If a distinction is drawn for the purposes of the law between single-party and two-party acts, the disabled person cannot commit suicide whereas the able-bodied person can, and this seems unjust since it undermines basic equality.

Note, however, that a distinction between single- and two-party paternalism is not necessary for this inequality of access to suicide. Such an inequality also occurs if suicide is completely illegal, whether assisted or not. Under these conditions an able-bodied person contemplating suicide is unlikely to fear legal sanction (since they expect to be dead and so not subject to prosecution), but it is likely that the disabled person will find it difficult to obtain a willing assistant (since the assistant will remain alive and thus vulnerable to the law). Such an inequality of access is true of all illegal acts. If an able-bodied person wishes to rob a bank, she can (attempt to) do so alone. However, if a seriously disabled or paralyzed person wishes to do so, she will have to find an assistant, and the fact that bank robbing is illegal may make this difficult. In other words, if actions are justly prohibited, it is not an objection that this makes them hard to perform, or that it is harder for some people than others. Bank robbing is harder for those who do not have a gun than for those who do, but this is of no normative consequence.

The fact that there is an inequality of access to suicide even where no distinction is made between single- and two-party paternalism suggests that the problem lies not in the distinction but in the very prohibition. Readers who feel that suicide should be illegal even for those people who act alone should not be overly troubled by the issue of unequal access, since as I have shown, it applies to all laws. If, on the other hand, suicide is justly permitted because there is an important human interest in being able to end one's life, it follows that assisted suicide ought to be permitted as well. I have not claimed that there ought to be a criminal prohibition against every potentially harmful act involving two parties. There are many harms, either potential or actual, that one party can justly inflict on other with her consent, such as risky surgery that may extend the patient's life but may kill her, or surgery (such as the amputation of a limb) that will deprive the patient of an important capacity but is necessary for her to survive. I have not argued that such acts should be prohibited, because in these cases the harms involved are outweighed by the benefits, and the benefits are not dependent on the existence of an unjust social norm. Instead, I have argued that there is a case for prohibition when a serious harm is counterbalanced only by benefits that rely on social norms. If there is a good argument in favor of permitting a practice, it should be permitted for all, whether assistance is need or not. However, where a practice merits prohibition, a useful guide is that the prohibition should apply to the person who inflicts the harm rather than the person who suffers it.

Hard versus Soft Paternalism

The last of Feinberg's distinctions to be considered is between hard and soft paternalism. He writes: "Soft paternalism holds that the state has the right to prevent self-regarding harmful conduct (so far as it *looks* 'paternalistic') *when but only when* that conduct is substantially nonvoluntary, or when temporary intervention is necessary to establish whether it is voluntary or not."[39] Feinberg's contention is that soft paternalism is not paternalism at all. So, if my approach is a species of soft paternalism, once again it will not have to face antipaternalist charges. Despite possible appearances, however, my approach is not a species of soft paternalism.

My approach might appear to fall under the category of proscribing "substantially nonvoluntary" conduct as a result of my arguments about social construction. While it is true that social construction renders conduct *in some sense* nonvoluntary, that sense is not of the sort required for soft paternalism. The most relevant sense is that, as I have argued, people might harm themselves in a way that runs counter to their first-order autonomous choices but in line with their second-order choices: they might make a second-order choice to alienate their first-order autonomy. I proposed that it is misleading to describe such a choice as being fully, or first-order, autonomous. However, this argument does not seem to merit the soft paternalism label, since the nonvoluntary conduct that Feinberg and others have in mind involves

---

39. Ibid., 12; emphasis in the original.

things such as "ignorance, coercion, derangement, drugs"[40] rather than the conscious choice to suffer a disadvantage for a greater goal.[41]

The second sense in which my approach might appear to be a variety of soft paternalism would involve a misunderstanding. It might be suggested that, according to my arguments about the social construction of preferences, all conduct is nonvoluntary because all conduct is the result of socially formed preferences. If, as Cass Sunstein argues, "autonomy should refer . . . to decisions reached . . . without illegitimate or excessive constraints on the process of preference formation,"[42] and if social construction were to constitute such a constraint on preference formation, my approach might seem to legitimate *any* restrictions on *all* preferences, on the grounds that *no* preferences are autonomously reached. Phrasing my argument in this way would be to invoke a nightmarish totalitarianism, with the state able to intervene in any and all preferences—far removed from my more limited proposals. Such a formulation would also obscure the fact that, as I argued in Part One, I reject the idea that there is a true subject behind social construction, that behind socially constructed "nonvoluntary" conduct there lies atomistic, purely "voluntary" conduct. Social construction does not mysteriously obscure real interests and choices, but is the basic requirement of choice. As Danny Scoccia points out:

> An acceptable theory of autonomous desire should have the consequence that desires based on brainwashing, knee-jerk conformism, and an unreflective response to natural impulses are nonautonomous. . . . On the other hand, such a theory would also have the consequence that few of our desires are or ever could be autonomous, for it is obvious that we (or our wills) cause few if any of our desires. Since "autonomy" in the sense being considered here surely is achievable, an acceptable theory will not say that autonomously formed values are created by the agent.[43]

Thus it is not part of my argument to suggest that paternalism is justified if and because the choice to be overridden is based on faulty rea-

40. Ibid.
41. On the other hand, as I discuss in the "Loyalty" section of Chapter 7, this argument may well render my approach nonpaternalist in the same way as Arneson's dueling example.
42. Sunstein, "Preferences and Politics," 11.
43. Danny Scoccia, "Paternalism and Respect for Autonomy," 327–28.

soning or irrationality, and it is not part of my approach to suggest that the individual concerned *would* consent to the paternalistic action *if* she were fully rational.[44] As I emphasized in Chapter 5, self-harming practices can be a fully rational response to the prevailing options and social context. If social norms demand that a second-order goal entails a first-order sacrifice, then no failure of rationality is involved. What may be involved is injustice.

This is not to argue that cases of soft paternalism cannot be identified. Clearly, there can be cases where individuals' decision-making abilities are particularly compromised by the sorts of phenomena that Feinberg describes; and in such cases, I tend to agree with the soft paternalist line. However, I do not seek to justify or excuse my approach by labeling it as a species of soft paternalism, and therefore not really a paternalist at all. Instead, I have sought to argue that proscription in the circumstances I have outlined is itself a contribution to, perhaps even a requirement of, liberal justice.

To conclude this brief discussion of paternalism: I have argued that my proscriptive proposals may escape the charge of paternalism via Arneson's definition and his dueling example, but not through the route of soft paternalism. If my proposals are paternalistic, then, the potential evil of their paternalism is mitigated by the fact that my proposals are harm-preventing rather than benefit-promoting, so that many options are left intact; and the fact that they should, wherever possible, be applied to the "other" individual, the individual who harms, in two-party cases. These considerations were adduced in this chapter; the most important arguments in favor of my proposals, however, are found in the book as a whole.

Autonomy

Here I consider the extent to which my theory promotes autonomy, and what kind of autonomy it promotes. Some theorists have argued

---

44. This proposal is advanced by Dworkin, who argues that "we would be most likely to consent to paternalism in those instances in which it preserves and enhances for the individual his ability to rationally consider and carry out his own decisions" ("Paternalism," 81). Arneson criticizes Dworkin on the grounds that his proposal fails "to safeguard adequately the right of persons to choose and pursue life plans that deviate from maximal rationality" ("Mill versus Paternalism," 474). Because my proposals are not based on rationality, Arneson's criticism does not apply to them.

that paternalism is justified if and because it *enhances* autonomy. Thus Dworkin argues that paternalism should be justified by "a concern not just for the happiness or welfare, in some broad sense, of the individual but rather a concern for the autonomy and freedom of the person."[45] Autonomy is enhanced, for Dworkin, because paternalism should be used to satisfy the person's own rational desires, a formulation that I have rejected.

Similarly, Scoccia sets out three conditions under which paternalistic action does not violate autonomy:

> Interfering with a person's choices for his own good does not violate his autonomy if: (*a*) the person has highly autonomous desires, but the choice made does not accurately express those desires, and the person would consent to the interference if he were fully rational, or (*b*) the person has low autonomy desires, and the interference is necessary to preserve his potential to develop it later . . . [or] (*c*) the person has low autonomy desires, the interference would increase the autonomy of his desires (e.g., by removing an obstacle like neurosis or false consciousness to autonomous desire formation), and the person would not object to the interference if he were rational and had high autonomy desires.[46]

These strategies may be successful. Cases (b) and (c) resemble the soft paternalism just described, which is at least initially plausible (I have not considered it in detail). The most relevant to my approach, though, is case (a). One might argue that paternalism is justified if and when one of the individual's second-order autonomous goals is thereby supported, so that the individual's "highly autonomous desires" are better met.

Thus, in the case of Jenna Franklin's breast implants discussed in Chapter 5, one might argue as follows:

1. Franklin has a second-order autonomous desire to be famous. (This premise is derived from her own statements.)

45. Dworkin, "Paternalism," 81.
46. Scoccia, "Paternalism and Respect for Autonomy," 330–31.

2. If Franklin is to be famous, she must have breast implants. (This premise is also derived from her own statements. For the purposes of argument, assume it to be true.)

3. Therefore, banning breast implants thwarts Franklin's second order desire to be famous.

4. Franklin has a (separate) second-order autonomous desire to be healthy. (This premise is imputed to her—possibly as a rational being.)

5. Breast implants will damage her health. (Arguments supporting this premise were given in Chapter 5. For the purposes of argument, assume it to be true.)

6. Therefore, allowing breast implants thwarts Franklin's second-order desire to be healthy.

7. Therefore, either banning or allowing breast implants will thwart one of Franklin's second-order desires.

8. Therefore, it is not an argument against banning breast implants that to do so would be to overrule her second-order autonomy.

This argument is valid. However, there are two problems. First, the argument as it stands provides equal support for allowing or proscribing breast implants. It simply states that either will both harm and promote her second-order autonomy. Second, the balance may be tipped against proscription by the following consideration: the antipaternalist defender of autonomy might argue that it should be *Franklin,* not the state, who decides which of her second-order goals—health or fame—to choose. (Such an argument might invoke some idea of third-order autonomy, according to which one chooses which second-order goal to follow.)

We can respond to these two problems by highlighting another plausible feature of the case, which I posited earlier:

9. Franklin would prefer to be famous without breast implants, if that were possible.

If this premise is added, the balance is tipped in favor of prohibition. For, as I have argued, banning breast implants will have the beneficial effect that it cannot, by definition, be a requirement of fame that one have breast implants (for no one would have them and so, if the requirement persisted, no one could be famous).[47] It follows, then, that only with prohibition will Franklin be able to achieve both her second-order goals of fame and health. As discussed earlier, premise 9 means that my proposals would not be paternalistic on Arneson's definition; the purpose here is to show that they might also be construed as autonomy-maximizing.

It will not be a good general strategy, however, to attempt to justify my proposals on the grounds that they are autonomy-maximizing. There are three potential problems. First, there might be people for whom (the equivalent of) premise 4 does not apply. Such people can be described as having unusual—we might want to say irrational—second-order goals. Second, there might be people for whom (the equivalent of) premise 9 does not apply. These people can be described as having unusual or irrational first-order goals. In either case, paternalist proscription may well reduce their second- or first-order autonomy. Third, however, autonomy-maximization is a bad goal. In the rest of this section, I consider each of these considerations in turn.

"Irrational" or Unusual Second-Order Goals

The first case to be considered is those people who have unusual or irrational second-order goals. In the breast implant example, we might describe these people as those who have no desire to be in good health. Since this condition seems implausible and, almost uncontroversially, irrational, it is better to describe them more sympathetically as people who are able to rank their second-order goals and for whom health has a lower priority than another of their second-order goals (in the Franklin case, fame). To describe them even more sympathetically (and thus in a way that poses even more problems for my argument), we could

47. It is possible, of course, that it might still be a requirement of fame for a woman that she has large breasts, so that prohibition of breast implants prevents small-breasted women from achieving fame. This seems unlikely, for several reasons already detailed (for example, that breast implants create as much as respond to a widespread desire for large-breasted women). However, if the requirement of large breasts were to remain for some particular careers (such as some sorts of topless or underwear modeling), it seems no more problematic that small-breasted women would not have access to such careers than it seems problematic that clumsy people cannot be brain surgeons—or at least, if the large-breast requirement is unjust (perhaps because there is no real *need* to have large breasts to perform the relevant functions), the injustice ought to be resolved by removing the requirement rather than by implanting silicone into women's bodies.

describe them as those for whom the *risk* of bad health is of less importance than the achievement of other goals.

This final, most sympathetic phrasing suggests a possible disanal-
ogy between breast implants and FGM. The harms of breast implants
are, by and large, *risks* rather than certainties, whereas the harms of
FGM (one might argue) are certain to occur as an intrinsic part of the
procedure. Against the argument we might say that for consenting
adult women undergoing FGM in clinical conditions many of the
harms of FGM (infection, death) become risks, and other harms (the
loss of the clitoris) might be described as the very purpose of the procedure and not as harmful for the women involved. Moreover, the Institute of Medicine found that many of the side effects of breast implants,
such as capsular contracture, are more or less certain to occur over the
course of an implanted woman's life. However, in favor of the argument it must be stated that the removal of the clitoris remains harmful
in the sense of destroying a bodily function (sexual pleasure), and that
infibulation brings with it other certain harms which are not the purpose of the procedure (hindering urination, menstruation, and childbirth; increasing the risk of infection; and so on).

My proposals must, then, respond to the challenge that for some
people, the disvalue of the risk of bad health is outweighed by other
second-order autonomous goals. Indeed, this seems to be true of all of
us who willingly drive a car, eat fast food, and so on. Dworkin takes an
uncompromising line with many such people: "Consider a person who
knows the statistical data on the probability of being injured when not
wearing seat belts in an automobile and knows the types and gravity of
the various injuries. He also insists that the inconvenience attached to
fastening the belt every time he gets in and out of the car outweighs
for him the possible risks to himself. I am inclined in this case to think
that such a weighing is irrational."[48] In this example, however, the
charge of irrationality relies on the imbalance between the tiny cost of
fastening one's seat belt and the huge potential damage that can be
done to a person in a car accident. It may not be possible to make such
an overwhelmingly clear judgment in other cases. Nonetheless, this
balancing act—what Feinberg calls the "balancing strategy"[49]—is pre-

48. Dworkin, "Paternalism," 76–77.

49. "To say that the need to protect people from their own foolishness is always a 'good
and relevant reason' for coercive legislation, is not to say that it is in any given case a decisive
reason. Rather, it leaves open the possibility that in that case reasons of a quite different kind
weigh on the other side, and that those other reasons (including respect for personal auton-

cisely what is called for in my proposals. It will be necessary, with each individual practice, to consider its overall harms and risks against the weight of the competing considerations, so as to discern where the balance of reasons lie. In this respect my proposals are no different from any other theory of justified paternalism.

Where they are different, however, is in their claim that one of the considerations that must be taken into account is the fact (if it is a fact) that the benefits of the practice result only from a social norm. If the practice is worth following only because a social norm decrees that it regulates access to some benefit, that fact should, I have argued, weigh very strongly against the practice in question. I have also argued that both physical *and* status harm ought to be placed on the scales, in favor of proscription.

That having been said, I do not wish to argue that this approach can never undermine individuals' autonomy. It would undermine a person's autonomy in the case where proscription serves no second-order goal of hers, or serves only a goal which she ranks as less important, but does prevent her from achieving her actual, or more important, second-order goal. Thus if a woman (1) wanted breast implants in order to be famous, *and* (2) ranked the risks to her health below her desire to be famous, *and* (3) would become famous with breast implants, *and* (4) would not become famous *if and because* she was unable to have breast implants, then proscribing breast implants *would* undermine her second-order autonomy. This undermining would, in turn, be one objection to proscription. Taken in the context of my arguments throughout this book, and the extreme particularity of the case, the objection is not decisive. However, it ought to be acknowledged; I take seriously Isaiah Berlin's point:

> It is one thing to say that I may be coerced for my own good which I am too blind to see: this may, on occasion, be for my benefit; indeed it may enlarge the scope of my liberty. It is another to say that if it is my good, then I am not being coerced, for I have willed it, whether I know this or not, and am free (or "truly" free) even while my poor earthly body and fool-

omy) may in the circumstances have still greater weight. Thus, it is possible to defend legal paternalism, as we have defined it, while arguing against paternalistic legislation in particular cases. We can call this approach 'the balancing strategy.' The anti-paternalist has a heavier argumentative load to carry" (Feinberg, *Harm to Self*, 25; emphasis in the original).

ish mind bitterly reject it, and struggle against those who seek however benevolently to impose it, with the greatest desperation.[50]

"Irrational" or Unusual First-Order Goals

The second case to be considered is those people who have unusual or irrational first-order goals. In the breast implant example, we might describe these people as women who want breast implants in and of themselves. Regardless of social norms or any other second-order goal, they just want breast implants.

I dealt with this issue much earlier in the book. Following Foucault, I argued that it would be impossible for someone to want to undergo a practice *regardless* of social norms—unless, perhaps, that desire were one that made no sense in the context of social norms, such as cosmetic knee implants. What would be possible, however, would be for a woman actively to consider a practice that makes sense only in the context of social norms (such as breast implants) and make an autonomous decision to conform to the social norm. However, for such a woman to fit into the category of someone with an unusual first-order desire rather than a second-order desire, that woman must *either* want to have breast implants in themselves, not as a means to a higher second-order goal (such as beauty or self-esteem), *or* prefer breast implants above all other alternatives (counseling, feminist consciousness-raising, a padded bra) as a means to that higher goal. The first possibility is at least odd and at most implausible since, by definition, such a woman could provide us with no reason for her desire. The second is more plausible. Many of the women in Kathy Davis's study of cosmetic surgery felt that cosmetic surgery was their only option for acquiring self-esteem, since alternatives had failed.[51] For these women, however, cosmetic surgery is not their *preferred* option so much as (in their eyes) their *only* option. If other options were available (and proscription might increase the effectiveness of other options by lessening the force

50. Berlin, "Two Concepts of Liberty," 25. I do not attempt to define either autonomy or paternalism in such a way as to make it true by definition that my proposals either promote autonomy or are not paternalistic, as Scoccia and Arneson respectively seem to do. Arneson's strategy for dealing with paternalism seems to be to decide what sorts of paternalism are justified, and then to construct a definition of paternalism that excludes them. The result is that the phrase "paternalistically justifiable" becomes oxymoronic.

51. Davis, *Reshaping the Female Body.*

of certain appearance norms), it seems likely that these women might prefer it.

Nonetheless, once again, it is the case that *if* a woman does in fact want breast implants in and of themselves, or as her preferred means to a second-order goal, then proscribing breast implants *will* hinder her first-order autonomy. Again, this consideration is an objection to my proposals that, though indecisive, should be acknowledged.

The Limitations of Autonomy

I have accepted, then, that under certain circumstances for certain individuals my proposals will limit either first- or second-order autonomy. I have also accepted that this limitation is a relevant objection to my proposals. It is not, however, a decisive objection, because there is no reason to think that autonomy is the only value, or that it is the most important value in a way that rules out trading it off for other values, or that it ought to be maximized.

My arguments hitherto are supported by Steven Wall's arguments against the idea of autonomy-maximization. Wall argues that autonomy is a "distinctive character ideal" that has "intrinsic and instrumental value" and should have a "privileged position in a sound account of political morality."[52] These claims notwithstanding, Wall argues that autonomy does not justify antiperfectionism (which would scupper my approach) because autonomy-maximization is not a coherent goal. He points out that autonomy simply cannot be maximized, because it is measured along several dimensions, and maximizing autonomy on one dimension may conflict with maximizing it on another. The dimensions that Wall cites are, first, the number of autonomous people in a society and, second, the amount of autonomy each one has. To these dimensions we might add that a person's first-order autonomy can conflict with her second-order autonomy (as in the case of a woman who wants to remain in her cultural community but not undergo FGM), and that two second-order autonomous goals may conflict (fame and health in the breast implants example). If autonomy contains conflicting dimensions, it cannot be maximized.

Even if it were possible to maximize autonomy, though, the most important objection to the idea of autonomy-maximization is that au-

---

52. Steven Wall, *Liberalism, Perfectionism and Restraint*, 183.

tonomy should not be the sole consideration of liberal justice. As Wall puts it: "*Autonomy is not all that matters.* It is one, but only one, component of a fully good life. . . . Sometimes the pursuit of maximal autonomy will obstruct the pursuit of other goods, and sometimes these goods will contribute more to a person's life than the increased autonomy."[53] Autonomy is not the only value, and cannot be the only value in a liberal theory of justice, because *equality* and *well-being* are also central (liberal) values. We must value things other than autonomy, for otherwise there is no value in the things we might wish to be autonomous *about*. Autonomy would seem to be without purpose or worth.[54] I have argued throughout that concerns for equality, coupled with the theory of social construction, must lead to a modification of the liberal prioritization of choice and of some liberal accounts of autonomy. I have also argued that we must take some account of well-being, which I have discussed in terms of the absence of harm. This argument is supported by Simon Caney, who argues: "We would like to live valuable lives and wish to avoid shabby, boring and worthless conceptions of the good. . . . [Thus] citizens also have an interest in wellbeing."[55] It follows that autonomy cannot be the supreme value in a way that rules out trade-offs with other values.

Moreover, the goal of autonomy-maximization would have extreme or bizarre implications that liberals are not willing to accept. The distinction between first- and second-order autonomy shows that it is quite possible for an individual to choose a way of life but not choose all its elements. If we were to attempt to maximize autonomy, we would have to say that second-order ways of life should entail no constraints whatsoever on first-order choices. In other words, it would have to be possible for individuals to be priests without believing in the basic tenets of the Church, or to be academics without marking exams. If autonomy were truly to be maximized, it would have to be open to each individual to choose precisely which elements of their second-order goals to pursue and which to reject. The equality tribunal would have to be replaced with an autonomy tribunal, in which any individual could complain that a group or institution's rules breached their first-order autonomy. Such a tribunal would not, I take it, be attractive. Indeed, as

---

53. Ibid., 185; emphasis in the original.
54. See Will Kymlicka, *Liberalism, Community, and Culture*, 48–50.
55. Simon Caney, "Anti-perfectionism and Rawlsian Liberalism," 260.

Will Kymlicka points out, it would be "perverse" to think there is always more value in making more autonomous choices rather than fewer: "We don't suppose that someone who has made twenty marriage choices is in any way leading a more valuable life than someone who has no reason to question or revise their original choice."[56]

Enhancing Autonomy

The arguments of the previous sections should not, finally, be taken to imply that my approach has only negative effects on autonomy. On the contrary, there are several ways in which my proposals enhance individual autonomy, all of which have been discussed previously. So as to end on a positive note, I briefly summarize them here.

First, my proscriptive proposals enhance an individual's first- *and* second-order autonomy when they destroy a norm that conflicted with the individual's first-order autonomy, but with which she complied so as to achieve some second-order goal. Thus proscribing breast implants increases the autonomy of the woman who does not want breast implants in and of themselves but feels she has to have them so as to be famous (if, after proscription, she can become famous without implants).[57] If the woman would merely prefer not to have the breast implants if possible, then her first-order autonomy is enhanced; if breast implants conflict with another of her second-order goals (such as health) then her second-order autonomy is also enhanced.

Second, my proposal of the equality tribunal, outlined in Chapter 4, should only enhance autonomy. As I argued, the equality tribunal leaves individuals' autonomy to live unequal lives intact since it affects only the rules that are imposed on them from above, not those which they set themselves from within. A woman who autonomously wished to have an unequal say in divorce, for example, could simply decide not to petition for divorce unless her husband consented. For individuals without such an autonomous desire to be unequal, the equality tribunal is even clearer in its enhancement of autonomy. The aim of the

56. Kymlicka, *Liberalism, Community, and Culture*, 49.

57. Similar examples from earlier in the book are that a woman's first- and second-order autonomy are enhanced if she does not have to undergo FGM to become marriageable and Rachel's first- and second-order autonomy are enhanced if she does not have to smoke so as to find success in her career. In the latter case I have not argued for state proscription; I do think, however, that autonomy would be better if Rachel could interact informally with her boss over tea rather than cigarettes.

equality tribunal is to undermine the degree to which second-order goals require individuals (unequally and therefore unjustly) to alienate their first-order autonomy, so that individuals have more scope to choose for themselves which aspects of their second-order goals they uphold and which they reject. This scope is not absolute—the equality tribunal is not an autonomy tribunal—but it is much wider than at present.

7

LIBERAL PERFECTIONISM AND THE AUTONOMY OF RESTRICTED LIVES

Is it possible to follow a restricted life and still be autonomous? To put the question more precisely, is it possible to submit to a form of life that is laid down by one's culture or religion, and which allows for little or no individual decision-making, innovation, or control, and for this submission to be compatible with autonomy? In the previous chapter I argued that a concern for autonomy does not rule out all forms of paternalism—in part because it does not make sense to attempt to *maximize* autonomy. Nonetheless, autonomy remains a key liberal and feminist value, and so in this chapter I consider the liberal perfectionist attempt to protect or enhance autonomy while using the coercive powers of the state.[1]

In Chapter 5, I identified two different sorts of autonomy, which I labeled first- and second-order autonomy. First-order autonomy pertains when one leads a daily life of active questioning, following only those norms one actively endorses. Second-order autonomy occurs when one chooses one's overall way of life. Liberal theories differ in their understandings of the *priority* of each order of autonomy and the *relationship* that holds between them. In this chapter I endorse the liberal perfectionist claim that a life of autonomy is more valuable than one without, and therefore that such a life is worthy of state promotion, protection, or even enforcement. However, several prominent liberal perfectionists attempt to render restrictive culturally defined ways of life compatible with autonomy. They can do so only by making problematic philosophical arguments concerning the concept of autonomy, arguments that must be rejected in the light of social construction. Throughout this chapter, I illustrate my argument with the general

---

1. For an account of autonomy's value to feminism, see Friedman, *Autonomy, Gender, Politics*, 3.

case of convent life, and with specific testimonies from several nuns drawn from interviews by Mary Loudon. Other sorts of restrictive lives that might also be considered include military life; life in traditional and restrictive cultures, religions, or marriages; and the example beloved of political philosophers of selling oneself into slavery.

In Chapter 5, I argued that political liberals such as Martha Nussbaum prioritize second-order autonomy over first. In response to convent life, a political liberal would say that nuns may well lack first-order autonomy, but that this lack is unproblematic from the point of view of justice if the choice to enter the convent was second-order autonomous. It does not seem possible for liberal perfectionists such as Joseph Raz to accept that such lives lack any sort of autonomy, since a key part of the liberal perfectionist claim is the idea that, in liberal societies at least, autonomous lives are more valuable than nonautonomous ones. Indeed, Raz goes further, claiming that we can prosper in a liberal society "*only* if we can be successfully autonomous."[2] From this point of view, it seems that perfectionists must say one of two things about convent life and other lives that lack first-order autonomy. Perfectionists could agree with political liberals that such lives do indeed lack autonomy, but would then have to part company from political liberals and conclude that such lives are *pro tanto* undesirable or incompatible with well-being. Given the perfectionist desire to use the state to promote autonomy, such an approach would invite state prohibition, discouragement, or regulation of convent life. Such a policy would be entirely consistent, but perfectionists do not seem to want to endorse it. Raz speaks approvingly or at least uncritically of monastic life, and Steven Wall explicitly endorses it, as we shall see shortly.

If convent life is to be acceptable from the perfectionist point of view, then, perfectionist liberals must follow a rather complex alternative. They must claim that convent life and other similarly restrictive lives are in fact compatible with autonomy. Thus, the reason that the perfectionist liberal state does not discourage or prohibit convent life is that convent life is autonomous life. At first sight, this strategy looks distinctly unpromising. After all, becoming a nun requires making two vows—poverty and chastity—that look at least potentially autonomy-reducing, and one vow—obedience—that seems paradigmatically so. How can a vow of lifelong obedience be compatible with autonomy?

2. Raz, *Morality of Freedom*, 394; emphasis added.

The simplest way in which one can argue that convent life is autonomous is by ignoring the idea of first-order autonomy and defining autonomy *per se* as second-order autonomy. Raz seems to follow this strategy when he claims "the autonomous life is discerned not by what
there is in it but by how it came to be."[3] This statement implies that
one might live a very restricted life in which one submits to others in
many areas and has no first-order autonomy (such as convent life),
without threatening Razian (second-order) autonomy. As long as the
life is the result of a conscious second-order autonomous decision, it
would be autonomous on Raz's terms. In Nozickian terms, autonomy
would be a historical concept, not an end-state concept.[4] In asking
whether a person is autonomous we should ask not "is she living an
autonomous kind of daily life?"—in other words, a life of first-order
autonomy—but rather "is she living her daily life as a result of prior
autonomous decision-making?"

This strategy, though internally consistent, is somewhat simplistic
on its own. After all, it seems to imply that autonomy is nothing more
than a once-in-a-lifetime choice; that one could be autonomous if one
had sold oneself into slavery or simply made some conscious decision
at some long-past point in one's life. Raz's theory is by no means simplistic, however. Behind this straightforward method of rendering convent life autonomous is a far more complex theory, one that combines
the two sorts of autonomy along with other concepts such as social
forms and loyalty. It is this more complex theory I want to examine. In
particular, I want to examine the idea that a second-order autonomous
choice of a way of life in some way *transforms* the first-order autonomy
status of that way of life. This idea of transformation is expressed by
Wall:

> People in modern western societies sometimes choose to lead
> relatively non-autonomous lives. For example, they join con-
> vents or enlist in the military for life. . . . Does this not show
> that one can live a fully good life in these societies without
> realizing the ideal of autonomy?
>
> This objection overlooks something important. People in
> modern western societies who lead relatively non-autonomous

3. Ibid., 370.
4. Robert Nozick, *Anarchy, State and Utopia.*

lives can choose to lead those lives. This fact is important, for *it transforms the nature of the way of life they engage in.* The self-conscious decision to become a nun or have a career in the military is not incompatible with the ideal of autonomy.[5]

The rest of the chapter considers whether the fact that one has chosen to live a nonautonomous life really does transform the nature of that life.

The Connection Between First- and Second-Order Autonomy

I have labeled a woman who wants to be a nun as having second- but not first-order autonomy. Her second-order autonomous choice to be a nun means that she will have to submit to the rules of the convent, and it is on that basis that I say she lacks first-order autonomy. But it might be objected that I have misdescribed the case. According to this objection, what it *means* to be a nun is that one must submit to the rules of the convent. A life as a nun is a life of obedience, to God and to the convent's rules and hierarchies. One cannot second-order autonomously choose to be a nun without, at the same time, autonomously choosing to submit to the rules of the convent. But, the objection continues, if one autonomously submits to the rules of the convent, one has first-order autonomy: in one's daily life, one is following rules that one actively wishes to follow, rather than following rules that are forced upon one or on which one does not reflect. It follows that the nun obeys the rules of the convent with first-order autonomy (albeit without negative freedom). Without these first-order desires, the second-order desire to live a life of obedience does not make sense. So, the objection concludes, one reason to defend a woman's autonomous choice to be a nun is that her choice does not involve alienating her first-order autonomy at all. It realizes that autonomy.

We now have two competing interpretations of convent life. According to the first interpretation, which I call the separation approach, the woman has second-order autonomy (because she has chosen to become a nun) but not first-order autonomy (because, once she is a nun, she must obey the rules of the convent, either without engaging in any

5. Wall, *Liberalism, Perfectionism and Restraint,* 170; emphasis added.

critical reflection on their value, or regardless of the results of such reflection). This is the approach taken by political liberals such as Nussbaum. According to the second interpretation, which I call the transformation approach, the woman has second-order autonomy (because she has chosen to become a nun) *and* first-order autonomy (because her choice to become a nun was in itself a choice to live a life of obedience, following the rules of the convent, so that the convent rules are *therefore* followed autonomously).

These alternative interpretations open up a number of complex issues, which will become clearer if we extend the example. At the time of the interviews which I quote from, Eva Heymann was a sixty-three-year-old nun in the Roman Catholic Holy Child Jesus Convent in Oxford Circus, London. She joined the convent at the age of thirty, and at that time there was a rule in the convent that incoming mail was read by the convent leaders. Eva recalls:

> The second year I was dead scared of being sent home. I really wanted to stay, even though it was a struggle and so much of our lifestyle was totally foreign to me.
>
> For instance, our letters were opened, and I thought that was horrendous. The incoming letters were read, and it smacked to me of the Nazi regime where letters and phone calls were intercepted. The whole business of somebody invading your life, your person, seemed to me appalling.[6]

Eva's discomfort concerning the rule is even more understandable when one learns that she converted to Catholicism from Judaism after fleeing from Nazi Germany as a child. So, is she autonomous? Even on the separation approach, once Eva is a nun she obeys many of the rules of the convent that confirm her commitment to Christ—rules governing times of prayer, for example—with both first- and second-order autonomy. Her second-order autonomy is realized because she wanted to be a nun; her first-order autonomy is realized because she has considered, questioned, and adopted wholeheartedly for herself the specific rules of prayer and the commitment to Christ.

What about Eva's submission to the rule that her incoming letters will be opened? Clearly, if this surveillance were part of what Eva val-

6. Mary Loudon, *Unveiled*, 64.

ued about being a nun, if she had thought about the rule and endorsed it, she would have first-order autonomy regarding it even on the separation approach. However, this is not her situation. Eva allows her letters to be opened and read simply so as to serve her second-order goal of being a nun, despite finding the rule unrelated to her religious motivations and beliefs and resonant of Nazi oppression. Nonetheless, she submits to the rule because, and to the extent that, it is a requirement of convent life. If she had been able, she would have remained in the convent without having her letters opened. Since there is a rule to the contrary, she submits to surveillance so as to be allowed to stay. Does she, then, submit with first-order autonomy?

According to the transformation approach, Eva does have first-order autonomy. On this interpretation, it is not possible to break down the rules of the convent and say that they have different implications for Eva's autonomy. The life of a nun must be considered as a whole, as a life of obedience to rules, regardless of the specific content of any individual rule. Surveillance of mail is a rule of the convent, part of what it means to be a nun, and so it is not possible for her to will autonomously to be a nun without at the same time autonomously willing that she submit to surveillance.

In effect, someone taking this transformation approach would deny the very possibility of any cases in which someone has second-order but not first-order autonomy.[7] Anyone with second-order autonomy would thereby have first-order autonomy with respect to all the norms that comprise the second-order goal. But this approach is problematic. First, it is conceptually impoverished. It ignores the philosophically coherent distinction between Eva's attitude to surveillance and her attitude to prayer, and does so in a way that flatly contradicts the definition of first-order autonomy. First-order autonomy, I argued, is when an individual lives a life in which one obeys only those rules that one endorses after reflection. If Eva's mail being opened counts as an instance of first-order autonomy, it undermines the meaningfulness of this definition, of the distinction between the two types of autonomy,

---

7. A trivial point in the name of precision: such a respondent would be denying the possibility of such cases only where the first-order choice is related to the second-order choice. One could still have second-order autonomy but lack first-order autonomy in an entirely unrelated matter. For example, a nun might have full autonomy as regards convent life but lack first-order autonomy with regard to her habit of biting her nails. In the discussion I am ignoring these kinds of cases and assuming that the two sorts of autonomy are related.

and of the distinction between how she feels about the surveillance and how she feels about committing herself to Christ.[8]

Note that at this point I am not making any normative claims about the relative importance of first-order autonomy. I am simply arguing that, in relation to her mail, Eva does not have it. Political liberals must agree. For political liberals, as we have seen, autonomy is valued in the political sphere partly because it is compatible with people being nonautonomous in private. But the transformation argument that we are considering effectively says that cases of freely chosen nonautonomous lives do not exist, as a matter of conceptual impossibility. Political liberals cannot follow this line of reasoning; to do so would mean that there can be no such thing as a freely chosen nonautonomous life. Imposing autonomy in the political sphere effectively imposes it in all spheres. However, such an outcome is not problematic for liberal perfectionists; indeed, that is their desired goal.

Raz and the Social Forms Thesis

Turn to liberal perfectionism, then, and to Raz's version of it in particular. A useful outline of Raz's theory is provided by David McCabe, and I largely follow his interpretation. According to McCabe, Raz's theory combines three "strategies of defense" of liberalism: "autonomy, value pluralism, and the appeal to social practices."[9] These strategies, which other theorists have viewed as competing, are combined in Raz's account. First, Raz argues that political arrangements must be judged according to their contribution to human well-being. Well-being, in turn, is determined by success in valuable comprehensive goals. These valuable goals "are determined by the social forms of one's commu-

8. Note that it remains possible for one to have first-order autonomy and regret, at one level, one's lack of negative freedom. For example, it might be convenient for me to be able to use my mobile phone while I am in the British Library, for then I could take important calls without having to interrupt my work by leaving the reading room. In this sense I regret the lack of negative freedom imposed on me by the library's rule forbidding mobile phones. However, I would be very annoyed if others made phone calls in the library. Moreover, I see that it would be unfair if only I were allowed to use my phone. So, although it would be far more convenient for me to disobey the rule, I obey willingly in the sense that I endorse the rule. The rule reduces my liberty but not my first-order autonomy.

9. David McCabe, "Joseph Raz and the Contextual Argument for Liberal Perfectionism," 493.

nity."[10] Thus the first strategy, the appeal to social practices, has been deployed. The second, autonomy, comes in next. Raz argues that "the social forms characterizing contemporary liberal states reflect the pervasiveness of autonomy and that success in the goals these forms make available requires the effective exercise of autonomy."[11] Finally, Raz argues that autonomy requires value pluralism. In order to be autonomous, one must have a range of valuable options to choose from. These options must not be in a clear, objective hierarchy, for then there would be no place for meaningful individual autonomous choice; individuals would simply have to adopt the best option. Instead, for autonomy to be meaningful, value pluralism must hold: different options must be equally, or incommensurably, valuable.[12]

This, then, is the basic structure of Raz's theory. The most relevant parts of it are the appeal to autonomy and the appeal to social practices, or what McCabe calls the social forms thesis.[13] The social forms thesis states that an individual can have a comprehensive goal of the sort that is required for second-order autonomous choice "only if it is based on existing social forms, i.e. on forms of behavior which are in fact widely practiced in the society." And since "success in one's comprehensive goals is among the most important elements of one's well-being," it follows that "a person's well-being depends to a large extent on success in *socially defined and determined* pursuits and activities."[14]

The problem at this stage is how we should understand the force of the social forms thesis. At one extreme, it could merely be the weak and trivial claim that individuals cannot invent comprehensive goals from nothing and with no social background. They cannot develop the necessary skills for living, or invent meaningful ways of life, without an upbringing in some sort of society. A baby abandoned on a desert island and kept alive by machines cannot develop the comprehensive goals necessary for well-being. As a trivial claim, this is probably true but certainly uninteresting, and it seems unlikely that this is Raz's intention. At the other extreme lies the claim that we cannot access the comprehensive goals necessary for well-being unless we accept spe-

10. Ibid., 498.
11. Ibid.
12. Ibid., 500.
13. Ibid., 497ff. Raz outlines the social forms thesis on pages 307–13 of *Morality of Freedom*, and again in his essay on multiculturalism in *Ethics and the Public Domain*.
14. Raz, *Morality of Freedom*, 308–9; emphasis added.

cific, developed, and particular cultural ways of life in their entirety: a claim that seems to prevent any exercise of autonomy whatsoever and seems as unlikely as its opposite. Between these unappealing extremes lies a wide range of complex alternatives that do have textual support.

Consider, for example, the following passage:

> A comprehensive goal may be based on a social form in being a simple instance of it [such as an] ordinary conventional marriage. . . . [But m]any marriages, perhaps all, are not that conventional. They are based on a shared perception of a social form while deviating from it in some respects. They are deviations on a common theme, and they can typically be that because the social form itself recognizes the existence of variations, or even their importance. A couple may evolve an "open" marriage even though this form is unknown to their society. But an open marriage is a relation combining elements of a conventional marriage and of a sexual pursuit which is kept free of emotional involvement. It is a combination of elements of two socially recognizable forms. The thesis that comprehensive goals are inevitably based on socially existing forms is meant to be consistent with experimentation, and with variations on a common theme and the like. It is no more possible to delimit in advance the range of deviations which still count as based on a social form than it is to delimit the possible relations between the literal and metaphorical use of an expression.[15]

In this passage, three alternatives can be discerned. According to the first, deviations in social forms are allowed if, perhaps only if, the social form itself allows for them. This option is expressed in Raz's claim that unconventional marriages can exist "because the social form itself recognizes the existence of variations." The second option is that deviations from a social form are possible if they are drawn from other recognized social forms (but not if they come from elsewhere, perhaps from individual experimentation). This option is expressed in Raz's claims that open marriage is possible because it is "a combination of elements of two socially recognizable forms." The third option is that

15. Ibid., 309.

deviations from social forms are allowed according to the autonomous choice of the individual concerned: she is free to pick and choose, to innovate, and to corrupt existing forms at will. This option might be supported by Raz's claim that the social forms thesis is compatible with "experimentation," and that it is not possible "to delimit in advance the range of deviations which still count as based on a social form."

It is, of course, possible to endorse all three options: to state that deviations from social forms are allowed or possible in any of the three ways. But such a position leaves little left of the social forms thesis except the trivial claim that humans need social interaction. As well as being trivial, this claim will not do the necessary work of justifying autonomy in relation to its connection with the social forms of liberal societies. If social forms are nothing more than some basic social context, there is no reason to protect or even notice the fact that liberal social contexts include autonomy. Indeed, this problem arises even if we adopt only the third option: that individuals may autonomously deviate from social forms as they please. If individual deviation from social forms is possible, then we have the principle of autonomy stated as a prior value, not as one dependent on the social forms of liberal societies. For individuals' ability to deviate from the social forms depends not on anything emanating from the social forms but from the value of deviation, of autonomy, itself.

We are left, then, with the first and second options: deviations may occur if, perhaps only if, the social form in question allows for them, or the idea that deviations may occur if they are drawn from alternative social forms. To take the second option first, the question that arises is whether these alternative social forms may be drawn from societies other than our own, a question that Raz raises but does not answer. McCabe argues that while it is in fact possible for individuals to draw on social forms from outside their own societies, this possibility ultimately undermines the social forms thesis and Raz's defense of autonomy. As McCabe puts it: "If individuals can pursue goals connected to the social forms of groups and cultures to which they do not belong, this undermines the connection, central to Raz's case for the special importance of autonomy in liberal societies, between social forms and the distinct character of one's own society."[16] There would be no reason to think that people living in liberal societies need autonomy, that they

---

16. McCabe, "Joseph Raz and the Contextual Argument," 510.

can succeed in comprehensive goals only via autonomy, or that the perfectionist defense of autonomy is based on its contextual, social value in liberal societies rather than on some more controversial account of the universal value of autonomy. In other words, if Raz is to accept that deviation in social forms can take place using forms from alternative cultures, his perfectionist defense of autonomy will have to be more far-reaching and universalist than he seems to want.[17]

The remaining option, then, is that deviation from social forms is permitted only when the social forms themselves allow for that deviation. This understanding is compatible with Raz's claim that autonomy is an important part of the social forms of liberal societies. Because liberal social forms contain within themselves the requirement that they be followed autonomously, it follows that one cannot succeed in a liberal society without being autonomous. Hence Raz writes: "Since we live in a society whose social forms are to a considerable extent based on individual choice, and since our options are limited by what is available in our society, we can prosper in it only if we can be successfully autonomous."[18]

We are now in a position to consider how Raz would respond to the case of Eva the nun. In the light of the quotation just given, it seems that Raz must reject the possibility of succeeding as a nun in a liberal society unless one can do so autonomously. In other words, Eva can successfully fulfill the comprehensive goal of being a nun within a liberal society *only if* she does so with full first-order autonomy, critically evaluating convent rules and rejecting those she finds wanting, such as the mail surveillance. However, this conclusion contradicts the conclusion that we reached concerning the possibility of deviation from social forms: that such deviation is acceptable only if the social form itself permits it. In other words, the existence of social forms that do not permit autonomous deviations (such as convent life) cause problems when they are found within liberal societies. The specific social form of convent life forbids first-order autonomy, whereas the broader social form of the liberal society requires it. The dictates of one social

17. See ibid., 494–95. McCabe considers the question of whether Raz holds a contextual view of autonomy, according to which autonomy is valuable only in certain social contexts, or a transcendent view, according to which autonomy is valuable for all people and places, and writes: "Raz's apparent slippage between autonomy's transcendent and contextual value can be maddening" (494 n. 3).

18. Raz, *Morality of Freedom*, 394.

form will have to be abandoned: either the liberal requirement that individuals are autonomous will have to be abandoned in favor of the convent requirement that individuals are not, or the convent requirement that individuals are obedient will have to be abandoned in favor of the liberal requirement of autonomy. Either option is controversial.

One way out of this dilemma is to attempt to retain *both* liberal autonomy *and* convent life by using the transformation approach outlined earlier and suggested by Wall: asserting that the second-order autonomous choice of a way of life *entails* first-order autonomy regarding the components of that way of life. This strategy would enable Raz to maintain the social forms thesis as regards both liberal societies and convent life. The social form of the convent requires obedience, so Eva must be obedient and allow her letters to be read. However, the social form of the liberal society requires autonomy, so Eva must allow them to be read autonomously. Her second-order choice to be a nun must become the first-order choice to submit to surveillance. Raz's discussion of the concept of loyalty lends support to the idea that he supports this strategy.

Loyalty

In order to maintain the social forms thesis concerning both liberal and convent life, Raz introduces the concept of *loyalty* as crucial to autonomy. This concept allows him to assimilate first- and second-order autonomy. For Raz, autonomy does not depend on the ability to change one's mind about one's way of life, or on the likelihood that one will do so by a continuing reassessment of ends. Raz advocates commitment to a way of life once it has been chosen. He argues that autonomy requires what he terms integrity or loyalty, stating: "To be autonomous one must identify with one's choices, and one must be loyal to them."[19] Raz describes loyalty as follows: "Our projects and relationships depend on the form they acquire through social conventions. This means, as we saw, that they depend on complex patterns of expectations, on the symbolic significance of various actions, and in general on remaining loyal, within the recognized limits set for improvisation and change, to their basic shape. Failure to do so is failure to

19. Ibid., 382.

succeed, or even to engage, in the pursuits one has set oneself to make the content of one's life."[20] On the one hand, Raz makes further reference to the social forms thesis: the social formation of preferences and the social meanings of practices. It is only within certain contexts that certain projects make sense and certain character traits are developed. But, on the other hand, the passage implies that there is no need to pay close attention to the nature of those social meanings, and prioritize those which are emancipatory over those which are oppressive. Rather than using our autonomy to question the practices recommended to us by our culture, the passage implies that we must protect our autonomy by adhering to those practices, remaining loyal to them. If we do not, we fail both to "succeed" and, in consequence, to be autonomous.

This is a counterintuitive approach. Autonomy implies that we do not commit unquestioningly to the social meanings presented to us. Rather, we should question those meanings and practices, and reject those which we find wanting. We should reject some social meanings and practices because we find them normatively unacceptable, others simply because we discover, in the course of adhering to them, that they are not best suited to us.

In order to allow for this possibility, Raz is quick to explain that the liberal nature of society means that loyalty is not required of everyone. It is required only of those who have chosen a social form that demands loyalty. In other words, as we have already seen, deviations from social forms are allowed if and only if the social form in question allows for them:

> Here another warning may be in place against thinking that the previous remarks embrace a rigid, planned life, lacking spontaneity and hostile to the possibility of changing one's mind and dropping the pursuit to embrace another. Nothing is further from the truth. While some pursuits, e.g. various forms of monastic life, involve complete advance commitment to a very regimented and routine style of living, most are not of this kind. . . . An autonomous person is free to choose pursuits which are more short-term, less comprehensive in na-

20. Ibid., 383.

ture, and which maximize opportunities for change and variety.

Once all that has been taken as read it remains the case that every pursuit has its form, according to which certain modes of behavior are disloyal to it, incompatible with dedication to it. These are the ones which signify more than a change of heart. They may come of that but they are, if persisted in, the marks of failure.[21]

If we are anxious to avoid failure, then, and if we cannot be certain that we will stick to a chosen way of life, we had better make sure that we choose one which does not demand commitment. If we do choose such ways of life, we can protect our autonomy only by sticking to them and adhering to all of their ingredients.

The problem with this argument is not Raz's assertion that abandoning some ways of life represents failure: clearly, if a nun leaves a convent, she has failed at being a nun. The problem is with Raz's equation of failure to fulfill certain goals with a failure of autonomy as such. For people who choose ways of life that demand commitment, autonomy becomes a once-in-a-lifetime affair: it depends not on the sort of life which they are living, or on their current attitude toward it and their ability to claim current authorship of it, but on whether they have, at some time in the past, consciously chosen or accepted their way of life. The fact that life may be restrictive, or may turn out to contradict the individual's fundamental beliefs, cannot be taken into account.

Consider nun Eva Heymann's thoughts about the Roman Catholic Church's attitude to homosexuality. This is an issue on which she has strong feelings, in part because she works with people who suffer from HIV and AIDS, many of whom are homosexual. She says:

> What never ceases to amaze me is the quality of love which many gay couples have for each other, and this is what makes me so angry about the stance of the Church. It *really* makes me angry. The phrase of the early Church, "See how these Christians love one another," is what I see, whether they're Christians or not in the formal sense. It's such an example to

21. Ibid., 384.

> a judgmental Church. . . . If I were challenged on this point—as I am sometimes—I hope I would have the courage of my convictions. I hope I would not be pushed to make a decision about whether to remain a member of the Roman Catholic Church with the views I have about homosexuality, because then in conscience I know I might have to make a decision which may or may not keep me within the institution. I *hope* it would never come to that.[22]

Eva hopes that she would not be made to choose between continued membership in the Church and the convent and her convictions on homosexuality. However, she implies that, if she were forced to choose, she would remain true to her convictions and leave the convent. Regardless of whether one agrees with her views on this issue, and regardless of whether leaving the Church and convent would mean that she had failed as a nun (for in one sense it clearly would), it seems difficult to say that she would not be acting autonomously. She may lack autonomy by being forced to choose, but Raz's views on loyalty seem to imply something further: that she would be nonautonomous if and only if she were to make the choice to leave. For, since convent life is life in which one must make a complete commitment to permanent membership and permanent obedience (like the monastic life to which Raz specifically refers), loyalty to that life requires that one neither questions nor leaves it. Loyalty this may well be, but loyalty in this sense seems incompatible with autonomy.

The issue at stake is the following. If an individual second-order autonomously chooses a comprehensive goal, knowing that powerful others, traditions, or social norms dictate that that comprehensive goal has certain ingredients, does it thereby follow that the individual in question can be said to have first-order autonomously chosen those ingredients? For Raz, it seems the answer must be "yes": second-order autonomous choice of a comprehensive goal must imply first-order autonomous choice of the individual practices that are part of that comprehensive goal, unless the goal itself allows for deviation. For if second-order autonomy is the choice of a comprehensive goal, and if a comprehensive goal is defined by Raz as a *socially defined* set of pursuits and activities, it follows that one cannot autonomously choose a sec-

---

22. Loudon, *Unveiled*, 81; emphasis in the original.

ond-order comprehensive goal that does not allow for deviation without *thereby* choosing the pursuits and activities that, according to social norms, define it. In other words, if Eva is to fulfill her second-order goal of being a nun, she must fulfill it in the manner in which it is defined by her social context. Since being a nun is a social form that does not allow for deviation, that means submitting to the rule that her letters be opened, and denouncing homosexuality as a sin. If she rejects these requirements, she is not conforming to social definitions and is not in fact a nun at all. She cannot be autonomous without submitting to surveillance and condemning homosexuality, because an autonomous desire to be a nun entails an autonomous desire to be obedient.

This strategy, the transformation approach, enables Raz to maintain the social forms thesis, the value of autonomy, and the possibility of individuals leading lives of obedience and advance commitments. Convent life does not have to be rejected as antithetical to autonomy. It can be embraced as part of that ideal, since an individual who chooses convent life can be understood as *maintaining* her autonomy.

The idea that second-order autonomous choice implies first-order autonomy is, then, a central part of the social forms thesis. But this strategy of transforming second-order autonomy into first-order autonomy is problematic in two ways. First, it is conceptually impoverished. People certainly can choose and endorse ways of life without endorsing every aspect of them. This feature is familiar to us all—we might autonomously choose our careers and yet not choose the hours we work,[23] or autonomously choose our religion and yet not endorse every tenet or religious leader. Second, the transformation of second-order autonomy into first-order autonomy is normatively impoverished, for it condemns individuals to accepting the interpretations of group leaders or

---

23. There clearly are some ingredients of a comprehensive goal that are necessary to that goal. It would not make much sense, for example, for a presenter of BBC Radio 4's breakfast-time *Today* program to say that she had autonomously chosen to present the program but had not autonomously chosen to get up extremely early, for it is an essential ingredient of that program that it is broadcast early in the morning. It is quite simply impossible to present a live breakfast-time program without rising early, and so the choice to be the presenter does seem to *imply* the choice to get up early. On the other hand, as the proponents of family-friendly and flexible working hours have long argued, it is not essential to many jobs that they be performed in traditional office hours. If this is the case, it is entirely possible to make the second-order autonomous choice to be a civil servant, for example, without at the same time making the first-order autonomous choice to work in an office from 9 a.m. to 6 p.m. Monday through Friday.

other entrenched interests as to the true meaning of their social form. If the social forms thesis were correct, there would be no grounds for reform of problematic, inegalitarian, or unjust ingredients, since, in endorsing the relevant comprehensive goal or social form writ large, individuals would be deemed to have autonomously chosen its socially defined ingredients. This result sits uneasily with liberal egalitarianism and, ultimately, with Raz's own normative commitments, since Raz does argue in favor of the cultural reform in the direction of liberalism. Something, then, has to give.

Indeed, it seems likely that many of the nuns interviewed in Loudon's book would not be happy with this normative conclusion, since they do express disagreement with the Church or certain rules of the convent. Several of the nuns feel that women should be able to be priests, for example.[24] Eva says:

> I just hope I live long enough to see the ordination of women. It makes such enormous sense to me. I feel equally strongly on the marriage of clergy in the Catholic church. . . . I remember watching the film of the installation of the first woman bishop, and it was a deeply moving experience. It filled me with enormous sadness that this is not a universal practice, particularly in terms of black women in the Church: the Church is still so white. So for me, being a woman or being black are not separate issues; they're both part of the whole issue of allowing God's creativity in the diversity of color, race, sex to be the Church. It's not for us to decide who we want to choose out of that medley of creativity. So I would campaign for the ordination of women.[25]

It is not only Eva, living as she does in an apostolic convent (one in which the nuns leave the convent to engage in community work) who has such progressive—one might even say heretical—views. Barbara

24. The fact that women cannot be priests also lessens the extent to which nuns can be thought of as autonomous, since it means that a woman who has a religious calling can fulfill it only by becoming a nun. A man who has a religious calling can follow it either by becoming a monk or by becoming a priest, but a woman is denied this choice. Thus we could describe a nun who would have preferred to become a priest as lacking first-order autonomy: she might have chosen to follow a religious life, but she was unable to choose how to follow it. I am grateful to Andrew Lewis for observations on this point.

25. Loudon, *Unveiled*, 78.

Anne, the member of a mixed apostolic and contemplative order in Oxfordshire, says:

> I think that the Church needs women who are able to be as fully functioning within the Church as men. I certainly don't think sex and gender should be determining factors in terms of ministry, and I sense a crisis in the priesthood, which is reflected in the kind of arguments men use to say that women should not be ordained. I feel strongly about it because the arguments say much more about the inadequate understanding of the priesthood than about the ordination, or lack of ordination, of women. So I think it's the priesthood that's in question rather than whether women should or shouldn't be ordained.
>
> Tradition is important, but tradition is not God.[26]

One of the few expressions of support for the Catholic ban on women priests in Loudon's collection of interviews comes from Angela Thérèse, a thirty-nine-year-old member of the enclosed Roman Catholic Carmelite Community in Darlington. Surprisingly, however, even she does not explain her opposition by saying that, as a nun, she must obey the rules laid down by the Vatican and her own convent. Instead she gives her own idiosyncratic explanation:

> The priesthood? No! Absolutely not! Absolutely not, no; anathema to me. It just seems totally wrong. The whole concept seems weird to me, the woman priesthood, I mean. I can't explain why, but I'll give you an example instead.
>
> We have an ecumenical service here every year, and a couple of years back there was a lady Methodist minister. She was an absolutely lovely person and she was great in the parlour and all that, but when I saw her trudging into the sanctuary, well I'm afraid most of us—I can't explain it, but it just does something to me, it's just weird. It's a butch image almost, with a dog collar and everything. It just has a strange effect on me. Ugh. No thanks.[27]

26. Ibid., 237.
27. Ibid., 39.

And yet even Angela Thérèse, with her traditional views on the male priesthood, does not hold that tradition and authority should be the guiding forces of convent life. She argues that convents in her Carmelite order, which Loudon describes as "the strictest of the female orders,"[28] must update and renew themselves so as to "make it acceptable to somebody of our day and age."[29] An example she gives of such renewal is the vow of obedience itself:

> Obedience is if one knows that one should be in a certain place at a certain time right through the day, which is why it is freeing rather than something which ties you up in knots. In days gone by, it was blind obedience, in the sense that even if the Prioress gave you three or four conflicting jobs to do you wouldn't have questioned it; you would have said "Yes, Mother." So there's much more of a personal responsibility angle that wasn't there before. And we have dropped the term "Mother" now, incidentally, [as the result of] a community vote round about 1984, 1985.[30]

What do these testimonies show us? Well, on the one hand they lend support to several of Raz's claims. Angela Thérèse's argument that her convent must update itself seems to support Raz's idea that one cannot be successful in a liberal society without autonomy—if the convent does not adapt to this fact, then it will fail. Indeed, the use of a community vote as one method of bringing about change surely epitomizes autonomy. But this case alerts us to the implausibility of saying that autonomy is nothing more than second-order autonomy, that autonomy is simply the choice of a way of life that is then determined by its own social form. For it surely makes sense to say that the nuns in Angela Thérèse's convent are more autonomous once the vow of obedience is interpreted in terms of personal responsibility rather than in terms of blind obedience, and that they are more autonomous if issues are decided by community vote rather than by the Mother Superior alone. If it does make sense to say that they are more autonomous after the changes, then it follows straightforwardly that they are less autonomous before the changes—*despite the fact that, before the changes*

28. Ibid., 9.
29. Ibid., 28.
30. Ibid., 35.

have been made, it is not part of the social form of being a nun that the nuns should have those sorts of autonomy. In other words, we can still identify first-order autonomy as something separate from second-order autonomy. This conclusion clearly supports the separation approach over the transformation approach.

Second, the fact that several of the nuns disagree with the position of the Church on issues such as the ordination of women priests and the acceptability of homosexuality shows that they would not be content with a philosophical approach that cast them as autonomous by definition. Despite the fact that all the nuns have taken a vow of obedience, and the fact that the Roman Catholic nuns are part of a church that is organized on the basis of hierarchy and authority, they still understand themselves as having legitimate disagreements with Church tenets. It follows, then, that their behavior is limited by rules with which they do not agree and which they do not endorse. Surely, then, it makes sense to describe them as lacking first-order autonomy in this regard.

If this argument is right, it does seem rather dangerous to take the line that the only autonomy worth the name is second-order autonomy, or the line that second-order autonomy thereby entails first-order autonomy (the transformation approach). Either line means that there can be no autonomy-based claim for changes in a way of life whose form is laid down by tradition and authority. A Catholic woman could not claim that her autonomy is restricted by the fact that she is unable to be ordained, and a nun could not claim that her autonomy is restricted by the facts that there are no community votes and that she must have her letters opened. Even if one thinks that Catholic women and nuns *should not* have autonomy regarding these issues, one must concede that they do not in fact have it.

My argument, then, may seem trivial and obviously true. It seems that way to me. But, for all its triviality, it has consequences for perfectionist arguments. If I am right that nuns, and other people living restricted lives that are laid down by authority and tradition, lack first-order autonomy, perfectionists must adjust their attitude toward them. They might adopt one of two strategies. First, they might agree with political liberals that nonautonomous ways of life are acceptable in certain circumstances (perhaps if they are chosen with second-order autonomy). This strategy would have several problems. It would undermine the distinctiveness of liberal perfectionism, along with its key claim that autonomous lives are better than nonautonomous lives. It would also mean rejecting Raz's claim that one cannot be successful in a liberal society without being autonomous, since autonomy is part of the social forms of liberalism.

Second, then, a perfectionist might argue that ways of life that lack first-order autonomy should be discouraged or even prohibited by the state. Such a strategy would be deeply controversial. It would also have philosophical implications. It could be justified by the abandonment of the social forms thesis and the defense of autonomy as a universal value. Or it could be philosophically justified by a refinement of the social forms thesis: the abandonment of the loyalty thesis, and the abandonment of the idea that individuals ought to participate in recognized ways of life with certain determinate structures. The only relevant social form would be the social form of autonomy itself, so that individuals would be able to—and indeed could flourish only if they did—mix and match and hybridize traditions and ways of life.

An Alternative Formulation

Liberal feminist Marilyn Friedman has a different strategy for dealing with restrictive lives. Friedman's strategy is to distinguish two types of autonomy and claim that only one is necessary for autonomy in general to exist. In this respect, her approach is similar to the transformation approach discussed so far. However, the two types of autonomy are not clearly defined.

Friedman's distinction is between substantive and content-neutral autonomy, and it is content-neutral autonomy that she favors. Content-neutral autonomy is very similar to second-order autonomy since it is concerned with "the manner in which [an individual] reaches and makes her choices. . . . The substance of her choices and commitments does not matter."[31] This definition leads Friedman to conclude that convent life is compatible with autonomy: "Someone can autonomously give up her own future autonomy, for example, by entering a religious order requiring unconditional obedience to church authority. She will become nonautonomous in her behavior after making and adhering to that sort of choice, but this does not mean that she was

---

31. Friedman, *Autonomy, Gender, Politics*, 19.

nonautonomous when first making the choice."[32] So far, Friedman's account looks very similar to Nussbaum's political liberal account discussed in Chapter 5, in that Friedman accepts that convent life is nonautonomous (in my terms, that it lacks first-order autonomy) but exonerates it so far as it was entered into with second-order/content-neutral autonomy.

However, Friedman's "substantive autonomy" is not the same as first-order autonomy. Substantive autonomy has features of both first- and second-order autonomy. Thus Friedman states that substantive autonomy (but not content-neutral autonomy) is "stable and enduring,"[33] since "someone choosing subservience would not be autonomous unless she did so for some higher nonsubordinate purpose which continued to be her own purpose even in the condition of her servitude."[34] This definition implies that substantive autonomy is the same as content-neutral autonomy, except that the former must persist whereas the latter can be a once-in-a-lifetime matter. Friedman implies that someone who autonomously entered a convent at time t only to regret that decision at $t + 1$ *still has* content-neutral autonomy at time $t + 1$ (even though she lacks substantive autonomy). This aspect of Friedman's account is closer to Raz's endorsement of loyalty than Nussbaum's prioritization of second-order autonomy; and since Friedman prioritizes content-neutral autonomy, her account is open to the objections raised against the requirement of loyalty.

Another similarity between Friedman and Raz is that Friedman attempts a version of the transformation strategy. For Raz, this consisted of the claim that a second-order choice of a way of life (e.g., to enter a convent) thereby transforms the nature of that way of life into one that is first-order autonomous, or autonomous in general. For Friedman, the transformation is in the other direction. She claims that a concern for substantive autonomy is, insofar as it is defensible, a concern for content-neutral autonomy. It is therefore preferable to prioritize content-neutral autonomy. This argument runs as follows:

> A substantive conception requires someone to be committed to autonomy itself as a value. . . . What exactly should someone be committed to when she is committed to autonomy as a

32. Ibid.
33. Ibid., 20.
34. Ibid., 19.

value? . . . She wants to be able to reflect on and discern her own values and concerns without manipulation or coercion and to be able to act accordingly and with some capacity to persist in doing so in the face of opposition from others. This commitment is a commitment to nothing other than *content-neutral* autonomy! . . . A substantive account would seem to imply, in its very own terms, that content-neutral autonomy is sufficient to count as genuine autonomy.[35]

However, this argument is inconsistent with the definition of content-neutral autonomy that Friedman gives. As we have seen, Friedman argues that a condition of servitude is compatible with autonomy even if it is no longer chosen or endorsed by the individual concerned. Content-neutral autonomy therefore becomes a once-in-a-lifetime affair for those who choose restricted lives. But if an individual is living a life of servitude that she no longer endorses, then it is *not the case* that she will "be able to reflect on and discern her own values and concerns without manipulation or coercion and to be able to act accordingly and with some capacity *to persist in doing so* in the face of opposition from others."[36] A person who cares about these capacities will not, therefore be happy with content-neutral autonomy.

The problem with Friedman's account is that there is a conceptual lacuna between the concepts of substantive and content-neutral autonomy, a lacuna which is filled by the concept of first-order autonomy that Friedman does not use. Her concept of substantive autonomy requires that individuals' choices "avoid conflicting in their *content* with the ideal of autonomy"; that an individual actively "aims to pursue" autonomy; and that a commitment to one's own substantive autonomy requires "valu[ing] my very valuing of my own activity of reflecting on my deeper concerns and acting accordingly."[37] These stipulations imply that it is never possible to be substantively autonomous while serving anyone else even for a moment, and that one's reason for valuing autonomy must be the value of autonomy in and of itself, not the goals which one uses one's autonomy to pursue. Friedman is right to suggest that such stipulations are not requirements of more defensible forms of autonomy. But it is important to note that they are not re-

35. Ibid., 21.
36. Ibid., emphasis added.
37. Ibid., 20–21, emphasis in the original.

quirements of first-order autonomy, and so substantive autonomy and first-order autonomy are not the same. Friedman has no correlative concept to first-order autonomy, and so her account provides insufficient space for the considerable value of being permanently able to question and separately endorse or reject the various ingredients of a way of life.

Perfectionism and Autonomy

Both Raz and Friedman, in their different ways, provide insufficient room for first-order autonomy—for questioning, reacting against, or reforming the social norms that constrain people, particularly those which are unequal and unjust—conceived of as separate from, not a necessary side effect of, second-order autonomy. Friedman's conceptual framework leads her to identify two forms of autonomy that are rather polarized. Neither captures what is of value in first-order autonomy, and so Friedman is compelled to endorse only the most limited version of autonomy. Raz attempts to package first-order autonomy with second-order autonomy but in doing so he too misses the distinctive value of the former.

The question of the compatibility of perfectionism and autonomy is one that exercises all liberal perfectionists. As liberals, they are keen to avoid the implication that perfectionism leaves no room for individual choice and freedom. Raz, Hurka, Sher, and Wall all devote considerable space to showing that perfectionism does leave room for autonomy. Two main strategies are used. First, the perfection for which liberal perfectionism aims may be defined as autonomy: the claim might be that the best possible life is one that is autonomous, or perhaps even maximally autonomous. This strategy has two main problems: first, how to distinguish perfectionism from other kinds of liberalism by giving autonomy some substantive meaning that is missing in alternative accounts but which does not controversially rule out things such as convent life; and, second, the fact that autonomy cannot be the only perfectionist value, since if it were, there would be nothing of value that people could autonomously choose and autonomy would have no real purpose.[38] These problems mean that few perfectionists adopt the

---

38. Thomas Hurka, *Perfectionism*, 148–52; Sher, *Beyond Neutrality*, 50, 57ff.

first strategy of defining autonomy as the perfection to be maximized by perfectionism.[39]

The second strategy, then, aims to solve these problems by showing that autonomy is one perfection or value among others, but that other perfections can only be fully realized if they are performed autonomously.[40] The problem with this second strategy, however, is that it seems to rule out perfectionist state action. For if other perfections or values are valuable only insofar as they are chosen autonomously, then state action aimed at overriding or directing people's choices will be self-defeating. To return to the example of breast implants: if it is more perfect or valuable for Jenna Franklin to respect her own body and gender equality by rejecting appearance norms that objectify women and not having breast implants, then, according to the second perfectionist strategy, that value will be lost if her lack of implants is the result of state coercion rather than autonomous choice. The issue, then, is how to retain the value of autonomy in a way that does not rule out perfectionist state action.

At this point, perfectionists might want to invoke a distinction between coercive and noncoercive perfectionist state action.[41] Whereas some perfectionist state action might be directly coercive, such as a ban on breast implants, other state action might leave more room for individual choice, such as an advertising campaign against breast implants. It is worth noting that perfectionists have worried about whether even noncoercive state action undermines the perfectionist idea that valuable things lose some or all of their value if they are not autonomously chosen. In an attempt to solve this problem, Sher uses the thesis of social construction to argue that individuals cannot be made autonomous simply by leaving them alone, since noninterference leaves social construction intact. As Sher puts it: "If all political arrangements do nonrationally shape preferences and provide incentives, a government will not *further* diminish autonomy simply by producing these effects intentionally."[42] Indeed, if the thesis of social construction is accepted, it cannot be an objection to noncoercive perfectionist action that it renders people's choices value-less. Consider

39. See Wall, *Liberalism, Perfectionism and Restraint*, 183–89, for more criticisms of the goal of maximizing autonomy, some of which were discussed in Chapter 6.

40. Hurka, *Perfectionism*, 152–53; Sher, *Beyond Neutrality*, 58–60.

41. See, for example, Caney, "Anti-perfectionism and Rawlsian Liberalism," 252.

42. Sher, *Beyond Neutrality*, 67; emphasis in the original.

the statement "X is influenced by Y to choose P." Y could be the state, but even if there is no deliberate state influence, the individual will still be influenced by nonstate forms of social construction. It therefore cannot be the case that the choice of P is valuable only if no Y exists. And, as Sher points out and as I have argued, perfectionist state action, if performed according to liberal principles, *benefits* the individuals whose actions are constrained by rendering their options more compatible with their own equality. Antiperfectionism is equivalent to arguing that the state should not take "(benign) advantage of a causal process that would occur anyhow,"[43] and this argument is rather perverse. If a process will occur anyhow, better that it does not undermine justice and equality.

It cannot be the case, then, that a putatively valuable practice or way of life loses its value if it is not autonomously chosen, where "autonomously chosen" means "chosen free from influence or encouragement." But a perfectionist might still want to argue that the value of a practice is lost if it is *coerced*. Sher's strategy for overcoming this problem is to argue that citizens may come to advocate the reasons for the state-imposed choice *after* it has been imposed on them and that if that happens, the choice becomes autonomous.[44] While such conversions may indeed occur, they do not undermine the fact that, at least at the point of state imposition, individual autonomy is overruled. My response is to argue that while it is *more* valuable if a practice is chosen, a practice need not lose its value entirely if it is coerced. The value will be lost in some cases but not in others. There may well be little value in a coerced apology or a coerced friendship, since apologies and friendship derive most (but not all) of their value from their freely given and sincere nature. But imagine that a violent husband is ordered by a court to attend a course on anger- and violence-management. While it would be more valuable if he had voluntarily attended such a course prior to the court's order, since he would be displaying a genuine wish to change his behavior (which might even make the course more likely to succeed), it does not follow that there is no value whatsoever in his attending the course by coercion. As long as the course has some effect in reducing his anger and violence, it has value

43. Ibid., 73.
44. Ibid., 63.

despite having been coerced. In such cases, it is more valuable that a practice is followed by coercion than that it is not followed at all.[45]

My approach differs in focus from contemporary liberal perfectionisms, then, in several ways. My focus is on proscription and discouragement (of injustice) rather than on prescription and encouragement (of perfection). More important, my approach recognizes social construction, but not the social forms thesis with its conservative and constraining normative implications. Finally, my approach recognizes the difference between first- and second-order autonomy (unlike perfectionism based on the social forms thesis)—and (unlike political liberalism) does not ignore the value of first-order autonomy.

---

45. Or, as in the breast implant example, it is sometimes more valuable that a practice is rejected *coercively* than not rejected at all.

CONCLUSION

Fashion followers are having collagen implanted into the soles of their feet and bones removed to wedge their tootsies into the latest Jimmy Choos or Manolo Blahniks. Some women have even requested toe removal, although most surgeons draw the line at this dramatic procedure. . . . Dr Sherman Nagler, who runs a practice in Houston, defends the wishes of these women: "Someone who's embarrassed or unwilling to wear an open shoe because their toe is crooked deserves the same respect and concern as someone who has a big bump on their nose and wants plastic surgery."

—AMY LAWSON, "Shoe Lovers Put Feet under the Knife"

Manolo Blahnik has a rare gift: he knows how to make women happy. Truly happy. Why else would a heavily pregnant Sarah Jessica Parker emerge from her nest to present the shoe designer with an award in New York last October? Despite the fact that she was due to give birth that day, she turned out in a black taffeta YSL dress, her miraculously unswollen ankles teetering on black, strappy Manolo stilettos.

—TAMSIN BLANCHARD, "High on Heels"

In the introduction, I compared the cases of the fraudulent Mexican plastic surgeon and the Oxfordshire foot survey. The first epigraph to this chapter suggests that the cases are even more similar than I suggested. A growing trend in America is cosmetic surgery on the feet, designed either to remedy the effects of constant high-heel wearing or to modify the feet so as to facilitate ever more extreme shoes. A number of cosmetic surgeons and podiatrists are performing operations for purely cosmetic reasons, ranging from toe straightening and bunion removal to collagen implants on the ball of the foot so as to cushion it when in high heels, shortening second and third toes which are "unattractively" longer than the big toe, and shortening or removing little toes so as to allow ever more pointy shoes to be worn.[1]

These practices share many features that I have discussed in this

1. See Beth Landman Keil, "Toe Job"; Kate Kelly and Shelly Branch, "Heels from Hell"; Lisa Tolin, "Foot Fault"; and Olivia Barker, "Cosmetic Toe Surgery Worries Some Doctors."

book. Like cosmetic surgery more generally, women engage in foot surgery to feel both normal ("Deborah Wilton was so embarrassed by her toes, she used to bury her feet in the sand when she lounged at the beach")[2] and extraordinary ("Wright Breece bought one wickedly tall pair after a salesman cooed 'just sit at the bar, cross your legs and reel in the fish'").[3] Women wear high heels despite the pain they experience so as to gain access to socially defined benefits or so as to comply with social norms. ("'I'm on my feet all day but I will not not wear high heels,' says Tracie Fiss . . . who rigs her pointy designer shoes with pads and special inserts. 'It's worth it. It's the price of fashion.'")[4] Feet, just as much as any other part of the body, are deemed worthy of repeated disciplinary attention. ("Exfoliate, exfoliate, moisturize, moisturize. . . . Everyday you should exfoliate and moisturize.")[5] Like many other beauty practices, high heels become pleasurable despite their disadvantages (Sarah Jessica Parker declares them more long lasting than marriages, Madonna claims they're better than sex).[6] Both high heels and foot surgery can be harmful (toe straightening can make previously painless feet painful, and high heels cause problems with the feet, legs, and back).[7] Finally, the availability of the practice and its growing normalization fuels demand and thus further normalizes the practice. ("In Houston, Dr Sherman Nagler says cosmetic surgeries make up 10 percent of his 200-patient-a-week practice. Five years ago, he says, such procedures were unheard of. He attributes the rise in numbers to advances in surgical techniques, a growing acceptance of plastic surgery and the foot-baring shoes now in fashion. 'The shoes they wear in "*Sex and the City*" probably make people more aware of their feet,' he says.")[8]

To make sense of these issues, I have argued that liberal justice—based on some form of autonomy and equality—cannot be realized without taking account of social construction. Social construction operates on both individuals and their surroundings. Individuals are socially constructed in the sense that their preferences and identities are

2. Tolin, "Foot Fault."
3. Kelly and Branch, "Heels from Hell."
4. Ibid.
5. Rebecca Rankin, "Get Your Winter Feet Fit For Summer."
6. Blanchard, "High on Heels."
7. Barker, "Cosmetic Toe Surgery."
8. Tolin, "Foot Fault."

formed in response to particular social contexts and norms. Social construction does not impurely impinge upon an otherwise fully autonomous, pure subject, but rather creates and constitutes that subject. There can be no subject without social construction. However, this is not to say that social construction is normatively neutral. Social construction can be more or less compatible with justice, as it can be more or less compatible with equality and autonomy. The sort of autonomy that is in question, then, is not an individual's ability to derive her principles, preferences, or way of life from the ground up, with no social influence—for that would be impossible—but rather the extent to which an individual's social construction is compatible with her choosing from a varied set of ways of life—her second-order autonomy—and the amount of choice that is available to her within any particular way of life or comprehensive goal—her first-order autonomy.

These considerations also apply to the second element of social construction: the social construction of options. I argued that even a perfectly rational, freely choosing individual is constrained by the fact that she must choose from the options that are available to her, and that are cast as appropriate for her. These options themselves may be limited; or they may violate an individual's well-being or her equality, since in order to access some benefit, the individual may be required to harm herself, and she may be required to harm herself when no such requirement is placed on other types of individuals seeking to access the benefit.

Moving to an argument of greater specificity, I then proposed the theory of the insufficiency of free choice as a way of responding to the general issues just outlined. Liberal theory tends to view choice as a normative transformer: a concept that renders an outcome just by its presence. In the light of social construction, however, choice often cannot be a normative transformer. Instead, the phenomenon of social construction should actively affect the legislative agenda when two factors are present: the disadvantage factor and the influence factor. The disadvantage factor occurs when an individual or group of individuals suffer disadvantage as a result of their own choices—particularly (though not only) if the disadvantage is severe, enduring, and related to the advantage of those who choose differently. The influence factor occurs when there are identifiable pressures on the choosers to make the disadvantageous choice. Where both factors are present, the disadvantaged suffer from an injustice, and the liberal state ought to intervene. State intervention in such cases could attempt to mitigate either the disadvantage factor, the influence factor, or both together. This general model is the basis for all the specific policy proposals I make in the book.

Moving to a yet more specific argument, I proposed the idea of the equality tribunal as a response to one sort of injustice identified by the insufficiency of free choice: the fact that individuals are sometimes treated unequally by their religious or cultural groups. This phenomenon is a clash between second- and first-order autonomy: one's second-order choice might be to remain a member of a particular cultural or religious group, but this need not mean that one has first-order autonomously chosen all of the specific norms and rules of that group. In particular, there should be no obligation on individuals to accept norms of gender inequality—norms that would, in other contexts such as employment—be rightly condemned by the liberal state.

As a remedy, I proposed that an equality tribunal should operate, run along lines similar to employment tribunals. Individuals would be able to go to the equality tribunal and argue that they had been discriminated against on grounds of sex[9] by their religious or cultural group: in other words, that the group had denied them some benefit or imposed some cost which did not apply to members of the other sex. If the case were upheld, the equality tribunal might impose a penalty such as a fine on the group, or require it to change its practice (with some more severe penalty for refusal); most important, the tribunal would publicly declare the practice to be unjust and unacceptable.

The equality tribunal is a way of mitigating both the disadvantage and the influence factors, and thus both equality and autonomy. Its direct purpose is to enhance equality and mitigate disadvantage via its rulings. It enhances autonomy and mitigates influence, moreover, by giving individuals more first-order autonomy, more ability to decide, within their second-order choice of a way of life, which elements of that way of life are of value to them. Individuals who genuinely wish to live according to inequality can do so, either by not attending the tribunal or, if previous tribunal rulings have given them equal rights, by choosing not to take up those rights. Their autonomy is not, therefore, affected. For those individuals who do wish to live equally within their groups, autonomy is greatly enhanced.

9. Discrimination along other lines might also be legislated for, but in this book I have focused on sex discrimination.

Finally, I argued that some cases of unjust social construction should be remedied by proscription. In particular, I proposed that practices that harm the choosing individual should be banned where, first, the harm involved is sufficiently severe that proscription would not be vastly disproportionate *and,* second, the only reason for the individual to choose the harmful practice is to comply with a social norm. The case for proscription is strengthened where the relevant social norm is unjust.

Again, this proposal is an attempt to counter the disadvantage and influence factors, and to enhance equality and autonomy. Harmful practices are clearly disadvantageous: by definition, harm is a disadvantage. The cases I discussed, however, are complex in that the disadvantage is the route to some further advantage. The disadvantage, then, can best be framed as the disadvantage of being able to access a benefit only by socially endorsed (and otherwise unnecessary) self-harm. Of course, where the social norm is unequal, the disadvantage is even clearer.

The connection between proscription of harmful practices, the mitigation of influence, and the enhancement of autonomy is more complex than in the case of the equality tribunal. The mitigation of influence is perhaps the easiest to see: by banning a previously socially endorsed practice, society thereby lessens the pressure it places on individual to undergo it.[10] In cases in which an individual follows the practice so as to achieve a second-order goal, but against her first-order autonomy, proscription enhances her autonomy overall. In other, limited and specific, cases, proscription might limit an individual's first- or second-order autonomy. However, as autonomy is neither the only liberal value nor worthy of maximization, these cases do not fatally undermine the proscriptive strategy.

In general, the principle behind my argument is that where social norms encourage individuals to harm themselves and to render themselves unequal, something is wrong. More specifically, what is wrong is best perceived not as an issue of individual choice, flawed reasoning, or psychology but of the society in question. Where the wrong is social,

---

10. To clarify: prohibition of a practice may not remove all pressure to undergo it, since there may be pressure on some individuals to undergo illegal, backstreet procedures such as breast implants, and since banning breast implants, for example, does not thereby remove all social pressure on individuals to conform to appearance norms. Nonetheless, some pressure has been removed.

moreover, it can be changed by social action. Kelly and Branch report a podiatrist who has the right idea: "A lot of times people come in and say, 'I need surgery to correct this,'" says Helena Reid, a Moline, Ill., podiatrist who recommends moderation for heel-wearers with sore soles. "And I say, 'No, you need different shoes.'"[11]

---

11. Kelly and Branch, "Heels from Hell."

BIBLIOGRAPHY

Abrams, Rebecca. "Nurseries Are Safe and Secure—But Are They Bad for Your Baby?" *Telegraph*, 12 June 2003.

American Society for Aesthetic Plastic Surgery, The. *Cosmetic Surgery National Data Bank Statistics 2005*, 2005. http://www.surgery.org/.

Adkins, Lisa. "Reflexivity: Freedom or Habit of Gender?" *Theory, Culture and Society* 20, no. 6 (2003).

Agencies via Xinhua. "Mexican 'Beautykiller.'" *Shanghai Star*, 31 October 2002.

Allen, Pamela. "The Small Group Process." In *Radical Feminism: A Documentary Reader*, ed. Barbara A. Crow. New York: New York University Press, 2000.

Altman, Irwin, and Joseph Ginat. *Polygamous Families in Contemporary Society*. Cambridge: Cambridge University Press, 1996.

Amnesty International, and Amnesty International USA. *It's About Time! Human Rights Are Women's Rights*. New York: Amnesty International USA, 1995.

Andersen, Elizabeth. "What Is the Point of Equality?" *Ethics* 109, no. 2 (1999).

Antommaria, Armand H. Matheny. "I Paid Out-of-Pocket for My Son's Circumcision at Happy Valley Tattoo and Piercing: Alternative Framings of the Debate over Routine Neonatal Male Circumcision." *American Journal of Bioethics* 3, no. 2 (2003).

Arendt, Hannah. "Communicative Power." In *Power*, ed. Steven Lukes. Oxford: Blackwell, 1987.

Arneson, Richard J. "Equality, Coercion, Culture and Social Norms." *Politics, Philosophy and Economics* 2, no. 2 (2003).

———. "Mill Versus Paternalism." *Ethics* 90, no. 4 (1980).

———. "Perfectionism and Politics." *Ethics* 111, no. 1 (2000).

Ayalah, Daphna, and Isaac Weinstock. *Breasts: Women Speak About Their Breasts and Their Lives*. London: Hutchinson, 1979.

Bacon, Michael. "Liberal Universalism: On Brian Barry and Richard Rorty." *Critical Review of International Social and Political Philosophy* 16, no. 2 (2003).

Barker, Olivia. "Cosmetic Toe Surgery Worries Some Doctors." *Lansing State Journal*, 9 May 2003. http://lsj.com/.

Barnett, Rosalind C., and Caryl Rivers. *She Works / He Works: How Two-Income Families Are Happy, Healthy, and Thriving*. Cambridge: Harvard University Press, 1998.

Barrett, Michèle, and Mary McIntosh. *The Anti-Social Family*. London: Verso, 1982.

Barry, Brian. *Culture and Equality: An Egalitarian Critique of Multiculturalism*. Cambridge: Polity Press, 2001.

———. *Justice as Impartiality*. Oxford: Oxford University Press, 1995.

———. *Liberty and Justice*. Oxford: Clarendon Press, 1990.

———. "Second Thoughts; Some First Thoughts Revived." In *Multiculturalism Reconsidered: Culture and Equality and Its Critics*, ed. Paul Kelly. Cambridge: Polity Press, 2002.

Bartky, Sandra Lee. "Foucault, Femininity and the Modernization of Patriarchal Power." In *Feminist Social Thought: A Reader*, ed. Diana Tietjens Meyers. London: Routledge, 1997.

Bartlett, Katherine T. "Feminist Legal Methods." *Harvard Law Review* 103, no. 4 (1990).

Beauvoir, Simone de. *The Second Sex*. London: Vintage, 1997.

Benatar, Michael, and David Benatar. "Between Prophylaxis and Child Abuse: The Ethics of Neonatal Male Circumcision." *American Journal of Bioethics* 3, no. 2 (2003).

Benhabib, Seyla. *The Claims of Culture: Equality and Diversity in the Global Era*. Princeton: Princeton University Press, 2002.

———. "Feminism and Postmodernism." In *Feminist Contentions*, ed. Seyla Benhabib, Judith Butler, Drucilla Cornell, and Nancy Fraser. London: Routledge, 1995.

———. *Situating the Self*. Cambridge: Polity Press, 1992.

———. "Subjectivity, Historiography and Politics." In *Feminist Contentions*, ed. Seyla Benhabib, Judith Butler, Drucilla Cornell, and Nancy Fraser. London: Routledge, 1995.

Benhabib, Seyla, Judith Butler, Drucilla Cornell, and Nancy Fraser, eds. *Feminist Contentions*. London: Routledge, 1995.

Bentham, Martin. "Working Mothers 'Damage Children's Education.'" *Telegraph*, 4 February 2001.

Berlin, Isaiah. "Two Concepts of Liberty." In *Liberalism and Its Critics*, ed. Michael Sandel. Oxford: Blackwell, 1984.

Blanchard, Tamsin. "High on Heels." *Observer*, 12 January 2003.

Blum, Virginia L. *Flesh Wounds: The Culture of Cosmetic Surgery*. Berkeley and Los Angeles: University of California Press, 2003.

Booth, William James, Patrick James, and Hudson Meadwell, eds. *Politics and Rationality*. Cambridge: Cambridge University Press, 1993.

Bordo, Susan. "Feminism, Foucault and the Politics of the Body." In *Up Against Foucault*, ed. Caroline Ramazanoğlu. London: Routledge, 1993.

———. *The Male Body: A New Look at Men in Public and in Private*. New York: Farrar Straus and Giroux, 2000.

———. *Unbearable Weight: Feminism, Western Culture, and the Body*. Berkeley and Los Angeles: University of California Press, 2003.

Bourdieu, Pierre. *In Other Words: Essays Toward a Reflexive Sociology*. Cambridge: Polity Press, 1990.

———. *The Logic of Practice*. Cambridge: Polity Press, 1990.

———. *Masculine Domination*. Cambridge: Polity Press, 2001.

———. "On the Family as a Realized Category." *Theory, Culture and Society* 13, no. 3 (1996).

———. *Pascalian Meditations*. Cambridge: Polity Press, 2000.

———. *Practical Reason*. Cambridge: Polity Press, 1998.

Bourdieu, Pierre, and Loïc Wacquant. *An Invitation to Reflexive Sociology*. Cambridge: Polity Press, 1992.

Boyd, Billy Ray. "The Loss." In *Men and Intimacy*, ed. Franklin Abbott. Freedom, Calif.: The Crossing Press, 1990.

Brown, Alexander. "Access to Educational Opportunities—One-off or Lifelong?" *Journal of Philosophy of Education* 40, no. 1 (2006).

Brownmiller, Susan. *Against Our Will: Men, Women and Rape*. Harmondsworth: Penguin, 1977.

———. *In Our Time: Memoir of a Revolution*. New York: Random House, 1999.

Bruley, Sue. *Women Awake: The Experience of Consciousness-Raising*. London: Sue Bruley, 1976.

Burkitt, Ian. "Social Relationships and Emotions." *Sociology* 31, no. 1 (1997).

Butler, Judith. "Contingent Foundations." In *Feminist Contentions*, ed. Seyla Benhabib, Judith Butler, Drucilla Cornell, and Nancy Fraser. London: Routledge, 1995.

———. *Gender Trouble*. London: Routledge, 1999.

———. "Performativity's Social Magic." In *Bourdieu: A Critical Reader*, ed. Richard Shusterman. Oxford: Blackwell, 1999.

———. "Restaging the Universal: Hegemony and the Limits of Formalism." In *Contingency, Hegemony, Universality: Contemporary Dialogues on the Left*, ed. Judith Butler, Ernesto Laclau, and Slavoj Žižek. London: Verso, 2000.

Butt, Daniel. *Rectifying International Injustice: Compensation and Restitution Between Nations*. Forthcoming.

Byrne, John A. *Informed Consent*. New York: McGraw-Hill, 1996.

Calderon, Alicia. "Fake Plastic Surgeon Accused of Harming Hundreds in Mexico." *San Diego Union-Tribune*, 13 October 2002.

Califia, Pat. "Feminism and Sadomasochism." In *Feminism and Sexuality: A Reader*, ed. Stevi Jackson and Sue Scott. Edinburgh: Edinburgh University Press, 1998.

Callan, Eamonn. "Liberal Legitimacy, Justice, and Civic Education." *Ethics* 111, no. 1 (2000).

Caney, Simon. "Anti-perfectionism and Rawlsian Liberalism." *Political Studies* 43, no. 2 (1995).

———. "Equal Treatment, Exceptions and Cultural Diversity." In *Multiculturalism Reconsidered: Culture and Equality and Its Critics*, ed. Paul Kelly. Cambridge: Polity Press, 2002.

———. "International Distributive Justice." *Political Studies* 49, no. 5 (2001).

Carling, Alan H. *Social Division*. London: Verso, 1991.

Carroll, Lewis. *Alice's Adventures in Wonderland*. In *The Complete Works of Lewis Carroll*. New York: Vintage Books, 1976.

Carter, Nicholas. *Routine Circumcision: The Tragic Myth*. London: Londinium Press, 1979.

Carter-Molney, Jess. "Tails of the Unexpected." *Guardian*, 21 April 2000.

Chambers, Clare. "Autonomy and Equality in Cultural Perspective: Response to Sawitri Saharso." *Feminist Theory* 5, no. 3 (2004).

———. "Nation-Building, Neutrality and Ethnocultural Justice: Kymlicka's 'Liberal Pluralism.'" *Ethnicities* 3, no. 3 (2003).

Charter, David. "Sugar Gel Breast Implants Banned." *Times*, 12 December 2000.

Chaudhuri, Anita, and Crystal Mahey. "The Silicone Generation." *Guardian*, 8 January 2001.

Cheal, David. *Family and the State of Theory*. London: Harvester Wheatsheaf, 1991.

Clarke, Simon. "A Definition of Paternalism." *Critical Review of Social and Political Philosophy* 5, no. 1 (2002).

Cohen, G. A. "Capitalism, Freedom and the Proletariat." In *Liberty*, ed. David Miller. Oxford: Oxford University Press, 1991.

————. *History, Labour and Freedom: Themes from Marx*. Oxford: Clarendon Press, 1988.

————. "Freedom and Money." Unpublished.

————. *If You're an Egalitarian, How Come You're So Rich?* Cambridge: Harvard University Press, 2000.

————. *Self-Ownership, Freedom, and Equality*. Cambridge: Cambridge University Press, 1995.

Cohen, Jean L. *Regulating Intimacy: A New Legal Paradigm*. Princeton: Princeton University Press, 2002.

Connell, R. W. *Gender and Power: Society, the Person and Sexual Politics*. Cambridge: Polity Press, 1987.

Connolly, William E. *The Terms of Political Discourse*. Oxford: Blackwell, 1993.

Coole, Diana. "Constructing and De-Constructing Liberty: A Feminist and Post-Structuralist Analysis." *Political Studies* 41, no. 1 (1993).

Cornell, Drucilla. *At the Heart of Freedom*. Princeton: Princeton University Press, 1998.

Cronin, Ciarin. "Translator's Introduction." In *Justification and Application*, by Jürgen Habermas, translated by Ciarin Cronin. Cambridge: Polity Press, 1993.

Cruz, Rio, Leonard B. Glick, and John W. Travis. "Circumcision as Human-Rights Violation: Assessing Benatar and Benatar." *American Journal of Bioethics* 3, no. 2 (2003).

Cudd, Ann E. *Analyzing Oppression*. Oxford: Oxford University Press, 2006.

Davies, Jessica. "Am I Damaging My Children?" *Times*, 5 December 2000.

Davis, Dena S. "Cultural Bias in Responses to Male and Female Genital Surgeries." *American Journal of Bioethics* 3, no. 2 (2003).

Davis, Kathy. *Reshaping the Female Body: The Dilemma of Cosmetic Surgery*. London: Routledge, 1995.

Deakin, Simon, and Gillian S. Morris. *Labour Law*. London: Butterworths, 2001.

Deckard, Barbara Sinclair. *The Women's Movement: Political, Socioeconomic, and Psychological Issues*. New York: Harper and Row, 1983.

Deleuze, Gilles, and Sean Hand. *Foucault*. London: Athlone, 1999.

Dench, Sally, Jane Aston, Ceri Evans, Nigel Meager, Matthew Williams, and Rebecca Willison. "Key Indicators of Women's Position in Britain." Women and Equality Unit, Department of Trade and Industry; Institute for Employment Studies, 2002.

Dennisten, George C., Frederick Mansfield Hodges, and Marilyn Fayre Milos, eds. *Understanding Circumcision: A Multi-Disciplinary Approach to a Multi-Dimensional Problem*. New York: Kluwer Academic / Plenum Publishers, 2001.

Dorkenoo, Efua. *Cutting the Rose: Female Genital Mutilation: The Practice and Its Prevention*. London: Minority Rights Publications, 1994.

Dowding, Keith. "Choice: Its Increase and Value." *British Journal of Political Science* 22, no. 3 (1992).

———. *Power*. Buckingham: Open University Press, 1996.

Doyle, Laura. *The Surrendered Wife: A Practical Guide to Finding Intimacy, Passion and Peace with Your Man*. New York: Simon and Schuster, 2001.

Dresser, Rebecca. "Standards for Family Decisions: Replacing Best Interests with Harm Prevention." *American Journal of Bioethics* 3, no. 2 (2003).

Dryburgh, Heather. "Work Hard, Play Hard: Women and Professionalization in Engineering—Adapting to the Culture." *Gender and Society* 13, no. 5 (1999).

Dworkin, Andrea. *Intercourse*. New York: The Free Press, 1987.

———. *Life and Death*. New York: The Free Press, 1997.

———. *Pornography: Men Possessing Women*. London: The Women's Press, 1981.

———. *Woman Hating*. New York: E. P. Dutton, 1974.

Dworkin, Gerald. "Paternalism." In *Mill's On Liberty: Critical Essays,* ed. Gerald Dworkin. Oxford: Rowman and Littlefield, 1997.

———. *The Theory and Practice of Autonomy*. Cambridge: Cambridge University Press, 1988.

Dworkin, Ronald. "Rights as Trumps." In *Theories of Rights,* ed. Jeremy Waldron. Oxford: Oxford University Press, 1984.

———. *Sovereign Virtue: The Theory and Practice of Equality*. Cambridge: Harvard University Press, 2000.

Ehrenreich, Barbara, and Arlie Russell Hochschild, eds. *Global Woman: Nannies, Maids, and Sex Workers in the New Economy*. New York: Metropolitan Books, 2002.

Elliston, Frederick, Jane English, and Mary Vetterling-Braggin, eds. *Feminism and Philosophy*. Totowa, N.J.: Littlefield Adams, 1977.

Elshtain, Jean Bethke. *The Family in Political Thought*. Brighton: Harvester, 1982.

Embry, Jessie L. *Mormon Polygamous Families: Life in Principle*. Salt Lake City: University of Utah Press, 1987.

Faludi, Susan. *Backlash: The Undeclared War Against Women*. London: Chatto and Windus, 1992.

———. *Stiffed: The Betrayal of the Modern Man*. London: Chatto and Windus, 1999.

Fein, Ellen, and Sherrie Schneider. *The Rules You Should Know for Capturing the Heart of Mr Right*. London: HarperCollins, 1995.

Feinberg, Joel. *Harm to Self: The Moral Limits of the Criminal Law, Volume Three*. Oxford: Oxford University Press, 1986.

———. *Offense to Others: The Moral Limits of the Criminal Law, Volume Two*. Oxford: Oxford University Press, 1985.

Firestone, Shulamith. "The Dialectic of Sex." In *Radical Feminism: A Documentary Reader,* ed. Barbara A. Crow. New York: New York University Press, 2000.

Ford, Paul J. "Physician Obligation, Cultural Factors, and Neonatal Male Circumcision." *American Journal of Bioethics* 3, no. 2 (2003).

Foucault, Michel. *The Care of the Self: The History of Sexuality: 3*. Harmondsworth: Penguin, 1990.

———. *Discipline and Punish: The Birth of the Prison*. Harmondsworth: Penguin, 1991.

———. "Nietzsche, Genealogy, History." In *The Foucault Reader,* ed. Paul Rabinow. Harmondsworth: Penguin, 1986.

———. "The Subject and Power." In *Michel Foucault: Beyond Structuralism and*

Hermeneutics, ed. Hubert L. Dreyfus and Paul Rabinow. Hemel Hempstead: Harvester Wheatsheaf, 1982.

———. *The Use of Pleasure: The History of Sexuality: 2.* Harmondsworth: Penguin, 1992.

———. *The Will to Knowledge: The History of Sexuality: 1.* Harmondsworth: Penguin, 1990.

Foucault, Michel, and Lawrence D. Kritzman. *Politics, Philosophy, Culture: Interviews and Other Writings, 1977–1984.* London: Routledge, 1988.

Foucault, Michel, and Paul Rabinow. *The Foucault Reader.* Harmondsworth: Penguin, 1986.

Foucault, Michel, and Duccio Trombadori. *Remarks on Marx: Conversations with Duccio Trombadori.* New York: Semiotext(e), 1991.

Frankfurt, Harry. "Equality as a Moral Ideal." *Ethics* 98, no. 1 (1987).

Fraser, Nancy. "Foucault on Modern Power: Empirical Insights and Normative Confusions." In *Michel Foucault (2): Critical Assessments,* ed. Barry Smart. London: Routledge, 1995.

———. *Justice Interruptus.* London: Routledge, 1997.

———. "Pragmatism, Feminism, and the Linguistic Turn." In *Feminist Contentions,* ed. Benhabib, Seyla, Judith Butler, Drucilla Cornell, and Nancy Fraser. London: Routledge, 1995.

Frazer, Elizabeth, and Nicola Lacey. "Politics and the Public in Rawls' Political Liberalism." *Political Studies* 43, no. 2 (1995).

Friday, Nancy. *My Secret Garden: Women's Sexual Fantasies.* London: Quartet Books, 1973.

Friedan, Betty. *The Feminine Mystique.* Harmondsworth: Penguin, 1983.

Friedman, Marilyn. *Autonomy, Gender, Politics.* New York: Oxford University Press, 2003.

Fuchs, Alan E. "Autonomy, Slavery, and Mill's Critique of Paternalism." *Ethical Theory and Moral Practice* 4, no. 3 (2001).

Galston, William. "A Liberal Defense of Equality of Opportunity." In *Equality: Selected Readings,* ed. Louis P. Pojman and Robert Westmoreland. Oxford: Oxford University Press, 1997.

———. "Two Concepts of Liberalism." *Ethics* 105, no. 3 (1995).

Gane, Mike, and Terry Johnson, eds. *Foucault's New Domains.* London: Routledge, 1993.

Gatens, Moira. "Power, Bodies and Difference." In *Destabilizing Theory: Contemporary Feminist Debates,* ed. Michele Barrett and Anne Phillips. Cambridge: Polity Press, 1992.

Gilman, Sander. "'Barbaric' Rituals?" In *Is Multiculturalism Bad for Women?* ed. Susan Moller Okin, Joshua Cohen, Matthew Howard, and Martha Nussbaum. Princeton: Princeton University Press, 1999.

Glick, Leonard B. "Jewish Circumcision: An Enigma in Historical Perspective." In *Understanding Circumcision: A Multi-Disciplinary Approach to a Multi-Dimensional Problem,* ed. George C. Dennisten, Frederick Mansfield Hodges, and Marilyn Fayre Milos. New York: Kluwer Academic / Plenum Publishers, 2001.

Gold, Michael Evan. *An Introduction to the Law of Employment Discrimination.* Ithaca: Cornell University Press, 2001.

Goodin, Robert. "The Ethics of Smoking." *Ethics* 99, no. 3 (1989).

Gornick, Vivian. "Consciousness." In *Radical Feminism: A Documentary Reader*, ed. Barbara A. Crow. New York: New York University Press, 2000.

Gray, John. *Two Faces of Liberalism*. Cambridge: Polity Press, 2000.

Green, Richard. "(Serious) Sadomasochism: A Protected Right of Privacy?" *Archives of Sexual Behavior* 30, no. 5 (2001).

Greenawalt, Kent. "Freedom of Association and Religious Association." In *Freedom of Association*, ed. Amy Gutmann. Princeton: Princeton University Press, 1998.

Greer, Germaine. *The Female Eunuch*. London: Flamingo, 1991.

————. *The Whole Woman*. London: Doubleday, 1999.

Grigg, Martha, Stuart Bondurant, Virginia L. Ernster, and Roger Herdman, eds. *Information for Women about the Safety of Silicone Breast Implants*. Report of the Institute of Medicine. Washington, D.C.: National Academy Press, 2000.

Guthrie, Randolph H., with Doug Podolsky. *The Truth about Breast Implants*. New York: John Wiley and Sons, 1994.

Gutmann, Amy. "Freedom of Association: An Introductory Essay." In *Freedom of Association*, ed. Amy Gutmann. Princeton: Princeton University Press, 1998.

Habermas, Jürgen. *Justification and Application*. Translated by Ciarin Cronin. Cambridge: Polity Press, 1993.

————. *Moral Consciousness and Communicative Action*. Translated by C. Lenhardt and S. W. Nicholsen. Cambridge: Polity Press, 1990.

Hall, Celia. "Mothers 'Prefer to Be at Home with Their Children.'" *Telegraph*, 5 April 2000.

————. "Sexy High Heels Are Worth the Agony, Say Women." *Telegraph*, 3 March 2001.

Hampton, Wayne F. "Nontherapeutic Circumcision Is Ethically Bankrupt." *American Journal of Bioethics* 3, no. 2 (2003).

Hare, R. M. *Moral Thinking: Its Levels, Method, and Point*. Oxford: Oxford University Press, 1981.

Hayek, F. A. von. *The Constitution of Liberty*. London: Routledge and Kegan Paul, 1960.

————. *The Road to Serfdom*. London: Ark Paperbacks, 1986.

Hekman, Susan J., ed. *Feminist Interpretations of Michel Foucault*. University Park: Pennsylvania State University Press, 1996.

Held, Virginia. *Feminist Morality: Transforming Culture, Society, and Politics*. Chicago: University of Chicago Press, 1993.

Helliwell, Christine. "It's Only a Penis: Rape, Feminism and Difference." *Signs* 25, no. 3 (2000).

Henry, Kristin, and Marlene Derlet. *Talking Up a Storm: Nine Women and Consciousness-raising*. Sydney: Hale and Iremonger, 1993.

Hill, George. "Can Anyone Authorize the Nontherapeutic Permanent Alteration of a Child's Body?" *American Journal of Bioethics* 3, no. 2 (2003).

Hill, Thomas E., Jr. "The Importance of Autonomy." In *Women and Moral Theory*, ed. Eva Feder Kittay and Diana T. Meyers. Totowa, N.J.: Rowman and Littlefield, 1987.

Hirschmann, Albert O. *Exit, Voice, and Loyalty: Responses to Decline in Firms, Organizations and States*. Cambridge: Harvard University Press, 1970.

Hirschmann, Nancy J. *The Subject of Liberty: Toward a Feminist Theory of Freedom.* Princeton: Princeton University Press, 2003.

Hirschmann, Nancy J., and Christine Di Stefano. *Revisioning the Political: Feminist Reconstructions of Traditional Concepts in Western Political Theory.* Boulder, Colo.: Westview Press, 1996.

Hitchcock, Tim. *English Sexualities, 1700–1800.* New York: St. Martin's Press, 1997.

Hite, Shere. *The Hite Report on the Family: Growing Up under Patriarchy.* London: Hodder and Stoughton, 1995.

———. *The New Hite Report: The Revolutionary Report on Female Sexuality Updated.* London: Hamlyn, 2000.

Hochschild, Arlie Russell. *The Managed Heart: Commercialization of Human Feeling.* Berkeley and Los Angeles: University of California Press, 1983.

Hochschild, Arlie Russell, and Anne Machung. *The Second Shift: Working Parents and the Revolution at Home.* London: Piatkus, 1990.

hooks, bell. *Ain't I a Woman: Black Women and Feminism.* London: Pluto Press, 1983.

Horley, Sandra. *The Charm Syndrome: Why Charming Men Can Make Dangerous Lovers.* Basingstoke: Macmillan, 1991.

Hoy, David Couzens, ed. *Foucault: A Critical Reader.* Oxford: Basil Blackwell, 1986.

Hughes, Paul M. "Paternalism, Battered Women, and the Law." *Journal of Social Philosophy* 30, no. 1 (1999).

Hurka, Thomas. *Perfectionism.* Oxford: Oxford University Press, 1993.

Jackson, Stevi, and Sue Scott, eds. *Feminism and Sexuality: A Reader.* Edinburgh: Edinburgh University Press, 1996.

Jaggar, Alison M. *Feminist Politics and Human Nature.* Brighton: Harvester, 1983.

Jeffreys, Sheila. *Anticlimax: A Feminist Perspective on the Sexual Revolution.* London: The Women's Press, 1990.

———. *Beauty and Misogyny: Harmful Cultural Practices in the West.* London: Routledge, 2005.

———. "'Body Art' and Social Status: Cutting, Tattooing and Piercing from a Feminist Perspective." *Feminism and Psychology* 10, no. 4 (2000).

Jenkins, Richard. "Language, Symbolic Power and Communication: Bourdieu's 'Homo Academicus.'" *Sociology* 23, no. 4 (1989).

———. *Pierre Bourdieu.* London: Routledge, 1992.

Johnson, Rebecca J., Kevin D. McCaul, and William M.O. Klein. "Risk Involvement and Risk Perception among Adolescents and Young Adults." *Journal of Behavioural Medicine* 25, no. 1 (2002).

Jones, Caroline McGee. "Neonatal Male Circumcision: Ethical Issues and Physician Responsibility." *American Journal of Bioethics* 3, no. 2 (2003).

Kanter, Hannah, Sarah Lefanu, Shaila Shah, and Carole Spedding, eds. *Sweeping Statements: Writings from the Women's Liberation Movement, 1981–83.* London: The Women's Press, 1984.

Katz, Michael. "The Compulsion to Circumcise Is Constant: The Reasons Keep Changing." In *Understanding Circumcision: A Multi-Disciplinary Approach to a Multi-Dimensional Problem,* ed. George C. Dennisten, Frederick Mansfield Hodges, and Marilyn Fayre Milos. New York: Kluwer Academic / Plenum Publishers, 2001.

Kaw, Eugenia. "Medicalization of Racial Features: Asian-American Women and Cosmetic Surgery." In *The Politics of Women's Bodies: Sexuality, Appearance and Behavior*, ed. Rose Weitz. Oxford: Oxford University Press, 2003.

Keil, Beth Landman. "Toe Job." *New York Metro*. http://newyorkmetro.com (22 October 2003).

Kelly, Kate, and Shelly Branch. "Heels from Hell: What's the Point?" *Wall Street Journal* (posted on http://www.twincities.com, 17 August 2003).

Kelly, P. J., ed. *Multiculturalism Reconsidered: Culture and Equality and Its Critics*. Cambridge: Polity Press, 2002.

King, Anthony. "Thinking with Bourdieu Against Bourdieu: A Practical Critique of the Habitus." *Sociological Theory* 18, no. 3 (2000).

Klosko, George. "Political Obligation and the Natural Duties of Justice." *Philosophy and Public Affairs* 23, no. 3 (1994).

Krais, Beate. "Gender and Symbolic Violence: Female Oppression in the Light of Pierre Bourdieu's Theory of Social Practice." In *Bourdieu: Critical Perspectives*, ed. Craig Calhoun, Edward LiPuma, and Moishe Posthone. Cambridge: Polity Press, 1993.

Kukathas, Chandran. "Are There Any Cultural Rights?" *Political Theory* 20, no. 1 (1992).

———. "The Life of Brian, or Now for Something Completely Difference-Blind." In *Multiculturalism Reconsidered: Culture and Equality and Its Critics*, ed. Paul Kelly. Cambridge: Polity Press, 2002.

Kymlicka, Will. *Contemporary Political Philosophy: An Introduction*. 2nd ed. Oxford: Oxford University Press, 2002.

———. *Liberalism, Community and Culture*. Oxford: Clarendon Press, 1989.

———. *Multicultural Citizenship: A Liberal Theory of Minority Rights*. Oxford: Oxford University Press, 1995.

———. *Politics in the Vernacular: Nationalism, Multiculturalism, and Citizenship*. Oxford: Oxford University Press, 2000.

———. "Rethinking the Family." *Philosophy and Public Affairs* 20, no. 1 (1991).

———. "The Rights of Minority Cultures: Reply to Kukathas." *Political Theory* 20, no. 1 (1992).

———. "Western Political Theory and Ethnic Relations in Eastern Europe." In *Can Liberal Pluralism Be Exported? Western Political Theory and Ethnic Relations in Eastern Europe*, ed. Will Kymlicka and Magdalena Opalski. Oxford: Oxford University Press, 2001.

Kymlicka, Will, and Magdalena Opalski, eds. *Can Liberal Pluralism Be Exported? Western Political Theory and Ethnic Relations in Eastern Europe*. Oxford: Oxford University Press, 2001.

Laden, Anthony Simon. "Radical Liberals, Reasonable Feminists: Reason, Power and Objectivity in MacKinnon and Rawls." *Journal of Political Philosophy* 11, no. 2 (2003).

Landes, Joan B., ed. *Feminism, the Public and the Private*. Oxford: Oxford University Press, 1998.

Lawson, Amy. "Shoe Lovers Put Feet under the Knife." *New Woman*. http://newwoman.co.uk (12 August 2003).

Lewis, Jon. *Hollywood V. Hard Core: How the Struggle over Censorship Saved the Modern Film Industry*. New York: New York University Press, 2000.

Lightfoot, Liz. "Too Long at Day Centres 'Can Disturb Children.'" *Telegraph*, 27 March 2003.

Lightfoot-Klein, Hanny. *Prisoners of Ritual: An Odyssey into Female Genital Circumcision*. Binghamton, N.Y.: Haworth Press, 1989.

Lkjaergard, Lise, and Bodil Als-Nielsen. "Association Between Competing Interests and Authors' Conclusions: Epidemiological Study of Randomised Clinical Trials Published in the BMJ." *British Medical Journal*, no. 325 (2002).

Lovelace, Linda, and Michael McGrady. *Ordeal*. Secaucus, N.J.: Citadel Press, 1980.

Lovell, Terry. "Thinking Feminism with and Against Bourdieu." *Feminist Theory* 1, no. 1 (2000).

Lovenduski, Joni, and Vicky Randall. *Contemporary Feminist Politics: Women and Power in Britain*. Oxford: Oxford University Press, 1993.

Lovibond, Sabina. "Feminism and Postmodernism." In *Postmodernism: A Reader*, ed. Thomas Docherty. London: Harvester Wheatsheaf, 1999.

Luciano, Lynne. *Looking Good: Male Body Image in Modern America*. New York: Hill and Wang, 2001.

Lukes, Steven. *Power: A Radical View*. Basingstoke: Macmillan, 1974.

———, ed. *Power*. New York: New York University Press, 1986.

Lund-Molfese, Nicholas C. "What Is Mutilation?" *American Journal of Bioethics* 3, no. 2 (2003).

MacCallum, Gerald. "Negative and Positive Liberty." In *Liberty*, ed. David Miller. Oxford: Oxford University Press, 1991.

MacIntyre, Alasdair. *After Virtue: A Study in Moral Theory*. London: Duckworth, 1981.

Mackie, Gerry. "Ending Footbinding and Infibulation: A Convention Account." *American Sociological Review* 61, no. 6 (1996).

———. "Ending Harmful Conventions: Liberal Responses to Female Genital Cutting." Unpublished.

———. "Female Genital Cutting: The Beginning of the End." In *Female "Circumcision" in Africa: Culture, Controversy, and Change*, ed. Bettina Shell-Duncan and Ylva Hernlund. London: Lynne Rienner, 2000.

———. "Female Genital Cutting: A Harmless Practice?" *Medical Anthropology Quarterly* 17, no. 2 (2003).

Mackie, J. L. *Ethics: Inventing Right and Wrong*. Harmondsworth: Penguin, 1990.

MacKinnon, Catharine A. "'The Case' Responds." *American Political Science Review* 95, no. 3 (2001).

———. *Feminism Unmodified*. Cambridge: Harvard University Press, 1987.

———. *Toward a Feminist Theory of the State*. Cambridge: Harvard University Press, 1989.

———. *Women's Lives, Men's Laws*. Cambridge: Harvard University Press, 2005.

MacKinnon, Catharine A., and Andrea Dworkin. *In Harm's Way: The Pornography Civil Rights Hearings*. Cambridge: Harvard University Press, 1997.

Maier, Charles. *Changing Boundaries of the Political: Essays on the Evolving Balance Between the State and Society, Public and Private in Europe*. Cambridge: Cambridge University Press, 1989.

Mason, Andrew. "Equality of Opportunity, Old and New." *Ethics* 111, no. 3 (2001).

———. "Imposing Liberal Principles." *Critical Review of Social and Political Philosophy* 1, no. 3 (1998).

———. "Meritocracy, Desert, and the Moral Force of Intuitions." In *Forms of Justice: Critical Perspectives on David Miller's Political Philosophy*, ed. Daniel Bell and Avner De-Shalit. Lanham, Md.: Rowman and Littlefield, 2003.

Maushart, Susan. *Wifework*. London: Bloomsbury, 2002.

McCabe, David. "Joseph Raz and the Contextual Argument for Liberal Perfectionism." *Ethics* 111, no. 3 (2001).

———. "Knowing About the Good: A Problem with Antiperfectionism." *Ethics* 110, no. 2 (2000).

McLaren, Angus. *Twentieth-Century Sexuality: A History*. Oxford: Blackwell, 1999.

McNay, Lois. *Foucault and Feminism*. Cambridge: Polity Press, 1992.

———. *Gender and Agency*. Cambridge: Polity Press, 2000.

———. "Gender and Narrative Identity." *Journal of Political Ideologies* 4, no. 3 (1999).

———. "Gender, Habitus and the Field: Pierre Bourdieu and the Limits of Reflexivity." *Theory, Culture and Society* 16, no. 1 (1999).

McNeil, Maureen. "Dancing with Foucault: Feminism and Power-Knowledge." In *Up Against Foucault*, ed. Caroline Ramazanoglu. London: Routledge, 1993.

Meek, James. "Drugs Could Put a Stop to Periods." *Guardian*, 27 July 2001.

———. "Prime Cuts." *Guardian*, 21 December 2001.

Mendus, Susan. "Choice, Chance and Multiculturalism." In *Multiculturalism Reconsidered: Culture and Equality and Its Critics*, ed. Paul Kelly. Cambridge: Polity Press, 2002.

———. *Impartiality in Moral and Political Philosophy*. Oxford: Oxford University Press, 2002.

———. *Toleration and the Limits of Liberalism*. Basingstoke: Macmillan, 1989.

Merquior, José Guilherme. *Foucault*. London: Fontana Press, 1991.

Meyers, Diana Tietjens, ed. *Feminists Rethink the Self*. Boulder, Colo.: Westview Press, 1996.

———, ed. *Feminist Social Thought: A Reader*. London: Routledge, 1997.

———. *Gender in the Mirror: Cultural Imagery and Women's Agency*. Oxford: Oxford University Press, 2002,

Mill, John Stuart. "On Liberty." In *Utilitarianism, on Liberty, Considerations on Representative Government*, ed. Geraint Williams. London: Everyman, 1993.

———. "The Subjection of Women." In *On Liberty and the Subjection of Women*. Ware: Wordsworth, 1996.

Miller, David. "Holding Nations Responsible." *Ethics* 114, no. 2 (2004).

———. "Liberalism, Equal Opportunities and Cultural Commitments." In *Multiculturalism Reconsidered: Culture and Equality and Its Critics*, ed. Paul Kelly. Cambridge: Polity Press, 2002.

———. *Social Justice*. Oxford: Clarendon Press, 1976.

Miller, Geoffrey. *The Mating Mind*. London: William Heinemann, 2000.

Millett, Kate. *Sexual Politics*. London: Hart-Davis, 1971.

Moghissi, Haideh. *Feminism and Islamic Fundamentalism: The Limits of Postmodern Analysis*. London: Zed Books, 1999.

Morgan, Kathryn Pauly. "Women and the Knife: Cosmetic Surgery and the Colonization of Women's Bodies." In *The Politics of Women's Bodies: Sexuality, Appearance and Behavior*, ed. Rose Weitz. Oxford: Oxford University Press, 2003.

Morris, Brian. *In Favour of Circumcision*. Sydney: University of New South Wales Press, 1999.

Moses, S., R. C. Bailey, and A. R. Ronald. "Male Circumcision: Assessment of Health Benefits and Risks." *Sexually Transmitted Infections* 74, no. 5 (1998).

Mottier, Veronique. "Masculine Domination." *Feminist Theory* 3, no. 3 (2002).

Mulhall, Stephen, and Adam Swift. *Liberals and Communitarians*. Oxford: Blackwell, 1992.

Mullen, Michelle A. "Who Speaks for Sons?" *American Journal of Bioethics* 3, no. 2 (2003).

Munro, Vanessa E. "On Power and Domination: Feminism and the Final Foucault." *European Journal of Political Theory* 2, no. 1 (2003).

Murphy, Timothy F. *Ethics in an Epidemic:* AIDS, *Morality, and Culture*. Berkeley and Los Angeles: University of California Press, 1994.

Nozick, Robert. *Anarchy, State and Utopia*. Oxford: Blackwell, 1980.

Nussbaum, Martha. "Aristotle, Politics, and Human Capabilities." *Ethics* 111, no. 1 (2000).

———. "Duties of Justice, Duties of Material Aid: Cicero's Problematic Legacy." *Journal of Political Philosophy* 8, no. 2 (2000).

———. *Hiding from Humanity: Disgust, Shame, and the Law*. Princeton: Princeton University Press, 2004.

———. "A Plea for Difficulty." In *Is Multiculturalism Bad for Women?* ed. Susan Moller Okin, Joshua Cohen, Matthew Howard, and Martha Nussbaum. Princeton: Princeton University Press, 1999.

———. *Sex and Social Justice*. Oxford: Oxford University Press, 1999.

———. "Sex Equality, Entitlements, and the Capabilities Approach." Paper presented at the London School of Economics, 13 March 2002.

———. *Women and Human Development: The Capabilities Approach*. Cambridge: Cambridge University Press, 2000.

Nussbaum, Martha, and David M. Estlund, eds. *Sex, Preference and Family: Essays on Law and Nature*. Oxford: Oxford University Press, 1997.

Oakley, Ann. *The Sociology of Housework*. Oxford: Blackwell, 1985.

Oakley, Ann, and Juliet Mitchell, eds. *Who's Afraid of Feminism? Seeing Through the Backlash*. London: Hamish Hamilton, 1997.

Obermeyer, Carla Makhlouf. "The Health Consequences of Female Circumcision: Science, Advocacy, and Standards of Evidence." *Medical Anthropology Quarterly* 17, no. 3 (2003).

Okin, Susan Moller. *Justice, Gender and the Family*. New York: Basic Books, 1989.

———. "Is Multiculturalism Bad for Women?" In *Is Multiculturalism Bad for Women?* ed. Susan Moller Okin, Joshua Cohen, Matthew Howard, and Martha Nussbaum. Princeton: Princeton University Press, 1999.

———. "Reply." In *Is Multiculturalism Bad for Women?* ed. Susan Moller Okin, Joshua Cohen, Matthew Howard, and Martha Nussbaum. Princeton: Princeton University Press, 1999.

Pang, Myung-Geol, Sae Chul Kim, and DaiSik Kim. "Male Circumcision in South Korea: History, Statistics, and the Role of Doctors in Creating a Circumcision Rate of over 100%." In *Understanding Circumcision: A Multi-Disciplinary Approach to a Multi-Dimensional Problem*, ed. George C. Dennisten, Frederick Mansfield Hodges, and Marilyn Fayre Milos. New York: Kluwer Academic / Plenum Publishers, 2001.

Parekh, Bhikhu. "Barry and the Dangers of Liberalism." In *Multiculturalism Reconsidered:* Culture and Equality *and Its Critics,* ed. Paul Kelly. Cambridge: Polity Press, 2002.

———. *Rethinking Multiculturalism: Cultural Diversity and Political Theory.* Basingstoke: Macmillan, 2000.

Parfit, Derek. "Equality and Priority." In *The Ideal of Equality,* ed. Andrew Williams and Matthew Clayton. New York: St. Martin's Press, 2000.

Pateman, Carole. *The Problem of Political Obligation: A Critique of Liberal Theory.* Cambridge: Polity Press, 1985.

———. *The Sexual Contract.* Cambridge: Polity Press, 1988.

Pettit, Philip. *Republicanism: A Theory of Freedom and Government.* Oxford: Clarendon Press, 1997.

Phillips, Anne, ed. *Feminism and Equality.* Oxford: Blackwell, 1987.

———. *The Politics of Presence.* Oxford: Clarendon Press, 1995.

———. *Which Equalities Matter?* Cambridge: Polity Press, 1999.

Pitt, Gwyneth. *Employment Law.* London: Sweet and Maxwell, 2000.

Platt, Steve. *Censored: The State of Film Censorship in Britain Today.* London: Channel 4 Television, 1999.

Pollitt, Katha. "Whose Culture?" In *Is Multiculturalism Bad for Women?* ed. Susan Moller Okin, Joshua Cohen, Matthew Howard, and Martha Nussbaum. Princeton: Princeton University Press, 1999.

Pook, Sally. "'Giving Up Work Was Best Thing I Did' [sic]." *Telegraph* 5 April 2000.

Ramazanoglu, Caroline. *Up Against Foucault: Explorations of Some Tensions Between Foucault and Feminism.* London: Routledge, 1993.

Rankin, Rebecca. "Get Your Winter Feet Fit For Summer." http://abclocal.go.com (22 October 2003).

Rawls, John. *Justice as Fairness: A Restatement.* Cambridge: Harvard University Press, 2001.

———. *The Law of Peoples.* Cambridge: Harvard University Press, 1999.

———. *Political Liberalism.* New York: Columbia University Press, 1993.

———. *A Theory of Justice.* Oxford: Oxford University Press, 1973.

Raz, Joseph. *Engaging Reason: On the Theory of Value and Action.* Oxford: Oxford University Press, 1999.

———. *Ethics in the Public Domain: Essays in the Morality of Law and Politics.* Oxford: Oxford University Press, 1994.

———. *The Morality of Freedom.* Oxford: Oxford University Press, 1988.

———. *Value, Respect and Attachment.* Cambridge: Cambridge University Press, 2001.

Reay, Diane. "A Useful Extension of Bourdieu's Conceptual Framework: Emotional Capital as a Way of Understanding Mothers' Involvement in Their Children's Education?" *Sociological Review* 48, no. 4 (2000).

Reeves, Richard. "If You Go Down to the Gender Ghetto Today." *Guardian,* 5 July 2000.

Rhode, Deborah L. *Speaking of Sex: The Denial of Gender Inequality.* Cambridge: Harvard University Press, 1997.

Richards, Janet Radcliffe. *The Sceptical Feminist*. Harmondsworth: Penguin, 1994.

Riley, Sarah. "A Feminist Construction of Body Art as a Harmful Cultural Practice: A Response to Jeffreys." *Feminism and Psychology* 12, no. 4 (2002).

Roemer, John E. *Equality of Opportunity*. Cambridge: Harvard University Press, 1998.

Rorty, Richard. *Contingency, Irony, and Solidarity*. Cambridge: Cambridge University Press, 1989.

———. "Moral Identity and Private Autonomy: The Case of Foucault." In Richard Rorty, *Essays on Heidegger and Others*. Cambridge: Cambridge University Press, 1991.

Sanchez, Laura, and Elizabeth Thomson. "Becoming Mothers and Fathers: Parenthood, Gender, and the Division of Labor." *Gender and Society* 11, no. 6 (1997).

Sandel, Michael J. *Liberalism and Its Critics*. Oxford: Blackwell, 1984.

———. *Liberalism and the Limits of Justice*. Cambridge: Cambridge University Press, 1982.

———. "The Procedural Republic and the Unencumbered Self." In *Communitarianism and Individualism*, ed. Shlomo Avineri and Avner De-Shalit. Oxford: Oxford University Press, 1992.

Santtila, Pekka, N. Kenneth Sandnabba, Laurence Alison, and Niklas Nordling. "Investigating the Underlying Structure in Sadomasochistically Oriented Behavior." *Archives of Sexual Behavior* 31, no. 2 (2002).

Scanlon, Thomas. "The Diversity of Objections to Inequality." In *The Ideal of Equality*, ed. Andrew Williams and Matthew Clayton. New York: St. Martin's Press, 2000.

Schaeffer, Denise. "Feminism and Liberalism Reconsidered: The Case of Catharine MacKinnon." *American Political Science Review* 95, no. 3 (2001).

Schneir, Miriam, ed. *The Vintage Book of Feminism*. Reading, UK: Cox and Wyman, 1995.

Schwartz, Pepper. *Love Between Equals: How Peer Marriage Really Works*. New York: The Free Press, 1994.

———. "Peer Marriage: What Does It Take to Create a Truly Egalitarian Relationship?" In *Family in Transition*, ed. Arlene S. Skolnick and Jerome H. Skolnick. Needham Heights, Mass.: Allyn and Bacon, 2001.

Scoccia, Danny. "Paternalism and Respect for Autonomy." *Ethics* 100, no. 2 (1990).

Segal, Lynne. "Lessons from the Past: Feminism, Sexual Politics and the Challenge of AIDS." In *Taking Liberties: AIDS and Cultural Politics*, ed. Erica Carter and Simon Watney. London: Serpent's Tail, 1989.

———. *Slow Motion: Changing Masculinity, Changing Men*. London: Virago, 1990.

———. *Straight Sex: The Politics of Desire*. London: Virago, 1994.

Segal, Lynne, and Mary McIntosh, eds. *Sex Exposed: Sexuality and the Pornography Debate*. London: Virago, 1992.

Shachar, Ayelet. *Multicultural Jurisdictions: Cultural Differences and Women's Rights*. Cambridge: Cambridge University Press, 2001.

Shanley, Mary Lyndon, and Uma Narayan, eds. *Reconstructing Political Theory: Feminist Perspectives*. Cambridge: Polity Press, 1997.

Shanley, Mary Lyndon, and Carole Pateman, eds. *Feminist Interpretations and Political Theory.* Cambridge: Polity Press, 1991.

Shapiro, Ian. "Democratic Justice and Multicultural Recognition." In *Multiculturalism Reconsidered:* Culture and Equality *and Its Critics,* ed. Paul Kelly. Cambridge: Polity Press, 2002.

Sheldon, Mark. "Male Circumcision, Religious Preferences, and the Question of Harm." *American Journal of Bioethics* 3, no. 2 (2003).

Shell-Duncan, Bettina, and Ylva Hernlund, eds. *Female "Circumcision" in Africa: Culture, Controversy, and Change.* London: Lynne Rienner, 2000.

Sher, George. *Beyond Neutrality: Perfectionism and Politics.* Cambridge: Cambridge University Press, 1997.

Simpson, Richard. "Demi Completes Cosmetic Makeover with £5,000 Knee Surgery." *Daily Mail,* 25 October 2006.

Singh, Dev. "Waist-to-Hip Ratio (WHR): A Defining Morphological Feature of Health and Female Attractiveness." *Journal of Personality and Social Psychology* 65 (1993).

Skanderowicz, Andrew. Answer to: "How Are Breast Implants Removed?" *Zest,* November 2001.

Sleator, Alex. *The Female Genital Mutilation Bill: Bill 21 of 2002–3.* House of Commons Library Research Paper 03/24, 2003.

Slosar, John Paul. "The Ethics of Neonatal Male Circumcision: A Catholic Perspective." *American Journal of Bioethics* 3, no. 2 (2003).

Smith, Joan. *Different for Girls: How Culture Creates Women.* London: Chatto and Windus, 1997.

———. *Misogynies: Reflections on Myths and Malice.* London: Faber and Faber, 1993.

Spinner-Halev, Jeff. "Feminism, Multiculturalism, Oppression, and the State." *Ethics* 112, no. 1 (2001).

Squires, Judith. "Culture, Equality and Diversity." In *Multiculturalism Reconsidered:* Culture and Equality *and Its Critics,* ed. Paul Kelly. Cambridge: Polity Press, 2002.

———. *Gender in Political Theory.* Cambridge: Polity Press, 1999.

Steinberger, Peter J. "Public and Private." *Political Studies* 47, no. 2 (1999).

Suarez, Troy, and Jeffrey Miller. "Negotiating Risks in Context: A Perspective on Unprotected Anal Intercourse and Barebacking among Men Who Have Sex with Men—Where Do We Go from Here?" *Archives of Sexual Behavior* 30, no. 3 (2001).

Sunstein, Cass R. "Neutrality in Constitutional Law (with special reference to pornography, abortion, and surrogacy)." *Columbia Law Review* 92, no. 1 (1992).

———. "Preferences and Politics." *Philosophy and Public Affairs* 20, no. 1 (1991).

———. "Should Sex Equality Law Apply to Religious Institutions?" In *Is Multiculturalism Bad for Women?* ed. Susan Moller Okin, Joshua Cohen, Matthew Howard, and Martha Nussbaum. Princeton: Princeton University Press, 1999.

Svoboda, J. Steven. "Circumcision—A Victorian Relic Lacking Ethical, Medical, or Legal Justification." *American Journal of Bioethics* 3, no. 2 (2003).

Taylor, Charles. "Atomism." In *Communitarianism and Individualism,* ed. Shlomo Avineri and Avner De-Shalit. Oxford: Oxford University Press, 1992.

――――. "The Politics of Recognition." In *Multiculturalism and "The Politics of Recognition,"* ed. Amy Gutmann. Princeton: Princeton University Press, 1992.

――――. "To Follow a Rule . . ." In *Bourdieu: Critical Perspectives,* ed. Craig Calhoun, Edward LiPuma, and Moishe Posthone. Cambridge: Polity Press, 1993.

――――. "What's Wrong with Negative Liberty." In Charles Taylor, *Philosophy and the Human Sciences: Philosophical Papers 2.* Cambridge: Cambridge University Press, 1985.

Taylor, J. R., A. P. Lockwood, and A. J. Taylor. "The Prepuce: Specialized Mucosa of the Penis and Its Loss to Circumcision." *British Journal of Urology* 77 (1996).

Tebble, Adam James. "What Is the Politics of Difference?" *Political Theory* 30, no. 2 (2002).

Temkin, Larry S. "Inequality." *Philosophy and Public Affairs* 15, no. 2 (1986).

Templeton, Sarah-Kate. "Girls Take to Surgery so They Can Face University." *Times.* http://www.timesonline.co.uk (10 July 2005).

Tolin, Lisa. "Foot Fault." http://stopgettingsick.com (22 October 2003).

Tomasi, John. "Individual Rights and Community Virtues." *Ethics* 101, no. 3 (1991).

――――. "Kymlicka, Liberalism, and Respect for Cultural Minorities." *Ethics* 105, no. 3 (1995).

Tuckman, Jo. "She Said She'd Make Us Look Like Barbie Dolls." *Guardian,* 9 December 2002.

Tully, James. "The Illiberal Liberal: Brian Barry's Polemical Attack on Multiculturalism." In *Multiculturalism Reconsidered:* Culture and Equality *and Its Critics,* ed. Paul Kelly. Cambridge: Polity Press, 2002.

Tyrrel, Rebecca. "Sexual Heeling." *Telegraph,* 4 November 2001.

United Kingdom. Department of Health. "Breast Implants: Information for Women Considering Breast Implants." Advisory leaflet no 21218 1P, 2000.

――――. "Health Minister Lord Warner Welcomes New Safety Measures for Breast Implants." Press release ref. 2003/0277, 25 July 2003.

United Kingdom. National Breast Implant Registry. *Annual Report 2002.* 2002.

United Kingdom. Office of National Statistics. "Marriage, Divorce and Adoption Statistics: Series FM2 No. 27 (2001)," 2001.

United Kingdom. UK Breast Implant Registry. *Annual Report 2004.* 2004.

United Kingdom. Video Appeals Committee. *Judgment of Appeals Numbers 15 and 16: Sheptonhurst Ltd and Prime Time (Shifnal) Ltd Vs. British Board of Film Classification,* 1999.

United Nations. "Harmful Traditional Practices Affecting the Health of Women and Children." Fact Sheet No. 23. http://www.unhchr.ch/html/menu6/2/fs23.htm (accessed on 25 July 2003).

United States. Bureau of Labor Statistics. "Occupational Outlook Handbook." Department of Labor, 2002–3.

Van Lenning, Alkeline. "The System Made Me Do It? A Response to Jeffreys." *Feminism and Psychology* 12, no. 4 (2002).

Vance, Carol S., ed. *Pleasure and Danger: Exploring Female Sexuality.* London: Pandora, 1989.

Waldeck, Sarah E. "Social Norm Theory and Male Circumcision: Why Parents Circumcise." *American Journal of Bioethics* 3, no. 2 (2003).

Waldron, Jeremy. "Minority Cultures and the Cosmopolitan Alternative." *University of Michigan Journal of Law Reform* 25 (1992).

———. "Special Ties and Natural Duties." *Philosophy and Public Affairs* 22, no. 1 (1993).

———, ed. *Theories of Rights.* Oxford: Oxford University Press, 1984.

Wall, Steven. *Liberalism, Perfectionism and Restraint.* Cambridge: Cambridge University Press, 1998.

Walzer, Michael. *Spheres of Justice: A Defence of Pluralism and Equality.* Oxford: Blackwell, 1985.

———. *Thick and Thin: Moral Argument at Home and Abroad.* Notre Dame: University of Notre Dame Press, 1994.

Watney, Simon. "AIDS, 'Moral Panic' Theory and Homophobia." In *Social Aspects of AIDS,* ed. Peter Aggleton and Hilary Homans. London: The Falmer Press, 1988.

Webber, Sarah. "Cutting History, Cutting Culture: Female Circumcision in the United States." *American Journal of Bioethics* 3, no. 2 (2003).

Weeks, Jeffrey. *Making Sexual History.* Cambridge: Polity Press, 2000.

Weitz, Rose, ed. *The Politics of Women's Bodies: Sexuality, Appearance and Behavior.* Oxford: Oxford University Press, 2003.

White, Stuart. "Freedom of Association and the Right to Exclude." *Journal of Political Philosophy* 5, no. 4 (1997).

———. "Republicanism, Patriotism, and Global Justice." In *Forms of Justice: Critical Perspectives on David Miller's Political Philosophy,* ed. Daniel Bell and Avner De-Shalit. Lanham, Md.: Rowman and Littlefield, 2003.

Wijngaards, John. *The Ordination of Women Catholic Internet Library.* http://www.womenpriests.org/.

Williams, Bernard. "The Idea of Equality." In *Equality: Selected Readings,* ed. Louis P. Pojman and Robert Westmoreland. Oxford: Oxford University Press, 1997.

———, ed. *Obscenity and Film Censorship: An Abridgement of the Williams Report.* Cambridge: Cambridge University Press, 1981.

Winter, Bronwyn, Denise Thompson, and Sheila Jeffreys. "The UN Approach to Harmful Traditional Practices." *International Feminist Journal of Politics* 4, no. 1 (2002).

Wolf, Naomi. *The Beauty Myth.* London: Vintage, 1990.

———. *Promiscuities: A Secret History of Female Desire.* London: Chatto and Windus, 1997.

Wollstonecraft, Mary. *A Vindication of the Rights of Woman.* London: Constable and Company, 1996.

Young, Iris Marion. "Breasted Experience: The Look and the Feeling." In *The Politics of Women's Bodies: Sexuality, Appearance and Behavior,* ed. Rose Weitz. Oxford: Oxford University Press, 2003.

———. *Inclusion and Democracy.* Oxford: Oxford University Press, 2000.

———. *Justice and the Politics of Difference.* Princeton: Princeton University Press, 1990.

———. "Reply to Tebble." *Political Theory* 30, no. 2 (2002).

Yuracko, Kimberley A. *Perfectionism and Contemporary Feminist Values.* Bloomington: Indiana University Press, 2003.

INDEX